I0124889

Homeless Voices

Homeless Voices

Stigma, Space, and Social Media

Mary L. Schuster

LEXINGTON BOOKS
Lanham • Boulder • New York • London

Published by Lexington Books
An imprint of The Rowman & Littlefield Publishing Group, Inc.
4501 Forbes Boulevard, Suite 200, Lanham, Maryland 20706
www.rowman.com

86-90 Paul Street, London EC2A 4NE, United Kingdom

Copyright © 2022 by The Rowman & Littlefield Publishing Group, Inc.

All rights reserved. No part of this book may be reproduced in any form or by any electronic or mechanical means, including information storage and retrieval systems, without written permission from the publisher, except by a reviewer who may quote passages in a review.

British Library Cataloguing in Publication Information Available

Library of Congress Cataloging-in-Publication Data

LC ebook record available at https://lccn.loc.gov/2021038096
Names: Schuster, Mary Lay, author.
Title: Homeless voices : stigma, space, and social media / Mary L. Schuster.
Description: Lanham : Lexington Books, [2022] | Includes bibliographical
  references and index. | Summary: "This book argues that the best sources
  for how to address the issues of homelessness are people experiencing
  homelessness themselves, particularly through their personal blogs and
  memoirs. Moreover, the author examines how stigmatization, metaphorical
  language, and spatial segregation relating to homelessness serve as tools
  for systemic oppression"—Provided by publisher.
Identifiers: LCCN 2021038095 (print) | LCCN 2021038096 (ebook) |
  ISBN 9781793635709 (cloth) | ISBN 9781793635716 (epub) | ISBN
  9781793635723 (paper)
Subjects: LCSH: Homeless persons. | Homelessness—Social aspects. |
  Social media.
Classification: LCC HV4493 .S358 2022 (print) | LCC HV4493 (ebook) |
  DDC 305.5/692—dc23
LC record available at https://lccn.loc.gov/2021038095

To all those who are experiencing or have experienced homelessness. Thank you for sharing your voices.

Contents

Acknowledgments

Too often people experiencing homelessness have no public voices despite the fine work that advocates and activists may do in representing them. I hope that with this book those voices are louder, more noticeable, and taken into consideration more frequently because they have much to teach us. In particular, I want to acknowledge those who wrote personal blogs and published memoirs to tell their compelling stories about homelessness.

The genesis for my own education about homelessness began with my attending a lecture on racially restrictive deed covenants held at the men's campus of Union Gospel Mission in St. Paul, Minnesota, and sponsored in part by the Mapping Prejudice program at the University of Minnesota. That education was greatly enhanced by my volunteer work with Tubman, which provides safe shelter and services for people who have experienced relationship violence and other forms of trauma. I also learned much about how victims of intimate violence are faced with homelessness through my volunteer work with WATCH, a court monitoring and judicial policy nonprofit organization that works to make the justice system more responsive to crimes of violence against women and children. Katherine Meerse, Ryan Berg, and Mason Persons introduced me to the work that Avenues for Youth and their ConneQT Host Homes program do to help youth experiencing homelessness achieve their dreams. Camille Gage kindly ensured that my analysis of "The Wall of Forgotten Natives" and her blog about the encampment was accurate and thorough. Jessie Tepper, Associate Acquisitions Editor with Lexington Books, offered professional help all through the various stages of bringing this book to publication. Colleagues within the Department of Writing Studies, the School of Law, and the College of Liberal Arts at the University of Minnesota also offered support. Amy Propen, Associate Professor and Director of the Writing Program at University of California, Santa Barbara, encouraged me throughout the writing and revising process. The Lay, Schuster, and Rhode families marked my progress with applause. Finally, my husband, Slade Schuster, proofread my many drafts, fixed dinner, walked the dogs, and attended to my need for quiet hours in my study. He has made my life a fulfilling and happy one indeed.

Introduction

Understanding Homelessness

In his memoir, Todd Murphy (2018) conveyed some common challenges as well as some unexpected advantages that he realized during his experience of being homeless. "On the one hand," Murphy admitted, "homelessness was a prison. . . . On the other, it was absolute freedom, so expansive that the normal points of references that mark most people's lives didn't exist for him." Murphy supported these notions with specific examples: "He wasn't free to buy a snack without first counting his coins. He wasn't free to insist on his rights. He didn't have the freedom or the luxury to crawl into a bed at night, pull the blankets over himself, turn out the lights and go to sleep." Murphy noted, however, "There was no alarm clock to wake him up at a specific time" (186–87). A veteran who was homeless for two and a half years, Murphy expressed in his memoir what any person experiencing homelessness might go through in a single day. Moreover, he offered the nuances of living homeless to his readers and in doing so challenged any inclination to essentialize or stereotype those experiencing homelessness. By listening to the voices of Murphy and such others, we can begin to understand and perhaps even remedy the personal and systemic crisis of homelessness.

Agencies report the growing population of people experiencing homelessness in the United States, now estimated to be over five hundred thousand on any given day. According to the National Alliance to End Homelessness (2020a), people experiencing homelessness are often "living in a place not meant for human habitation, in emergency shelter, in transitional housing, or are exiting an institution where they temporarily resided." They also include those who are "losing their primary nighttime residence," families with children, unaccompanied youth "who are unstably housed and likely to continue in that state," and people who are "fleeing or attempting to flee domestic violence, have no other residence and lack the resources or support networks to obtain other permanent housing." In 2020, 21 out of every 10,000 veterans experienced homelessness, and 90 percent of these homeless veterans were men. Moreover, Black veterans made up about one-third of all veterans dealing with unstable housing, even though they constituted only 12 percent of the total veterans' population (Shane 2021). These statistics represent a social and economic crisis across the country as affected by gender, race, and health conditions such as post-traumatic stress disorder (PTSD) and depression.

To better understand this crisis of homelessness, I apply and build upon transdisciplinary research on the stigmatization and marginalization as well as spatial segregation of people experiencing homelessness. By transdisciplinary research, I mean the work of scholars who might identify with the following areas: rhetoric and communication studies, rhetoric of science and of health and medicine, public health and public policy, disability studies, law and society studies, cultural studies, sociology, and urban geography. Moreover, the very term spatial segregation was created and employed by a variety of scholars in these fields (see, for example, Reardon and O'Sullivan 2004; Stern 2021; Wong 2008). I offer this transdisciplinary perspective in the context of several case studies that illuminate past and current conditions of homelessness. In doing so, I provide a glimpse into how space and land were historically and often legally denied to certain racial and ethnic groups who remain marginalized and traumatized today. I focus on two vulnerable groups who often deal with unstable and unsafe housing: female victims of domestic violence, particularly those who must leave the home of their abusers, and unaccompanied youth, particularly those who struggle with gender identity. I analyze three common sites of shelter for those experiencing homelessness—"welfare" or "spill-over" hotels, homeless shelters, and tent encampments—an analysis beginning with the situation decades ago and ending with the effects of the 2020–2021 novel coronavirus (COVID-19). Throughout these case studies, I offer my observations of public meetings and symposiums and the substance of my personal interviews with advocates and activists. Finally, I review what public health and public policy representatives as well as the homeless themselves recommend to ease the homelessness crisis.

More specifically, I examine the frequent rejection of night homeless shelter options by people experiencing homelessness in favor of temporary tent encampments, and I find that city and state statutes and ordinances have, in some cases, contributed to or criminalized homelessness. Also, I analyze how intersectionality, such as age, race, sexual and gender identity, and ethnicity, plays a part in understanding homelessness. To accomplish this, I argue that metaphorical language can function as a tool of systemic oppression by reducing individuality and leading to a biased consideration of people experiencing homelessness. Scholars of rhetoric and communication studies, with whom I identify, often analyze such strategic uses of language, especially as it pertains to the stigmatization of marginalized groups. I find that those who struggle with homelessness at times adopt these same strategies to expose, resist, or impose that bias onto others. Finally, I use as a primary source of data and analysis the personal blogs and other social media as well as the published memoirs created by people who are struggling or have struggled with homelessness. (See Appendix A for a list of such social media sources and my citation style in referring to them.) My overall objective is to capture what people experiencing homelessness, such as Todd Murphy, want us to understand about their situation as expressed in these primarily unmediated and unmoderated genres. Thus, I attend to rhetorician Jenny Rice's (2021) caution "against theorizing a single universal subject at the experience of all others who are denied entrance into the single public sphere" (44; see also Warner 1991). I conclude that only by recognizing homelessness as a complex crisis and by attending to the diverse voices of those who experience homelessness can we begin to remedy this crisis.

THEORETICAL STANCE

Although the theoretical perspectives that scholars from a variety of fields have created to understand stigmatization of marginal groups as well as creation of spatial boundaries to contain these groups, my primary goal is to use these theoretical perspectives to illuminate how homelessness is rightly considered a social, economic, and public health and policy issue. Again, my initial means of interpretation is often rhetorical, such as was rhetorician Amy Koerber's (2018b) as she exposed the enthymematic result of modern medicine's focus on female hormones, a focus that shaped the frequent belief that "women's bodies are fundamentally irregular and much more difficult to manage than men's bodies" (183). Such beliefs, found Koerber, were "embedded in the same expert scientific discourses that we have always treated as neutral and authoritative in the Western tradition" (188). Similarly, our attitudes toward people experiencing homelessness often reflect the biases that link homelessness to personal laziness and incompetence rather than to the failure of socioeconomic systems. And so, I agree with Koerber's (2018a) stance that rhetorical analysis "should accomplish multiple shifts, disruptions, and reorientations. After a good rhetorical analysis, the world should never look the same as it did before" (199). Moreover, I believe that scholarship might help us to not only understand but also improve the lives of research participants and specify an effective means of addressing a social problem—a kind of scholarly advocacy or activism.

These two roles, advocacy and activism, are distinct and yet highly related. According to Heather Zoller (2005), particularly from the field of health and medicine, advocacy focuses on education and existing systems and relies on expert knowledge rather than inserting "lay knowledge in expert systems." Activists "tend to engage in direct action," such as challenging the medical paradigm and insisting on "democratic participation in knowledge production" (344; see also Brown et al. 2004; Fabj and Sobnosky 1995). Zoller herself focused primarily on community activism, which can be fostered by scholarly work in a variety of disciplines and research perspectives, work that can help interpret causes and identify solutions that such activists chose as "targets for change" (354). And yet, advocacy might lead to activism and vice versa, and so both stances are not static and seldom silent. (See the second half of Appendix B for a description of my own advocacy and activism on curtailing domestic violence and sexual assault.) In turn, Karma Chávez (2011) studied the ways in which rhetoric might function within the "enclaves" or spaces into which activist groups initially withdraw publicly to create strategies for their social movements. The two groups that Chávez studied, one that promoted queer rights and the other that supported migrant rights, first interpreted "external rhetorical messages" that were created about them. Then they invented rhetorical strategies to challenge the oppressive rhetoric they encountered, and they created new images for the groups and issues they represented and wanted "to bring into coalition" (3; see also Chávez 2013; Chávez 2015). Thus, I analyze how those experiencing homelessness may follow that same pattern of identifying external messages and then resisting and replacing them.

Throughout this book, I take the stance of both scholar and advocate, hoping that readers will not only learn more about the systemic bias that fuels homelessness but also create or extend their understanding and their own advocacy and activism in addressing homelessness (see, for example, the scholar-advocate stance explained in Propen and Schuster 2008; Schuster 2006). Similarly, Jenny Rice (2012) took the position of advocate in her study of development and public spaces in Austin, Texas. In her book on *Distant Publics*, Rice's goal was "to interrogate the techniques and technologies used to help people see themselves as beings-in-the world. This interrogation is a rhetorician's way to intervening firsthand in the public crises around us" (6). And as Rice noted, Elenore Long (2008) proposed that rhetoricians could serve as activists "to improve the quality of public deliberations about our local and global spaces that are increasingly under pressure from thoughtless, harmful, and simply excessive development" (7). Therefore, Rice herself found that "interrogating the underlying discourses of public subjectivities is the best way rhetoricians can intervene into actual crises" (15). I share this goal, but my initial challenge was to uncover the voices of people experiencing homelessness who could provide a close and personal look at the crisis, voices from which we may in turn learn.

We learn from these voices that the tools of systemic oppression, such as stigmatization of people experiencing homelessness, are often openly realized and either accepted or resisted and may lead not only to intergroup conflict but also to intragroup conflict, power struggles, and even violence. We learn that spatial boundaries that exclude people experiencing homelessness become social, political, and legal tools to maintain capitalism, privacy, and sometimes ill-perceived safety among the empowered. Social media, such as personal blogs, and published memories, capture the unmediated and unmoderated voices of those experiencing homelessness—and become sites of resistance and of personal testimony and even confession about the plight of the homeless. In his memoir, for example, Murphy offered a simple but memorable description of how newspaper was "a great insulator on cold nights," using the third person point of view to describe his own efforts: "You could line your sleeping bag, but he usually stepped behind a dumpster, dropped his pants, but not his long underwear, wrapped newspaper around his outer thighs between his pants and his 'skivvies,' and left it at that" (46). Such was one of Murphy's contributions to our understanding of the harsh circumstances of life without stable housing. Ultimately, I try to offer a complex and nuanced understanding of homelessness but argue that through stigmatizing the marginalized "other" and creating spatial boundaries to exclude and contain that other, we have not only created but also maintain the homelessness crisis—but with this understanding and to use Koerber's (2018a) terminology again, I hope that after reading this book the homeless world will never look the same as it did before.

THE VOICES OF PEOPLE EXPERIENCING HOMELESSNESS

Authors of scholarly and popular sources have covered the history of homelessness in specific cities, such as did journalist Antero Pietila (2010) who studied homelessness in Baltimore, Maryland; they have described how men, women, and families experiencing homelessness select different places to shelter, such as did sociologists Jason Wasserman and Jeffrey Clair (2010); they have suggested how to curtail homelessness, such as did Donald Burnes (2016), founder of the Burnes Center on Housing and Homelessness Research at the University of Denver; and they have noted how some people experiencing homelessness have resisted spatial segregation, such as did sociologist Talmage Wright (1992). Some authors have examined in depth the causes of homelessness, such as did sociologist Matthew Desmond (2016) in his analysis of evictions, while others have described the lives of particular individuals experiencing homelessness, such as did attorney and law scholar

Jody Raphael (2000) and journalist Lauren Sandler (2020). Finally, organizations and agencies have broken down the statistics on homelessness by type and population throughout the nation or in certain locations (see, for example, the Coalition for the Homeless 2020 report on New York City).

These studies are excellent in their coverage, but as Wright (1992) lamented, although many of these researchers have recognized that the individual stories of people experiencing homelessness provide an essential way to contextualize statistics and demographics, homelessness remains

> an objective reality for many Americans, and indeed for many people in other countries. It is also a social construction that has functioned in policy circles by displacing attention away from social inequality, social-economic justice, and property relations. This has been accomplished through the academic separation of homeless bodies and in "speaking for the other." Rarely have the voices of the homeless . . . been allowed to speak for themselves. (299)

In turn, Randall Amster (2008), a professor of Peace Studies and Social Thought, offered that "the homeless are generally viewed as a problem in need of a solution." This perspective portrays "the homeless as either defective units to be replaced or removed, or as unwitting victims of social circumstances," which results in "stripping homeless individuals of rights of agency and autonomy" (7). Again, throughout this book, I extend our understanding of homelessness by listening to the voices of individuals experiencing homelessness, particularly those voices expressed in social media and in memoirs—allowing, as much as possible, people experiencing homelessness "to speak for themselves." I avoid referring to people experiencing homelessness as one entity or essentializing them as "the homeless"—because their voices remind me to celebrate their individuality. I agree, for example, with the perspective of communication scholars Barbara Schneider and Chaseten Remillard (2013) "that language shapes what can be known and therefore what can be done about a problem like homelessness and the people who experience it. That is, language does much more than simply describe the world; it constructs the world as we come to know it" (95–96). Bloggers, memoir writers, and even video storytellers or interviewees often describe their experiences while being homeless—their individual challenges and decisions, the causes of their situations and the effects on their wellbeing, their desire to protect or reconnect with their families, their search for stable shelter, and, for some, their struggles with mental illness and substance addiction. As expressed in these sources, their voices are usually unaltered and conveyed in a personal and direct tone.

Sociologist Forrest Stuart (2016), on the one hand, astutely studied the theoretical "criminology of the other," a social stance that "essentializes differences" and sustains the perspective that if the so-called other cannot reintegrate into society by making the right choices, then that other will not only remain quarantined or exiled but will also "deserve to be punished harshly" (122). Certainly, Forrest exposed a dominant social perspective that might essentialize those experiencing homelessness. On the other hand, T. Ray Verteramo (2019) revealed in her memoir how she came to be living on the streets of Las Vegas:

> I believe stupidity is the main cause of homelessness. Making a bad choice like committing a crime, drugs, or not leaving a bad partner can land you on the street. Bad legislation, dumb housing rules, discrimination can floor you, too. . . . I'm guilty of stupid. I'm guilty of working without pay for . . . too long. I'm guilty of not pressing through my education fast enough to be able to live. I'm guilty of putting sentimental value above practical means. I'm guilty of putting food above everything else. (126–27)

Verteramo not only identified the primary reason she thought that many people find themselves without stable housing, but she also reflected on why she ended up on the streets or "living rough," such as by not pursing her education or a well-paying job and by being so hungry that food took precedence over everything else. She assumed responsibility for making these choices, and in reading her memoir thoroughly, we learn so much more. Verteramo remembered, for example, the worst parts of her childhood: "It's a toss-up between getting molested by my dad's former best friend and just crying alone in my crib over and over and over until my [m]other reluctantly picked me up as if I was bothering her" (56). Such early neglect and abuse contributed to her loss of agency and most likely contributed to her becoming homeless. When people experiencing homelessness share these very personal histories, we understand much more about their challenges and needs.

Similarly, in her video interview seventeen-year-old Michelle explained the reason that she became homeless and then reminded her viewers that every such story is unique: "My family and I were trying to escape an injurious situation, so we left the home that we were in. There are situations that can cause homelessness—you really can't stereotype it. You really can't" ("Homeless Teenagers" May 26, 2011). These individual voices help us understand the complex and unique causes and problems of being homeless. However, as blogger "George" (B9) related, "you can find a bowl of soup or a sweater, but try getting somebody to listen to you for 5 minutes. . . . Telling one's story is a very important part of the healing journey." According to George, we do best when we "provide a listening ear" (8.20.2006). George maintained his blog from March 2005 to September 2017 and told of being homeless since age fifteen. Although he lived primarily on the streets, he went on to graduate from a Canadian university and joined a project to count the number of individuals experiencing homelessness in that location. Thus, throughout this book, I try to find and refine that "listening ear" by conveying how individuals, such as Ray, Michelle, and George, use social media and published memoirs—as well as what such individuals can achieve via these media, how they envision their readers and viewers, and how they may heal from the effects of homelessness by expressing their voices.

Overall, analyzing the voices of people experiencing homelessness through social media and memoirs becomes a type of rhetorical listening. As Krista Ratcliffe (2005) explained such a strategy, rhetorical listening is a matter of understanding another's cultural and social logics rather than focusing on already shared interests in order to accept, judge, or persuade the other. The goal of rhetorical listening is to understand how others hold a belief or have made choices given their personal circumstances, what Ratcliffe called a "shared way of reasoning" (33). In turn, Elizabeth Britt (2018) distinguished among three types of rhetorical listening: identification, disidentification, and nonidentification. Identification, or establishing a shared way of reasoning or understanding another's personal logics, may be the most difficult for any researcher whose participants are experiencing homelessness, although some listeners or researchers may position themselves by relating their own encounters with poverty or unstable housing. (See my own such positioning in Appendix B.) Disidentification leads to the unfortunate conclusion that the researcher has nothing or little in common with her research participants, and therefore she might dismiss or even judge them. Nonidentification, however, can help the researcher question any initial rejection of or miscommunication with the other person and "lead a listener to new identification" and understanding (75–76). Thus, admitting that "gaps" exist in identification can be productive, as Ratcliffe (2005) put it (75). Blogger "Patrick" (B3), for example, recommended that when someone complains about "homeless people," the response should be "'which homeless people?' [And] point out that there are many types of homeless people, and that he is over generalizing, which is a sign of being disingenuous" (6.23.2015). Patrick began his blog in 2002 and ended it in 2016. In his fifties, Patrick was a native of California, who usually functioned well even though he was on the Asperger's spectrum and struggled to develop the skills necessary to live independently. Nonetheless Patrick offered his readers insight into the lives of people experiencing homelessness. I aimed for such productive nonidentification throughout this book, the position that provides an opportunity for understanding, for altering one's vision of the world of homelessness, and for contributing to necessary systemic change.

STIGMATIZATION AND MARGINALIZATION

Quite simply, stigmatization involves biased othering, essentializing, or marginalizing an individual or a group, often to justify distinction from or discrimination by so-called normal or legitimate citizens, including exclusion from social and economic resources. Stigmatization restricts and haunts people experiencing homelessness, so much so that they frequently assume that they are failed and lesser people. They may, however, also rebel against such stigmatization, or they may themselves marginalize or stigmatize other individuals and groups experiencing homelessness. Verteramo (2019), for example, contrasted people experiencing homelessness in her memoir: "There are homeless and then there are *hooomeless* [sic]. The former are those like myself; victims and architects of their own demise. The latter are slathering in the filth of their bodies, wandering around aimlessly in someone else's clothes, further and further away from someone else's love or memory" (emphasis in original, 10). Therefore, the impulse to separate oneself from the other seems almost universal—either from another group or within a group. Moreover, inheriting such a stigma diminishes one's credibility, that trustworthy identity assigned to an individual or group, such that the very term "homeless" becomes a metaphorical term or rhetorical trope to assign any number of negative characteristics to people experiencing homelessness and to dismiss their individuality. The rhetorical strategy of stigmatization limits our understanding of and sympathy for people experiencing homelessness and curtails systemic efforts to help them.

Definitions and Classifications of Stigma

Aristotle laid the groundwork for our understanding of stigma by way of his studies of *ethos*, more specifically the credible stance cultivated by the virtuous habits of the speaker or rhetor and exhibited through that rhetor's display of practical wisdom, expertise, and goodwill toward an audience (*Ethics* 1103a17; *Rhetoric* 1356a4). This stance can be endangered or lost in a variety of ways, including stigmatization. Sociologist and social psychologist Erving Goffman (1963), for example, is well known for drawing renewed attention to the rhetorical strategy of stigmatization as reducing "a whole and usual person to a tainted, discounted one" and therefore "deeply discrediting" that person by assigning him or her a negative virtual or social identity (3). Goffman listed three different types of stigma, all of which pertain to how people experiencing homelessness may be stigmatized: (1) "abominations of the body," such as a physical deformity; (2) "blemishes" of character, such as weak will; and (3) dishonesty, such as a "known record" of unacceptable behavior (4). Thus, according to Goffman's categories, people experiencing homelessness might be seen frequently as having poor hygiene (an abomination of the body), lacking the will to remedy their situation through employment (blemishes of character), and succumbing to substance abuse, panhandling, and theft (dishonesty).

Epidemiologist and sociologist Bruce Link and research scientist Jo Phelan (2001) further sophisticated Goffman's theory by identifying the following sequential components of stigmatization: (1) People "distinguish and label human differences"; (2) dominant cultural beliefs "link labeled persons to undesirable characteristics—to negative stereotypes"; (3) such labeled persons are placed in linked categories "to accomplish some degree of separation of 'us' from 'them'"; (4) labeled persons "experience status loss and discrimination that lead to unequal outcomes"; and finally (5) "stigmatization is entirely contingent on access to social, economic, and political power that allows identification of differentness, the construction of stereotypes, the separation of labeled persons into distinct categories, and the full execution of disapproval, rejection, exclusion, and discrimination" (367). Stigmatizing, therefore, is a tool of power and a reflection of hierarchy—and a common challenge to people experiencing homelessness regardless of the cause of their condition. Specific to Link and Phelan's (2001) third component, separation of us from them, is the phenomenon that "stereotyping can be smoothly accomplished because there is [supposedly] little harm in attributing all manner of bad characteristics to 'them'" (370). And again, excluding others is rationalized and implemented through power and status. Blogger "Lawrence" (B4), for example, in his mid-fifties, had been homeless for thirteen years and had blogged since 2013. He concluded: The sight of a person with a shopping cart who "presents" as homeless

> triggers a kaleidoscope of conflicting ideas and emotions: social inequity, the welfare state, the gap between the rich and the poor, contempt and pity, compassion and revulsion, empathy and fear. . . . Hence, I really believe a major driver behind policies to get homeless people off the street may be that the very sight of us makes non-homeless people so uncomfortable. (6.29.2014)

Thus, stigmatization not only includes the interrelated components that Goffman (1963) and Link and Phelan (2001) proposed but also masks the disturbing reminder that the housed can easily become homeless.

Such disturbance is also evident in not only such potential similarity but also the tenuous and rather odd contrast between those labeled homeless and those labeled poor. On the one hand, in a national survey regarding attitudes toward poverty in the United States, sociologist Joe Feagin (1975) found his respondents stressed that, overall, housed impoverished people displayed poor money management; lack of effort, ability, and talent; and loose morals and substance abuse. On the other hand, Phelan and Link along with Robert Moore and Ann Stueve (1997) confirmed that, despite these similar aspects of stigmatization, people experiencing homelessness were usually viewed more severely than housed poor people for the following reasons:

> Because many homeless people live in public spaces, homelessness is often more visible and more disruptive than other forms of poverty; because of the difficulties involved in cleaning and grooming themselves, many homeless people also may be aesthetically unappealing. Moreover, homelessness is associated in the public mind with other stigmatizing conditions such as mental illness and substance abuse. (325; see also Link, Phelan, Stueve, Moore, Bresnahan, and Struening 1995).

However, most of Feagin's survey respondents failed to stress the systemic causes of either poverty or homelessness. These respondents, for example, did not recognize the effects of low wages, lack of employment opportunities, or racial discrimination on homelessness as well as on poverty. And again, those experiencing homelessness were more stigmatized than the housed poor, often on the basis of personal appearance and perceived mental abnormalities. In turn, communication studies scholar Melanie Loehwing (2010) offered an analysis of the film *Reversal of Fortune*, the story of a man who was given $100,000 and still does not escape homelessness. Loehwing concluded that the popular discourse of homelessness

> is blind to the ways in which structural inequalities contribute to the lack of universal housing, that stifles opportunities for identification between homeless and housed individuals, and that tacitly lends support to the continued disenfranchisement and exclusion of people experiencing homelessness from a shared political future. (382)

Although systemic failures plague both groups, housed people experiencing poverty are viewed more positively than poor people experiencing homelessness, and critics and observers may fail to identify poverty as a primary cause of homelessness.

Additionally, individuals experiencing homelessness may face a kind of dissociation as a result of their extreme stigmatization—not only an acceptance of how they are othered but also a self-stigmatization. As Verteramo (2019) said in her memoir about her own homelessness, "I have a real problem with self-sabotage, whether it be illness or just me . . . simply because I just don't believe I deserve anything better than [simply] 'good'" (221). Thus, psychologists Patrick Corrigan, Amy Kerr, and Lisa Knudsen (2005) distinguished between public stigmatization, which is based on negative stereotypes, and self-stigmatization, which is based on internalization of that public stigma (see also Schneiger and Remillard 2013). Those who self-stigmatize, according to Goffman (1963), may struggle to learn, accept, and even imitate the "normal point of view," even though they themselves feel "disqualified" according to that point of view (80). People experiencing homelessness may also attempt to "pass" as normal by hiding their home-less condition, another type of acceptance of their stigmatization. Blogger "Ralph" (B7), for example, advised others who were homeless:

> Holding down a job may require that you camouflage your homelessness, though, depending on what kind of work you do. If you are a white collar worker or a service industry worker, you must keep your secret hidden. . . . Get a mailbox at a UPS store or similar establishment, and use that as your home address. . . . Keep clean, wear a smile, and market the skills you have. You can add finishing touches to your look by keeping a nice haircut, and getting a $6 manicure at your nearest nail salon. (10.28.2004)

Ralph blogged between 2004 and 2011, and his blog garnered several reader responses as he described some advantages of homelessness, including the sense of freedom that Murphy expressed in his memoir. His advice to his readers included everything from how to maintain hygiene while on the road to how to address periods of personal depression. Thus, as Goffman (1963) pointed out, people may not only develop "in-group alignments," such as with other individuals experiencing homelessness, but also attempt to see themselves according to "out-group alignment" (112), by passing or imitat-ing the so-called normal and acceptable in the way that Ralph described. Goffman predicted, however, that the stress caused by balancing these two alignments might lead to a "psychiatric" condition (114). All in all, people experiencing homelessness are confronted with stigmatization that is very difficult to resist, to accept, or to hide, and that may contribute to the stress of being homeless in the first place.

Rhetorical Tropes and Metaphors

Rhetorical tropes, such as those used in stigmatization, consist of figurative language, including metaphors, similes, allegories, analogies, hyperboles, paradoxes, puns, rhetorical questions, satires, and synecdoche. In deviating from the common or main use of language, tropes often endure and thus support specific appeals and means of persuasion to an audience, long after the first use of the trope. "Homelessness" itself, for example, often serves as a trope for moral, economic, and personal failure, or as Wright (1992) amplified this concept, "Homeless persons wearing soiled clothing are a trope for the margins of society, a symbol of abjection, or the combination of revulsion and intense attraction" (71). Rhetoricians of science have focused primarily on the metaphor as the primary persuasive strategy in scientific thinking and development. Jeanne Fahnestock (1999), for example, proposed that metaphors and analogies have long dominated scientific argument and pedagogy; thus, the trope was a primary persuasive strategy in science. In his study of metaphor in the multidisciplinary scientific think tank at the Santa Fe Institute, Ken Baake (2003) identified the heuristic power of the metaphor in science and argued that such metaphors generated and controlled scientific practice. In turn, Timothy Giles (2007) found that the metaphor was also "communal" as it was "passed from scientist to scientist, from groups of scientists to groups of scientists" (2). Although the metaphor was "epistemologically generative," according to Giles, it could also misdirect science and stagnate scientific thinking (6). A trope, particularly the metaphor, is a powerful and assumptive directive of cognition as well as acceptance or rejection of alternative thinking.

In turn, rhetoricians of health and medicine, such as Lora Arduser (2013), have proposed that critical metaphor analysis can be "emancipatory" by examining "prevailing social problems" and by highlighting the perspectives of those who live with a challenging condition or situation (97). In her study of the online diabetes community of TuDiabetes (https://tudiabetes. org), Arduser found that "control" metaphors often alluded to such illness as battles, wars, storms, and journeys and were imposed upon people living with diabetes—and countering these metaphors could expose stigmatization and marginalization among those living with and being treated for diabetes. Overall, the metaphors or tropes have the potential to control and marginalize the other, and examining them can illuminate the strategies of systemic oppression that challenge marginalized people. In his study of such figurative language, Jonathan Culler (1978) reconciled two primary functions of rhetoric, the second of which I explore more throughout this book: (1) persuading and (2) creating, conveying, and discovering tropes. Culler noted that the first function of rhetoric, persuasive strategies or discourse have "the power to produce events: events of persuasion, understanding, revelation." The second function, rhetorical analysis, "attempts to account for these events, and it does so by identifying structures, patterns, figures [including tropes], which then constitute rhetoric" (608). The rhetorical trope of homelessness may constitute social discourse about homelessness, but it might also stall personal and systemic ways to address the problem. The very recognition of the trope among people experiencing homelessness and their advocates—and I hope among the readers of this book—may also set the stage for productive change.

To realize such change, it is necessary to recognize and admit that homelessness, as a rhetorical trope, represents all that is perceived as wrong with such individuals or groups, the result of stigmatization, as conveyed and examined within the comments and stories by and about people experiencing homelessness. Professor of social work James Forte (2002), for example, examined a newspaper campaign that used homelessness as a rhetorical trope to justify the closing of a homeless shelter. Using a social constructionist approach, Forte found that those opposing the shelter depicted people experiencing homelessness as "panhandlers, drunks, and drug addicts" or described the health hazards of having such a shelter, warning of a potential "alarming surge of tuberculosis" because "one drop of sputum from a sneeze, or a cough, or a mere conversation can infect many people in the proximity to the carrier" (151). Thus, as Ratcliffe (2000) noted, "when bodies are troped and tropes are embodied" (89), personal and cultural change may be limited. These tropes, concluded Ratcliffe, may so inform our own attitudes and actions to "foster stasis" (98; see also Cohn 2016; Van Ness 2001). And, such stasis prevents understanding and deconstruction of the trope and, as a result, curtails productive change in our social responses to people experiencing homelessness.

Individuals experiencing homelessness, however, offer their own rhetorical tropes to "claim legitimacy" or establish their own "subject position," as communication studies scholars Corey Anton and Valerie Peterson (2003) defined such a position—a place where "people stand from which to encounter the world" (406–7). Additionally, James Arnt Aune (1983) speculated in his review of rhetorician Kenneth Burke, "Rhetorical strength is seen more fully when a writer transumes a previous trope and makes it his/her own" (339). Thus, people experiencing homelessness may expose the tropes used to discredit them as a first step to establish their own subject position or personal authority. Dick Murphy-Scott (2019) in his published blog, for example, used a metaphor for how his own homeless condition was unfairly perceived by the empowered "normal": "I am a leaf in the breeze, not even worthy of note as you step on me" (1.15.2017; note that although Murphy-Scott's blog was eventually published, he used dates rather than page numbers throughout). Similarly, in his memoir, Jesse Thistle (2019) used a metaphor to describe how he was discounted: "I am now one of those shadow people" (117). Todd Murphy (2018), however, used a somewhat unique trope—a chiastic inversion, or a reversal of the order of words, particularly a parallelism—to challenge a common belief about homelessness: "People are more willing to believe the myth of the 'rags to riches' than the truth that riches can turn into rags" (100). Even though they did not identify this language as such, Murphy-Scott, Thistle, and Murphy recognized how their stigmatization might be expressed in and maintained by rhetorical tropes—tropes often difficult for them to counter or overcome, and yet such recognition of these tropes seemed an initial step to resist discrimination and othering. In summary, as blogger George emphasized, "Homelessness is a CIRCUMSTANCE, not a characteristic" (emphasis in original, 4.21.2013).

Finally, by calling for individualization, bloggers, memoir writers, and video interviewees and narrators attempt to deconstruct and refute the tropes that reinforce their rhetorical disabilities as well as their subsequent stigmatization for being homeless. As Michael Gaulden (2017) said in his memoir about growing up homeless, "When the impoverished are together no one can see individuals. All they see is darkness. All they see is, 'the homeless.' I grew up in that darkness" (33). Similarly, a homeless girl who had lived in fifty-seven different foster homes pointed out in her video interview, "People walk around and look down on you. Look through our eyes. . . . We are not even after money; we are looking for acceptance" ("Young Homeless Girl" 2013). Both of these young people learned early on that they were invisible because they were homeless. And so, in her published memoir, Rose Lamatt (2011) called for understanding of the circumstances of "homelessness": "Nothing you can call your own, nothing that's yours, to cook your meals on, no table of your own, to eat meals off, no bed of your own, to sleep in. No door of your own. I want them to read my words, and listen to my voice, and *help*" (emphasis in original, 237). Lamatt spent much of her memoir describing her life in a women's shelter as a consequence of not being able to pay medical bills for a necessary surgery, not being able to cover her rent, and not being able to take care of herself given persistent dizziness and inability to pay for a restorative surgery. People experiencing homelessness, such as Lamatt, often call for understanding and help, but the first step to their agency or subject position may be a recognition of their own stigmatization and marginalization.

Kakoethos or Lack of Credibility

Illuminating my study of stigmatization and marginalization are not only the concept of *ethos* but also *kakoethos*, the perceived lack of credibility of the speaker or writer, in particular the barriers that prevent audiences from accepting a rhetor's strategies to establish credibility. According to Jenell Johnson (2010) in her rhetorical study of the stigma of mental illness, for example, stigmatization may not only subtract from a speaker's *ethos*, but it may also create *kakoethos*, a kind of spoiled *ethos* or anti-*ethos*—in other words, "rhetorical disability" (461). Thus, according to Johnson, "Stigma's defining characteristic [as identified by Aristotle] was to render its bearer's bad character permanently visible," perhaps again by marks on the body or by a perceived threat to community values (463–64). And so, as memoir writer

Murphy (2018) described his own homeless identity, he was "an untouchable; a pariah. He knew it, and he tried not to let his shadow fall on a yuppie's food, lest it be polluted" (86).

Along with Johnson (2010), a number of other scholars in the area of rhetoric of health and medicine have explored *kakoethos*, particularly regarding those living with a physical and mental disability, traits often assigned to people experiencing homelessness. According to Elisabeth Miller (2019), for example, former Governor of New Jersey Chris Christie encountered *kakoethos* because of "fat stigma," which was rhetorically disabling for him because of the cultural messages regarding the obesity epidemic. At the time, being overweight was linked to individual failure, failing health, and even lack of morality. Specifically, said Miller, "Rhetorical disability, and rhetoric in general, help to reveal how this individual framing perpetuates stigma— and the implications of that stigma—for individuals perceived to have abnormal bodies and minds" (67)—and as such those without persuasive and explanatory skills are judged incompetent and untrustworthy (see also Lewis et al. 2011). Similarly, Nicole Quackenbush (2011) explored the rhetorical performance of actor and activist Michael J. Fox, a performance that allowed him to "speak both *as* stigma—because his rhetorical issues from and through his body as he experiences Parkinson's disease—and *of* stigma—because Fox performed disability not just to provide an exigency for research into cures but also to challenge the cultural norms that dehumanize the disabled subject" (emphasis in original). In particular, according to Quackenbush, Fox spent several years passing as nondisabled, but during that time he experienced not ease or escape but instead "an embodied submersion in fear, pain, and psychic damage" because of the social pressure to pass as so-called normal. Even after Fox revealed his struggles with the disease, he faced possible *kakoethos* because some viewers thought his physical movements distracted from his message about disability. These viewers speculated as to whether Fox purposely exaggerated those movements or had deliberately not taken medication to control them in order to stress the effects of his condition and so to support his message about needed research on Parkinson's disease. Moreover, as much as stigmatization may be based on real or perceived physical disability, stigmatization based on mental disabilities or challenges also may lead to *kakoethos*. Johnson (2010) herself, for example, explored how those diagnosed with mental illness experience *kakoethos*—or a perceived bad character based on their challenges to communicate.

Finally, Cathryn Molloy (2019), from the perspective of disability studies and rhetoric of health and medicine, identified how bias contributes to *kakoethos*. In particular, Molloy distinguished between *implicit bias*, or the prejudice against or for a particular group that a person holds without conscious awareness, and *anchoring bias*, or the reluctance to consider alternative approaches to a problem or diagnosis "even when new evidence suggests alternative etiologies" (see also Molloy 2015). In fact, according to Molloy, both *ethos* and *kakoethos* are based on bias of some sort, and neither are static but are "constantly in the state of being made and remade" (3). It is anchoring bias, according to Molloy (2019), that is more difficult to alter because it may have "origins in racial/ethnic, gender, and/or socioeconomic status judgments" (31). However, what Molloy calls recuperative *ethos* holds the potential for "displays of astuteness" that include "social insight, displays of experiential knowledge, and references to book and scholarly knowledges" (125). The experiential knowledge, offered by people experiencing homelessness such as memoir writer Murphy, include what Molloy calls "valuable sets of life experiences—incidences from which they have undergone significant personal growth and out of which they have gotten new forms of knowledge that would otherwise be inaccessible" (126). The voices of those living without stable housing, such as Murphy, often display not only experiential knowledge but also work to counter *kakoethos*, as seen throughout this book.

And so, people experiencing homelessness often readily identify and describe their challenges in ways that they hope their readers or viewers might understand and appreciate—in some cases both to deconstruct stigmatization and to challenge medical authority. In his published blog, for example, Murphy-Scott (2019) told his readers that his problem was "psychosis and hallucinations": "Modern medicine hasn't advanced to the point where they can find out what exactly is wrong with my brain" (12.27.2018). Instead of accepting stigmatization based on his mental illness, Murphy-Scott accused the medical establishment of causing his problems because of its failure to diagnose and treat him properly. In turn, blogger George speculated that undiagnosed and untreated ADHD "may be one of the largest causes of homelessness" and then explained that this "invisible disability" had caused him to "frequently find myself in awful situations for no real good reason why" (3.13.2015). Not only did George accept his condition, as he told his blog readers, but he also encouraged those readers to laugh with him about it (and so develop a more critical eye), such as in the common intake interviews for social assistance that required documents such as current identification, income tax assessment, and a sixty-day bank statement. George concluded, "For many of us, homelessness is the only way to find peace from the relentless demands of systems and institutions" (3.13.2015). Because both the medical and the social services systems failed to help him, blogger Lawrence also summarized the problems with such social assistance programs for his readers. One such program, Lawrence concluded, did not offer much more than "warehousing drug-addicted and mentally ill homeless people at perpetual government expense than actually empowering them to become self-supporting members of society" (11.27.2016). And so, those people experiencing homelessness may struggle to assess their own health and medical complaints but attempt to restore their *ethos* by way of their own experiential knowledge.

SPATIAL SEGREGATION

Spatial formations, including the protean boundaries that separate public and private space, are created by discursive and material efforts and effects. In other words, the ways in which the empowered discuss and designate space—as well as the ways in which the disempowered encounter social, political, and legal discourse about space and the physical presence of that space—dictate who might live, work, play, and rest in space. Moreover, not only the physical objects but also the bodies that occupy a space constitute material rhetoric, a kind of embodiment in that people are invited to make use or are prevented from making use of that space. In her study of the conflicting visions for Wilson Yard, a vacant lot in a diverse Chicago neighborhood called Uptown, rhetorician Candice Rai (2016) proposed that Wilson Yard became a metaphor for democracy and "took on a powerful force all its own because people with very different sensibilities invested it with their own contradictory dreams, evoking it to fight for justice as they understood it, and twisting the metaphor this way and that to accommodate various uses" (5). This force and conflict were both rhetorical, according to Rai, and related to materiality—bodies, structures, locations, and space—out of which shared meanings were invested, facilitated, inspired, grown, debated, and/or inhibited. Rai examined how topoi or stock formulas such as tropes and metaphors were used to debate the possibility of affordable housing being built in Wilson Yard. In turn, new media scholar Jeff Rice (2012) defined topoi as strategies to "maintain commonality, predictability, expectation" (11). Thus, the topoi, as expressed by way of tropes and used to support affordable housing in Uptown, identified such housing as a democratic right to help eliminate the systemic inequality produced and perpetuated by capitalism. In contrast, the topoi used to oppose affordable housing included the visual evidence of poverty as the primary cause of the deterioration of the neighborhood overall. Thus, spaces inhabit and convey meaning and are dynamic and often disputed.

In turn, communication studies scholar Greg Dickinson (2020) built upon the exploration of space and rhetoric as Raka Shome (2003) proposed: "Space is not merely a backdrop . . . against which the communication of politics occurs. Rather, it needs to be recognized as a central component of that communication" (40). And so, Dickinson himself concluded, "Writing about material places whether sublime, quotidian [or concrete], or somewhere in between, localizes our attention, demands that we critically evaluate power, and requires that we think carefully about bodies, selves, others, and identity" (300). Thus, space, place, power, and *ethos* are coupled, and rhetorical analysis explores and exposes that coupling. Moreover, movement within places and through spaces is a form of "everyday rhetoric" (301) where spatiality and the body are "absolutely connected," according to Dickinson (303; see also Bachelard 1992; Code 1995; Mountford 2001; Mountford 2003; Ruddick 1995). Throughout my study of the spatial segregation of people experiencing homelessness, I focus on the places in which such people might dwell, such as homeless shelters or tent encampments, as well as the public and private spaces from which they are excluded not only because of their habits and appearances but also because of the tropes that essentialize and marginalize them. I necessarily identify with what Dickinson called "rhetorical critics of space" who "do their work by exploring" physical structures or places, in my case homeless shelters and tent encampments, and "the spatial practices these environments encode, enable, and constrain" (302), such as the rules that regulate bodily movement of those who seek refuge in homeless shelters and the city ordinances that exclude these bodies from public spaces.

Rhetorician Carole Blair (1999) provided a heuristic for examining these material components of place and space, suggesting that such components could be read as "texts": "(1) What is the significance of the text's material existence? (2) What are the apparatuses and degrees of durability displayed by the text? (3) What are the text's modes or possibilities of reproduction or preservation? (4) What does the text do to (or with, or against) other texts? (5) How does the text act on people?" (23). French Marxist theorist Henri Lefebvre (1991) had proposed that instead of approaching these material components as text, they should be considered texture, "made up of a usually rather large space covered by networks or webs," including "a specific or indefinite multiplicity of meanings, a shifting hierarchy in which now one, now another meaning comes momentarily to the force, and by means of—and for sake of—a particular action" (222). To understand the material rhetoric that people experiencing homelessness encounter, we must add the powerful voices and actions of those who have stable housing in private space and those who promote businesses in public spaces by way of spatial boundaries. In his memoir, for example, Murphy (2018) described in detail how physical barriers were created to dislodge homeless bodies and exclude them from particular spaces: "Any ledge that was the right height to sit on had turned hostile. Now they had metal strips with ragged teeth so it was painful to sit on them. Now there were cobblestones embedded in the concrete beneath the highway overpasses, making it impossible to sleep there" (165). Also, blogger Lawrence concluded that a wall of interlocking concrete blocks laid alongside a thoroughfare was meant "to deter" people experiencing homelessness from camping there (11.13.2018). These structures act as durable and significant material texts (or textures) meant not only to displace people experiencing homelessness but also to make them invisible to those who travel on the thoroughfares and walk the streets—and to justify that invisibility. Thus, two women in their video interview described how a simple and temporary structure took on great significance: "All we have is a tent, and that's some place to call home" ("Escaping" March 3, 2016). For these women experiencing homelessness, the existence of that tent not only signified home but also countered any actions that prevented them from resting elsewhere.

Finally, spatial boundaries reflect attempts to contain or confine this homeless population, attempts designed to ease the fears of dominant social, economic, and political factions. However, as with hunger, cold or heat, and personal safety, finding acceptable and permitted space in which to rest constitutes survival for people experiencing homelessness. Memoir writer Liz Murray (2010), for example, explained how available and sanctioned space determined much of her existence while homeless: "I never get too comfortable in my accommodations. . . . I am afraid all the time lately. I wonder where I will sleep tomorrow—at another friend's apartment, on the train, in some stairwell?" (2). Murray was homeless on the streets from the age of fifteen but eventually returned to high school and won a scholarship to Harvard. As public spaces become more and more restricted, however, young Murray's options become uncertain. Thus, how people experiencing homelessness are restricted by spatial boundaries provides a context in which to understand their thoughts and actions.

As Wright (1992) concluded, "Space is produced and space is consumed" (46). People experiencing homelessness may occupy a particular location, such as under a bridge or on a sidewalk, and that space becomes, even temporarily, a place in which to sleep or even to form a community. However, according to Danielle Endres and Samantha Senda-Cook, scholars in the field of environmental studies (2011), that space is "semi-bounded, a combination of material and symbolic qualities, and embodied" (259). In essence, designation of space, either open or closed to those experiencing homelessness, refers to "a more general notion of how society and social practice are regulated (and sometimes disciplined) by spatial thinking (for example, capitalist modes of production or gendered notions of private and public spaces)" (260; see also de Certeau 1984, who proposed that users could find their voice and agency by using space in unpredictable ways; Foucault 1986, who identified heterotopias as spaces that were not freely accessible, that required permission to enter, and that expressed the state's power to manage social life; and McKerrow 1999, who concluded that space was so political and ideological that it reflected many ideologies). Space, then, results from and creates stigmatization and marginalization, and in the midst of economic, political, and social entities that determine the use of space, access to safe and permissible places are of primary concern to people experiencing homelessness. Memoir writer Verteramo (2019) distinguished between the housed and the homeless, between the privileged and the disadvantaged: "Seriously, it wasn't the Mercedes or the Tiffany jewelry that was the luxury; it's personal space. That's what it's all about. The rich just have more of it" (164). And, as Dickinson (2020) cautioned, "Keeping our attention steadily engaged on the organization of power arrayed in, though, and on space gives rhetorical criticism a crucial mode for engaging the materiality of our world. Power, bodies, movement, the environment are not accidental or tertiary concerns for rhetorical critics of space; instead they take center stage" (308). Space becomes a necessary construction and possession, as important as food and clothing, to those experiencing homelessness, and a necessary perspective for those who do research on homelessness.

Classification and Categorization of Space

Because the survival of people experiencing homelessness is complicated by access to physical space and because those who are housed and/or empowered restrict that access to space, scholars have attempted to categorize how individuals and groups are controlled in their interactions with space. Quite simply, public and private spaces are distinct, but as Amster (2008) stated, public spaces are "shrinking or disappearing altogether as they are being privatized and as access is limited" often by redevelopment or gentrification (46). And such privatization of public spaces, noted journalist Shirley Kressel (2000), "enables large-scaled property owners to exclude 'undesirables,' the homeless, the non-shoppers, from places of investment and privilege intended to attract up-scale suburbanites, the urban elite, and tourists with disposable income." Therefore, people experiencing homelessness often have less access to public space but are not welcome in private space.

These spatial boundaries are justified by a belief that they maintain the safety of the housed and empowered. According to sociologists David Snow and Michael Mulcathy (2001),

[T]he growth of the homeless population and its spread into spatial domains traditionally reserved for domiciled citizens and their activities implies a rupture of the spatial bedrock and the associated cultural imagery on which the urban order rests and thus accounts, in large part, for the alarm and unease that many domiciled citizens and officials feel about homelessness. (154)

Snow and Mulcathy studied what they called the sociospatial dynamics of homelessness, a phenomenon represented during a campaign in Tucson,

Arizona, to not only shut down a homeless camp but also to control more strictly people experiencing homelessness. As a result of their study, Snow and Mulcathy identified three categories of space: (1) prime space, which is used by "domiciled citizens for residential, recreational, or navigational purposes," by commercial entrepreneurs, and by politicians and their agents for "political and symbolic purposes"; (2) marginal space, which has little value to most residents, entrepreneurs, and political agents, and so might appear to be abandoned and open to be "ceded, whether intentionally or unwittingly, to the marginalized—that is, to the powerless and property-less"; and (3) transitional space, which has ambiguous use in that it might be populated by either the marginalized or the domiciled citizens, and "sits a buffer" between a marginal area and another that is "more fully prime" (157). When prime space increases and transitional space decreases, people experiencing homelessness are more confined to marginal space. According to these categories, prime space might be reserved for the financially, socially, and politically empowered, but people experiencing homelessness often must cross prime space to get to marginal space, despite the boundaries set up to exclude them and to the alarm of private property owners. In turn, people experiencing homelessness might reject marginal spaces reserved for them, such as homeless shelters, because of lack of freedom and privacy and the ongoing problems with poor food, infestations and disease, restrictive schedules, and aggressive residents in such shelters. Consequently, those experiencing homelessness might set up places such as tent encampments in transitional and generally unstable spaces—or, as Lefebvre (1991) described them, material spaces that suggest symbolic associations, such as freedom, and cause occupants "to form relationships with each other and the space through its structures," such as a supportive community among the people experiencing homelessness who reside there (quoted in Mountford 2001, 49).

Wright (1992) added her own categories of space, based on gentrification or the movement of wealthier people into a poor urban area to improve housing and attract new businesses, a movement that displaces the current residents—or as Wright called it, "the vehicle through which displacement and concentration are accomplished" (92). According to Wright, there are "pleasure spaces," "refuse [pronounced reFUSE] spaces," and "functional spaces." Functional spaces are those through which people move to get to a certain destination. Pleasure spaces "reify social, cultural, and economic inequalities" where people experiencing homelessness are stigmatized and excluded. Refuse spaces are those in which people on the low end of spatial hierarchies are refused services, human rights, dignity, food, shelter, medical care, and such, "often stigmatizing its inhabitants even more than the label *poor* " (emphasis in original, 106). Memoir writer Verteramo (2019) seemed to confirm Wright's contrast of refuse and pleasure spaces, respectively, when she mused, "One can be in the open with not enough space and one can have space and not be open" (250). Overall, these categories of space either reflect or restrict how people experiencing homelessness find a place to rest, and one might question, as did Verteramo, how to balance the benefits of space and resources.

Furthermore, marginal and transitional spaces may be reclaimed for economic or political purposes and therefore become prime space. Blogger George, for example, noted how the designations of space are dynamic rather than static, often to the disadvantage of people experiencing homelessness in his hometown: "Every nook and crannie [sic] on every street downtown has been gated, locked, or is patrolled by security guard companies. It seems that many business owners and municipalities are taking a more active role, cementing up sleeping spots and using any creative method they can to prevent 'undesirables' . . . from 'polluting the landscape.'" George went on to contrast these recently reclaimed spaces to those in the 1980s when "a street sleeper could sneak into a back alleyway, curl up beside a garbage can, and nobody would be the wiser, except maybe the guy who takes the garbage out in the morning" (9.23.2006). Thus, Snow and Mulcathy (2001) confirmed that "social control agents" attempt to contain, displace, and exclude people experiencing homelessness by reducing their visibility and removing them from a place they might have previously used to hang out, panhandle, or simply sleep. Individuals experiencing homelessness, such as blogger George, soon discover how space is fluid but frequently redefined and restricted to their disadvantage. Another important rhetorical event, however, is resistance—conflict over spatial exclusions, repressions, and displacements.

Resistance to Spatial Boundaries

Wright (1992) identified as spatial *exclusion* those actions and events created to keep out certain populations "from particular areas, discourses, narratives, and any given means of communication"; as *repression* those actions or events to forcibly remove, punish, or harass those populations for "occupying space or communication in ways not sanctioned by authority"; and as *displacement* "strategic actions that relocate the causes of conflict from one source to another source that is perceived by authority as less threatening to their interests" (emphasis added, 183). People experiencing homelessness may resist exclusion from a space as well as repression of their voices. Displacement, as defined by Wright, also seems more difficult to identify and analyze—and it may be supported by internalized stigmatization by people experiencing homelessness. Memoir writer Verteramo (2019), for example, commented about the need for homeless encampments, ultimately shifting disputes about space from the empowered to the homeless themselves:

"There are so, so many of us. . . . We have scruples. We have instincts. And sometimes we even have each other. We don't steal another's food. We share our water, our cigarettes, our makeshift instant coffee in warm bottles. *But for space, we fight*" (emphasis added, 168). People experiencing homelessness might fight among themselves for space, not only when space is considered prime and restricted by the empowered, the so-called normal or legitimate citizen, but also when marginal space is taken up by other people experiencing homelessness, in the latter case perhaps a displacement of anger over imposed spatial boundaries and segregation. Moreover, people experiencing homelessness must not only protect their space but also their bodies from those who live and travel among them—again a displacement of stigmatization and marginalization.

As Alayna, a twenty-four-year-old woman who had lived on the streets for five months, conveyed in her video interview, "Living down here, there is not a time when you can be relaxed. You are always on guard because you never know what is going to happen. I have had not only females trying to fight me . . . but I have had men trying to get at me" ("Alayna's Story" November 8, 2016). Moreover, blogger "Norman" (B10) described how conflict and aggression were to be expected among people experiencing homelessness, not faulting the empowered but the homeless themselves: "Don't get me wrong, I'm not saying that I purposefully go looking for fights or I fight because I enjoy it, but on the street if you can't fight even to defend yourself a lot of streeties [sic] target you and make your life very hard to enjoy . . . they will fly of the handle at the merest slight, imagined or real, so violence becomes part of your everyday life . . ." (7.18.2004). Norman was twenty-seven years old when he began his blog and had lived on the streets in Australia since he was six years old. In the banner to his blog, he noted that the blog "chronicles my life journey through foster care, homelessness, drug addiction, prison and my new life off drugs and off the streets" and thus established his authority or *ethos* to speak. The strategies of repression and displacement can become embodied in homeless communities, and violence among people experiencing homelessness may at times seem more threatening than aggression by the empowered and the housed.

Some individuals and groups who experience homelessness, however, more openly and actively resist the discourse and spatial boundaries established by the politically, socially, and economically empowered. As social geographer Jessie Speer (2016) found in her study of Fresno, California, homeless communities today are "challenging dominant notions of the meaning of home, [even] while state intervention continues to police these expressions of domesticity" (521). Speer calls the action of "home making and remaking," a necessarily fluid rather than static process and space itself, albeit marginal, as "central to the experience of homelessness" (519). However, so-called legitimate homeowners might see homeless encampments as "illegitimate" because they are appropriated from prime and/or public space rather than owned, and therefore these encampments are considered to be "challenging the legitimacy of capitalistic private property and the distinction between public and private space" (524). And, yet even these conflicting stances are complicated by individual experiences shared by people experiencing homelessness. Memoir writer Leo Gnawa (2016), for example, resisted an eviction notice placed on his donated tent in a park in Washington, DC. He read the notice to mean, "I had to move my tent and all belongings by the date on the notice, otherwise the city Department of public works would remove my belongings, which would be considered trash" (59). Gnawa never moved his tent and so challenged this threat to his home, a threat that the city never carried out. Moreover, blogger Lawrence (B4) critiqued what appeared to him to be arbitrary laws both in Los Angeles and in parts of Canada. These laws regulated how, when, and where people experiencing homelessness could store personal belongings and erect tents and makeshift shelters in public spaces. One such law dictated that tents "must be taken down between the hours of 6:00 a.m. and 9:00 p.m., except when it's raining or the temperature is below 10 degrees Celsius," a regulation he called "an extreme law, driven by extreme and chronic homelessness," but one that was hard to enforce and even harder to obey (11.27.2016). Few people experiencing homelessness carry with them a temperature gauge and can discern where they can store their personal belongings without those belongings being stolen or confiscated.

Although these examples might seem somewhat mild forms of resistance, such as Gnawa in deciding not to remove his tent, resistance among people experiencing homelessness can take more and more radical forms. Rhetorician Richard Marback (1998), on the one hand, found that in Detroit, Michigan, so-called public space improvements took the form of displacement and gentrification. As a result, Marback concluded, "On the receiving end, ghettoization, homelessness, and sudden bursts of anger in the form of riots . . . [are] some of the ways that these changes find expression in public spaces" (44; see also Mandanipour 2019). On the other hand, although cultural historian David Fleming (2008) did not have people experiencing homelessness specifically in mind, he proposed an alternative to resistance, a kind of nonidentification to use Britt's (2018) terms or rhetorical listening to use Ratcliffe's (2005) terms. Fleming concluded that we unfortunately tend to believe that "we must either separate or assimilate, either avoid difference, turning our back on people unlike us, or purify it, pretending that conflicts are mistakes and that we can live in harmony only if we see the errors of our ways." Fleming suggested a third alternative to the impulse to either separate or assimilate and to resist: A "practice that acknowledges, even celebrates conflict but also attempts to resolve that conflict through debate, deliberation, and adjudication." Although people experiencing homelessness have been disadvantaged by adjudication, particularly regarding spatial segregation, to accomplish this third alternative, Fleming suggested that we need to establish *"commonplaces* where people can literally come together to discuss and negotiate their differences" as well as "a public philosophy that says: difference is normal and good" (emphasis in original, 16). In the meantime, people experiencing homelessness are assumed to follow errant ways and therefore need to be confined by spatial boundaries, and they often describe their resistance to stigmatization and spatial segregation in social media and other sources.

SOCIAL MEDIA AND OTHER SOURCES
OF DATA AND ANALYSIS

In large part, the internet is an unregulated space, where traditional gatekeeping and hierarchies (such as editors and publishers) have been excluded or "flattened" in a way, which allows people to communicate with an audience of millions at little to no cost. Before the shift from print, radio, and television as the primary sources of communication among large public groups, the people experiencing homelessness who authored the blogs that I studied would never have been visible. Thus, within this book, social media, in particular blogs, serve as the essential source of data and interpretation for my case studies, a means of confirmation or extension of other scholarly work on stigmatization and spatial segregation, and a primary area of my understanding of homelessness. My study generally falls into the research category identified by David Wilkinson and Mike Thelwall (2011) as "using the web as a data source for nonweb issues" (389). Therefore, I conducted a qualitative, inductive study of the conditions and effects of homelessness, and I employed a descriptive and exploratory orientation that was content- rather than hypothesis-driven. From my inductive coding, certain words and phrases emerged in social media and published memoirs to help me identify and describe both implicit and explicit ideas on homelessness (see Guest, MacQueen, and Namey 2012 for a more thorough explanation of this method of interpretation). Overall, I followed the advice of rhetorician Barbara Warnick (1998), who suggested that rhetorical analysis on the web "should 'sample' systems of texts, rather than try to thoroughly analyze individual websites in the way that rhetorical scholars have traditionally aimed to 'master' the printed texts they had examined" (74–75). Moreover, although I brought transdisciplinary perspectives to this study, it is primarily rhetorical, or as Laura Gurak (1997) noted, it "combines empirical analysis . . . that has real evidence to support its claims" with "the critical and somewhat broad lens of a narrative or literary critic" (4–5).

There are over six hundred million blogs in the world today, and in the United States over thirty-one million active bloggers (Byers 2019; *HostingTribal.com* 2020), but as Wilkinson and Thelwall (2011) cautioned, in such research "people who do not use the web are almost certain to be excluded from the sampling frame" (389). Therefore, my means of triangulation included published works, such as memoirs, to extend my access to the voices of people experiencing homelessness. The sixteen blogs that I discovered and consequently studied (one of which was published) consisted primarily of the bloggers' personal thoughts. These blogs were somewhat "free-style," which as Blood defined them are often "nothing less than an outbreak of self-expression," and some were continued for many years. Blogger "James" (B1), for example, lamented, "I hope that I can continue to write great blogs for all to read and sometimes i [sic] feel as though nobody really cares. I still continue to write because for me it is very therapeutic and it helps me to carry on with what i would say has been a very difficult life at times" (7.15.2010). I appreciated that, as Koerber (2001) pointed out in her work on feminist mothers on the web, the reality we perceive "in the 'new world' of cyberspace depends largely on the concepts we carry with us from the 'old world' of offline reality" (219), insight first offered by communication studies and cultural scholars David Gunkel and Ann Hetzel Gunkel (1997). Finally, I remembered that, as social studies of science and technology scholar Sherry Turkle (1995) noted, the internet "has contributed to thinking about identity as multiplicity. On it, people are able to build a self by cycling through many selves" (178). Therefore, these sixteen blog writers have the freedom to narrate their stories and even fictionalize to some extent their entries, but they bolster their *ethos* by way of detailed descriptions of the homeless life, by sharing with their readers transitions in their identity and agency through blogging as well as through experiencing that homeless life, and, at times, by confirming the conclusions about homelessness that empirical research has revealed.

Therefore, in doing this study I was heartened by social media scholars Dawn Wichowski and Laura Kohl (2013) who concluded that personal blogs allowed researchers "to identify sources who speak at length in their own words, and bring perspectives that might ordinarily be lost or unavailable" (238–39). Or as blogger Rebecca Blood (2002) noted, "The appeal of each weblog is grounded thoroughly in the personality of its writer," no matter the extent to which that writing might reidentify that person. Additionally, Jeff Rice (2012) concluded in his study of digital networks, that the blog can serve "as an attempt to work out the ways our personal responses to things, events, moments, and so on function within networks as encounters. . . . [or]

engagements with more than one body of information [including] spatial encounters beyond personal engagement" (167–68). Certainly, the blog of someone experiencing homelessness provides a rare opportunity for understanding a personal stance and individual experiences. Thus, my explorations began with those personal blogs—people experiencing homelessness who owned or borrowed laptops; who found WiFi available in such places as public libraries, coffee shops, or fast food establishments; who could use computers in homeless shelters; who were computer and digitally literate enough to produce a blog; and who had enough stability to create blog entries on a fairly regular basis.

Finally, in their blogs, the voices of people experiencing homelessness are unrestricted by questions and imposed topics, such as they might be in formal interviews, and the observations offered by people experiencing homelessness are not affected by their mobility and fluctuating willingness to be observed, such as they might be in ethnographic studies. Therefore, according to Linda Eastham, a family practitioner in the School of Nursing at University of Virginia (2011), the "unsolicited narrative data from blogs is free from the influence of the research process itself, such as responses given to please the interviewer" (354; see also Jones and Alony 2008). In essence, social media constitute a practice that goes beyond, according to sociologist Ashlee Humphreys (2016), "private, dyadic communication between two people" because that practice "usually happens in a public or semipublic forum" (7). Therefore, personal bloggers such as James, who might retreat into enclaves given their experiences with homelessness, still want the broadest possible audience to hear their voices and understand their concerns—and avoid a mediator directing that conversation.

Blogs by People Experiencing Homelessness

The blog might very well constitute a rhetorical genre because it is an asynchronous and relatively permanent form of asymmetric communication that usually offers a title and date, welcomes or even solicits responses to an entry, and is organized in reverse chronological order with the most recent entry given priority. Rhetoricians Carolyn Miller and Dawn Shepherd (2004), however, concluded that so different is the blog that it represents, instead of a genre, "a technology, a medium, a constellation of *affordances*"—or views of objects given their uses rather than their physical properties (emphasis added, 282). Moreover, communication studies scholar Erin Hollenbaugh noted in 2011 that affordances constituting the personal blogs are the least researched of social media, and in responding to questions that Hollenbaugh posed to bloggers, many offered that their blogs provided a variety of uses: "To record my thoughts and feelings so I can reflect on them"; "To share information that may be of use to others"; and "To show others encouragement" (16). Finally, computer science scholar Jenny Bronstein (2013) found that because blogs often exhibit "high amounts of self-disclosure," some bloggers felt both satisfied and drained when posting a new blog entry (161) and felt "honored and valued" when their readers commented on an entry or agreed with an opinion (174). The voices of such bloggers come as close to face-to-face communication as one might get but require the rhetorical listener.

Recently, more scholars and advocates have studied the community blogs that address specific groups, fulfill specific functions, and raise awareness of the challenges a group might face, such as those experiencing homelessness. The blogs "Let's End Homelessness Together" (homeless.org.UK) and "Picture the Homeless" (picturethehomeless.org), for example, provide their readers with suggestions on how to survive homelessness. The range of community blogs is large and dynamic, as Koerber (2001) discovered when she studied women who frequented the online community of feminist mothering and alternative parenting to "enact resistance by exploiting the inconsistencies inherent in mainstream discourses on motherhood and feminism, thereby producing new meanings that incorporate elements of these discourses, but, at the same time, refuse to obey them" (218; see also Koerber 2018a). In turn, political scientist Juan Sánchez-Villar (2019) studied how community blogs were used to encourage activism, mobilization, and political and social engagement, at the time of an election or when promoting a "new type of citizen journalism, political communication and a more transparent, interactive and open creation of public opinion" (40). The potential of these blogs, even more than other social media concluded Sánchez-Villar, was to "denounce reporting bias in the mass media" by "bringing to light issues of public interest deliberately omitted" and by doing so, create "dense networks of contact which serve as influencer platforms, information nodes, and content amplification" (50; see also Tremayne 2007). Additionally, British medical researchers E. Staite et al. (2018) revealed how three key themes emerged in blogs written between 2012 and 2017 by people with both type I diabetes mellitus and eating disorders—their relationship with insulin, including motive for omitting insulin; their experiences with diabetes complications; and their strategies for recovery and triggers for relapse, which involved self-management and a support system (1329). Knowing these three themes via the blog could enlighten medical caregivers on how to better treat their clients. Finally, the scholars and advocates who contributed to Keisha Edwards Tassie and Sonja Brown Givens (2012) edited collection, *Women of Color and Social Media Multitasking*, focused on minority women who have written blogs, well exceeding the number written by White women and minority men. In this collection, Alexa Harris (2012) explored the blog Theybf.com created by Natasha Edwards, which was designed to enhance intraracial connections in the Black community and not only bridge the gaps "between class, age, and academic achievements through technology and digital media" but also to use blogging "as a form of protest rhetoric by sharing their perspectives" (72). In the same collection, Minu Basnet (2012) looked at the blog WindowSexProject.com, created by Sydney Mosley, which incorporated written entries, videos, and links to other social media outlets to interrogate street harassment, such as catcalling and other unwanted attention, as "an exigence or an event that necessitates action." Through incorporating dance performance into the blog and focusing on the body as a site for harassment, Basnet's blog attempted "to have women assert their confidence and work through the challenges of harassment in the form of humiliation experienced on the streets" and "to help women find the courage to stand up against it and prepare themselves from within to challenge the harassment" (122). Thus, the community blog may take on one purpose of the personal blog in addressing groups experiencing a common challenge, and certainly those experiencing homelessness would have access to both community and personal blogs. Personal blogs, however, offer an opportunity for the creator to realize *ethos*, to work through social challenges, and to meet expressive needs, and yet to transition from an initial identity or sense of agency to a new one.

Thus, the personal blogs that I studied offer detailed descriptions of the challenges and successes in experiencing homelessness, including stress and safety issues; ways to obtain food, clothing, and employment; stigma and marginalization by the so-called normal members of society; and an array of housing options, including tent encampments, emergency or transitional homeless shelters, subsidized public or single room occupancy (SRO) housing, mobile or immobile cars and vans, or life on the street. The entries also vary from political statements and critiques about the state of homelessness in the writer's location, a sort of framing of issues, to narratives about failure or success in escaping homelessness or grappling with mental illness or substance abuse. The bloggers welcomed comments from their readers although generally they received very few given the hardships that their readers also faced, and some reveal their identities and even email addresses to solicit contributions. Indeed, *Digital Magazine* (2010) recognized more than a decade ago that technology in general can benefit people experiencing homelessness (see also Roberson and Nardi 2010; Taylor 2011). As Kristen, who was interviewed by the magazine, related, "It's scary out there. Taking small comforts through technology can mean more than most people know. I don't have anyone I can reach out to in real life, but someone there will always take a minute to say something encouraging and it helps, even if just a tiny bit." Thus, these blogs may be based on the writer's desire to connect with others and engage in conversations about homelessness as a personal and societal crisis—a kind of *communitas* or the feeling of being in a social group or part of a collective of like-minded individuals. Or, as Sherry Turkle (2021) defined *communitas,* "new ideas . . . formed in the crucible of broken hierarchies" (216). The potential for personal and social change via blogs remains great.

Ultimately, I found that the personal blogs of many people experiencing homelessness seemed therapeutic and were almost confessional in their nature, and bloggers often requested understanding, support, and even forgiveness from their readers. The blog entries regarding substance abuse, for example, resembled the sort of statements that might be offered in Alcoholics Anonymous (AA) or Narcotics Anonymous (NA) support groups. A string of entries offered by blogger James exemplified this characteristic. In the first such entry, James admitted that

> I really screwed by last Friday night, I ended up going out and having a few beers and then wound up using crack again after actually having 3 and a half months of clean time. I can tell you first hand that addiction is very powerful and it got a hold of me and I wound up falling. I now need to pick myself up and try to learn from my mistakes. I really thought that I was doing well and that I was becoming cured, and boy was I wrong. (4.24.2010)

Later on, James celebrated his sobriety with his blog readers:

> I just started another addiction program . . . and I'm only meters away from where I used to use quite frequently so so many times. . . . I have actually now been clean from Crack for just over three months, and although it's a great accomplishment, I still feel I have a long, long way to go. (6.10. 2010)

A month later, James seemed to argue with his blog readers that a recent use of marijuana was not a complete loss of sobriety:

> For the most part of the last couple of weeks i [sic] have managed to stay clean and sober, however there was a few times i went out and used. Now i know your [sic] probably thinking i went and used crack cocaine but it was actually only marijuana. Yes i smoked some weed. . . . Its [sic] not been that bad lately, and I have not used in the last week. I am however still beating myself up over my past usage of weed and i really shouldn't be. (7.15.2010)

James reported other such "slips" on September 15, 2010, October 2, 2010, November 29, 2010, and February 11, 2011. Then he entered another treatment program, and reported on March 14, 2011: "I can't believe I actually have 32 days in clean and sober. . . . Wow! I feel really proud of myself the way I have changed the way of thinking, I am able to cope with my emotions without the use of drugs or alcohol." However, James next wrote an entry in which he admitted that he drank alcohol and shared his reason for writing this entry: "The only reason I am telling you this is because if I lie to you, I will not be the better person I am trying to be" (6.22.2011). Finally, almost two years later, James shared with his blog readers:

> I actually had myself a big slip and started using crack for the umpteenth time. I can tell you that I have currently been clean since Christmas past. I am actually doing very well and I even got back into an addiction program about 2 months ago, and things are going very well for me. I am now again currently considered homeless once again, even though I do reside in a room that is paid for by the government. (5.21.2013)

James created almost an imaginary dialogue with his blog readers, which appeared to be very important to his sobriety. His confessions about when he used drugs and alcohol and his celebrations of the times when he was sober, as he wrote, kept him "honest" about his struggles and status. A part of that honesty was also reflected in his conclusion that although he longed to see his children again, "I will always be an addict whether I stay clean or not" and they might be better off if James "just let them live out there [sic] life with just there mother" (10.15.2010).

Finally, these confessional blog entries, such as those offered by James, do raise the challenge of establishing *ethos* by gauging how much emotion to display in the personal blog—and almost a social media exception granted to bloggers who are experiencing homelessness. As information science researchers Soo Young Rieh et al. (2014) discovered in their interviews with twenty-two independent bloggers (not affiliated with a business or organization) the most important way to establish credibility in a blog was to exhibit transparency or the "honest disclosure in terms of who the bloggers were, what their affiliations were, and why they were posting content" (441). In terms of expressions of emotion in a blog, on the one hand, new media scholars Sophie Waterloo et al. (2018) noted that social media encouraged emotional self-expression but that "overly emotional" expressions are considered "norms violations" because such expressions seemed too intimate (1815). On the other hand, many social media users found both the display of positive and negative emotions acceptable in that "authentic self-presentation" was in line with presenting one's "true self" (1827; see also De Choudbury, Counts, and Gamon 2012). Certainly, bloggers such as James displayed a range of emotions—from loneliness to anger, from frustration to joy. They might apologize for such displays to their blog readers, but to the blogger they seemed necessary to establish their *ethos* and to transume stigmatization and marginalization.

Video Interviews with People Experiencing Homelessness

To these blog sources I added another type social media—video interviews such as those offered over YouTube and by such organizations as Invisible People. These video interviews may seem to depart from the spontaneity and the unrestricted comments of bloggers, but they offer another opportunity to "listen to" or engage in, to use Britt's (2018) terms again, productive nonidentification with those experiencing homelessness. Although video interviews can be governed by the questions asked by the interviewers, in particular I sought interviewees who seemed to ignore or resist that mediation and whose comments appeared to be immediate and unsolicited. Overall, such video interviews provide "features of a social networking site, including profiles, private messages, and the ability to 'follow' others" (Humphreys 2016, 31; see also Tolson 2010). A video interview with a fifty-four-year-old homeless man who had been homeless since he was seventeen, for example, allowed him to related his own story, somewhat reminiscent of that of blogger James: "My life has jumped off the tracks, right? You can't put it back. It's a cycle that's nasty to get out of it. I can't be with my family. Maybe that's one of the reasons why I do like to have my beer . . . to wipe that out" ("Homeless Interview" July 22, 2011). In a way, video interviews do offer an intimate look at people experiencing homelessness either because someone initially interviews them, or, perhaps with the help of another, they tell their own stories.

Memoirs by People Experiencing Homelessness

Memoirs written by people experiencing homelessness, although likely edited and proofread before publication, are often as fresh and open as a blog, particularly self-published memoirs. By definition, a memoir is an account written from personal knowledge by someone having intimate experience with the events depicted and based on the writer's own observations. Cultural commentator George Fetherling (2001), for example, described the memoir as "tightly focused," "daring in construction," and "penetrating" (vii). Thus, memoirs written by people experiencing homelessness convey the story of a life, including the "facts" of that life, and memoirs focus on the intimate experiences, thoughts, feelings, challenges, and successes that characterize the life.

Maria Fabian (2013), for example, expressed the advantages of writing her memoir about experiencing homelessness: "I do know that talking about what I've endured has made me stronger. Speaking about my past has helped me overcome shame. It's helped me beat hunger. It's helped me put aside anger. It's made me so I'm no longer afraid" (105). Fabian lived with unwelcoming and sometimes abusive relatives beginning at age six and as a teenager in an apartment without electricity and heat. Eventually, however, she became an advocate for homeless youth. In turn, Justin Reed Early (2013) described his memoir as "inspired by my life," and the events he depicted as "recreated in the spirit of raising awareness of various issues including (but not limited to) homelessness, child trafficking, drug awareness and racism," all to help homeless street children find a "successful path" out of homelessness ("Note from the Author," 2, 5). He became a foster child at a very young age and eventually sought out a new family on the streets, and like Fabian he became an advocate for young people experiencing homelessness. The memoirs of Fabian and Early, like many others, offer an intimate portrayal of the events that led them in and out of homelessness, and therefore supplement the social media sources that I analyzed. (See Appendix B for fair use and privacy concerns regarding my use of social media).

OVERVIEW OF THIS BOOK

This book is organized around a number of case studies and informed by scholarly perspectives and data sources that I have shared thus far. Several of these cases stem from events in Minnesota or in the Midwest, simply because I had extensive access to these data. Journalism and composition scholars Yanira Rodriguez and Ben Kuebrich (2018) have described the opportunity to have such a local focus: "Like holding an object close enough that one begins to see it both as a whole and for the fragments that constitute its makeup, proximity provides the necessary context and experiences that inform the knowledge- and decision-making processes of organized resistance [as well as organized oppression]" (163). Moreover, Amster (2008) agreed that "an investigation of a single piece of a whole reveals something of the nature of that whole" and "lessons learned from a micro-exploration illuminate our understanding of macro trends" (xi). On the average nearly twenty thousand people are homeless on any given night in Minnesota, according to a study by Wilder Research (Furst 2020), and the state is slightly above average in a nationwide comparison. Washington, DC, for example, has the highest estimated rate of homelessness while Mississippi has the lowest rate (Statista. com 2019). Moreover, the gap in racial homeownership in the Twin Cities is the highest in the nation and has only widened over the past two decades, according to journalists Jim Buchta and Mary Jo Webster (2021). Thus, Minnesota provides a solid opportunity for a study of homelessness and unstable housing.

In the first two chapters, I analyze how space, land, and place affect the lives of people experiencing homelessness, and in chapters three and four, I illuminate how stigmatization diminishes the sense of identity and agency among those people experiencing homelessness and how the tropes of home and homelessness contribute to that diminishment. Specifically, in both chapters one and two, I begin by looking at some historical roots of homelessness as they pertain to spatial segregation—first the hodgepodge of treaties, court decisions, and acts that justified the seizure of Native lands in the United States, and then the redlining, racial zoning, and restrictive deed covenants that segregated racial and religious minorities in major cities across the country. This history reveals the capitalist impulse to link land with wealth, particularly privately owned land, and forms a foundation for the more current effects of stigmatization and spatial segregation of people considered other, abnormal, and/or dangerous because of their race, ethnicity, and socioeconomic identities. In chapter one, I rely on the blog created by Camille Gage as managed by the Metropolitan Urban Indian Directors to follow the emergence of a tent encampment called the "Wall of Forgotten Natives" in the Twin Cities in Spring 2018. Of particular importance to my analysis is the intragroup conflict created when the organization Natives Against Heroin began to evict those encampment residents whom they considered drug dealers and users. Such conflict both belies the essentialist or collective identity often assigned both by authorities and the public to individuals experiencing homelessness and the spaces they occupy—as well as offers the opportunity for a nuanced analysis of the discursive and material rhetoric surrounding *communitas*. In chapter two, I offer a similar case study, this time of the Five Points community in Denver, Colorado, in which the Black population grew during the Great Migration to northern states, culturally flourished in the 1920s through the 1940s, was spatially segregated by housing restrictions in the 1950s and 1960s, and then was threatened by gentrification in the 1990s. Then, in a somewhat surprising parallel case, I study the city ordinances governing the housing and movements of convicted sex offenders that were recently created in three Minnesota cities and, based on unsubstantiated fear, contribute to homelessness among this group. I end this second chapter by exploring the increasing number of regulations, called "quality-of-life" ordinances, that people experiencing homelessness may be forced to violate in order to sleep, sit, rest, and eat in public spaces. All in all, these past and current ordinances and regulations have created a sense of safety and dominance among majority homeowners and may belie attempts to ease the homelessness crisis.

In chapters three and four, I focus on two groups experiencing homelessness who are particularly vulnerable and stigmatized—female victims of domestic violence and unaccompanied youth—and on options those experiencing homelessness often pursue or reject, including so-called welfare or spill-over hotels, day or night homeless shelters, encampments, or life on the streets. In both chapters, I explain how those experiencing unstable housing or homelessness express their need to create a sense of identity, *ethos*, and agency in the face of stigmatization and marginalization by way of social media and published memoirs. Specifically, in chapter three I ground my analysis on the home as a rhetorical trope and explore the housing complications and legal responses that female victims of domestic violence encounter, and I reveal the complexities and failures of the law's attempt to protect them. In exploring the challenges faced by unaccompanied youth, I rely not only on social media and memoirs but also on personal interviews with advocates and youth who reveal what efforts might ease their situation. Then in chapter four, I return to the "Wall of Forgotten Natives" to describe the Minneapolis Navigation Center created to accept "Wall" residents and to offer them shelter, services, and transition to stable housing once the encampment was dismantled, not a completely successful effort. I also look in depth at the resistance among people experiencing homelessness to established homeless shelters, the stigmatization and spatial segregation caused by seemingly unreasonable rules and regulations at those shelters, and the rhetorical and hierarchical features of the "total" institution in those shelters that negate agency, *ethos*, and identity among people experiencing homelessness. I end this fourth chapter by analyzing the debates between neighbors and city officials regarding the creation of a new day homeless shelter in St. Paul, reveal the reactions to a fire at a spill-over hotel in Minneapolis, and examine how the novel coronavirus (COVID-19) affected people experiencing homelessness in 2020 and 2021 across the county.

Those people experiencing homelessness, advocates and activists helping them, and public health and policy officials studying and guiding them have shared their recommendations on how to address the homeless crisis. I end this book by summarizing their recommendations in chapter five. Overall, I hope that this book illuminates, by applying the perspectives of spatial segregation and stigmatization, and by capturing the voices of those people experiencing homelessness, how historically and currently our political, legal, and socioeconomic systems create and sustain homelessness—and how we might ease or even eliminate that homelessness crisis.

Chapter One

The "Wall of Forgotten Natives"

Contested Land and Space

In his memoir, once homeless Jesse Thistle (2019) explained what it meant to him to identify as Métis, a people living primarily in North American and Canada who descended from both Indigenous people and European settlers and who maintained their own culture and language. When Thistle's grandfather taught Jesse about the relationship between the Métis people and the land, he related stories about "how our people once had lived in large communities in handmade houses just like his all over Saskatchewan, living off the land, but that was before the government attacked us and stole our land during the resistance, before our clans fell apart" (11). Apropos of the lessons that Thistle's grandfather passed on, collaborators Shawn Wilson, who identifies as an Opaskwayak Cree, and Margaret Hughes, who identifies as a "White Settler American" and an Indigenous researcher (2019), concluded that for Native people, "Reality as relationships includes our relations to ancestors, family, and Place, as well as ideas and cultural understandings that make us who we are" (8). Wilson and Hughes found that among Native people their ancestral history, including life on their own land, formed not only their past but also their current sense of identity and self-worth. In this chapter, I reveal how the loss of that historic relationship with the land contributed to the current state of stigmatization, spatial segregation, and resulting homelessness among many Native people in urban spaces.

For Thistle's grandfather, the loss of land led to instability, as it did among most Native people. In contrast, for those who stole that land, acquisition of it meant gaining status, wealth, and power. When the government seized Native land, such as that belonging to the Métis, it conquered Native people—removing them from their ancestral land, placing them in reservations, and attempting to assimilate them into a colonialist and capitalistic culture. Resistance from Native people was often met with violence, ethnocide, and genocide. Thus, those Natives who once had homes became homeless—and generations were traumatized by that homelessness. In response, Native people were expected to assimilate, individually and collectively, into White civilization as well as to pursue private ownership of land, a perspective counter to their customs, values, and beliefs. Attention to and appreciation of past and current Native voices, however, helps to enable not only advocacy and activism but also more nuanced social and scholarly recognition, or as Métis social worker and educator Lindsay DuPré (2019) defined such an effort, "Reconciliation needs intersectional analysis and theories of change that reflect the diverse identities and realities of people living on these lands" (2). Success in this reconciliation effort may also create for Native people what Molloy (2019) called recuperative *ethos*, or the appeals "woven into" the interactions of stigmatized and marginalized individuals and groups that indicate they are now "worthwhile and reliable speakers, thinkers, lovers, friends, and community members," perhaps a counter to anchoring or racial and ethnic bias (122). I hope that in this book I help identify how such recuperation might take place.

Although the Métis themselves identified separately from both their Inuit and their European forebears, Thistle reflected on the stigma and *kakoethos* that he bore as a child. He was singled out, for example, by his classmates and friends: "For as long as I could remember, people had teased me about being a half-breed 'Indian,' and I hated it." Thistle resisted this stigmatization by directing it toward others: "When I acted the same way toward others, nobody focused on who I was" (86). If he won in a fight, however, he was still likely to be told, "You're just a dirty Indian, like the rest of them. . . . You'll probably die drinking like they all do" (87). And so, Thistle claimed to be of Italian descent throughout his school days in order to escape stigmatization and establish *ethos*, particularly within his childhood environment in which he heard songs about "killing Indians and selling them whiskey and destroying the buffalo," songs in which he was sure that "the Indians had to run away" (77). Similarly, Vietnam War veteran Evan Haney of the Seminole Nation recalled, "When I was a child, watching cowboys and Indians on TV, I would root for the cavalry, not the Indians. It was that bad. I was that far toward my own destruction" (quoted in Dunbar-Ortiz 2014, 192). Historically, according to historian and activist Roxanne Dunbar-Ortiz (2014), the continuing stigmatization of Native people was not based on *inherent racism* toward them but instead on the *race hatred* fueled by "extreme violence of unlimited warfare" against Native people to remove them from their land (59). In this chapter I focus on the spatial segregation of Native people as I focus in the next chapter on the exclusion of Black people from neighborhoods and communities—both of which were linked to land ownership and contribute to homelessness.

IMPLICATIONS OF TERMINOLOGY

As a non-Native researcher, I am aware that scholars, such as Wilson and Hughes (2019), recommend that such research be "grounded in reality as relationships and relational accountability" and in accomplishing this, I strive to go beyond validity or reliability to reach the "authenticity and credibility" that these scholars suggest (15). Listening to and capturing the voices of Natives experiencing homelessness, as expressed in social media and memoirs, as well as using the techniques of "nonidentification" as Britt (2018) explained them, I hope to achieve that authenticity and credibility as well as scholarly and personal openness and understanding. To work toward that, I carefully chose my terminology in this chapter as it pertains to Native people. Such choices vary within popular and scholarly literature and throughout organizations and activist groups. Alex Westerfelt and Michael Yellow Bird (1999), for example, chose to use the term Indigenous because, as they reminded their readers, labels such as Native American are problematic because they "obscure" the diversity of such groups and "may refer to most native born Americans whose ancestors are not indigenous to these lands" (146). In turn, Dunbar-Ortiz (2014) used Indigenous, Indian, and Native interchangeably, as did David Treuer (2019), an Ojibwe from the Leech Lake Reservation, who added American Indian to his list. The title of Donna Martinez, Grace Sage, and Azusa Ono's *Urban American Indians: Reclaiming Native Space* (2016) reflects their choices as do those of prominent Native organizations, such as the American Indian Movement, the National Indian Youth Council, the Minnesota Indian Women's Resource Center, and the Native American Community Development Institute. Ultimately, I decided to use the term Native or Native people to conform to the name of the Minneapolis homeless tent encampment, the 2018 "Wall of Forgotten Natives," which constitutes the case study within this chapter and to acknowledge that my social media and scholarly sources include Native people from Canada as well as Alaska Native nations (AIAN) (see, for example, Grandbois 2005). However, in using the singular "people," I do not mean to essentialize Native people; they are among the most diverse groups that one could study.

Moreover, the term "tribe" is controversial among many Native people. Bruce Johansen, a professor of Communication and Native American Studies, in his foreword to Joy Porter's *Land and Spirit in Native America* (2012), recommended the use of "nations or confederacies" instead of "tribes" to avoid "the nineteenth-century diminishment of Native American political economies" (xi). In turn, in an article in *Indian Country Today*, journalist Steven Newcomb (2004) concluded that the contrast between the terms nation and tribe was "striking" because "tribe" is "degrading" to Native people. In particular, treaties were formal agreements between Native people and the US government, both sovereign entities, as Newcomb reminded his readers, and these treaties never mentioned the word tribe "because such demeaning terminology is outside of formal international diplomatic relations." A nation, comparable to a state, realm, or independent political unit, has the unity to possess a government "peculiarly its own" and common to "the whole people of a country," noted Newcomb. Thus, throughout this chapter and book, I use the term nation unless the specific identities are used by my sources. This second option, however, is somewhat complicated. I learned, for example, in referring to the Red Lake Band of Chippewa, that "Chippewa," according to Treuer (2019), is an older mispronunciation of Ojibwe, that the Ojibwe people presently live in at least fifteen groups called bands, and that the Ojibwe are allied with Natives such as the Odawa and Potawatomi to form the Anishinaabe Nation. Again, I follow the lead of my sources and acknowledge that these identities are often tied to the historical relationship between Native people and the land.

HISTORICAL RELATIONSHIP BETWEEN NATIVE PEOPLE AND THE LAND

Everything in the history of the United States, according to Dunbar-Ortiz (2014), is "about the land—who oversaw and cultivated it, fished its waters, maintained its wildlife; who invaded it and stole it; how it became a commodity ('real estate') broken into pieces and sold on the market" (1). In turn, historian Francis Jennings (2010) reminded his readers that the Europeans "did not settle a virgin land. They invaded and displaced a resident population" (15). The Europeans who invaded such lands saw Native people as obstacles in their plans to take advantage of the land and its productive potential. Therefore, in order to understand the complications and conflicts regarding the "Wall of Forgotten Natives" homeless tent encampment in Minneapolis in 2018, it is necessary to rehearse the historical relationship between land and space for Native people, a relationship that remains. After all, as DuPré (2019) cautioned her Native readers, "Who we are and our experiences in the world are shaped by the history of the land that we are on" and "reclaiming our stories and cultural knowledge presents pathways to belonging" (2). I begin this chapter by reviewing the historical treatment of Native people, primarily in the United States and Canada, and illuminating the hodge-podge of federal acts and state ordinances that spatially segregated Native people.

If indeed everything in the history of the United States is related to land, Native people, in particular, saw that land as a living part of their ancestry as well as their current residences, just as Thistle's grandfather did. This perspective was revealed, for example, after Native people were uprooted from that land, forced to move elsewhere, and subsequently were allowed to tell their stories before a wider forum. In 1879, Chief Joseph of the Nez Perce gave a speech in Washington, DC, after he surrendered in his attempt to return to the Nez Perce's ancestral lands. Chief Joseph noted that his father had taught him that "no man owned any part of the earth, and a man could not sell what he did not own" and made Chief Joseph promise the following: "This country holds your father's body. Never sell the bones of your father and mother" (quoted in Treuer 2019, 119). In essence, one cannot sell what one cannot own—the land and its ancestral relationship. Similarly, Chief Standing Bear of the Ponca Tribe was captured as his people attempted to walk back to their ancestral land in Nebraska, land that had been given to the Lakotas in a treaty arrangement. In *United States ex rel. Standing Bear v. Crook* (1879), Chief Standing Bear revealed his vision of his homeland to the judge: "At last I see a rift in the rocks. A little way beyond there are green prairies. The swift-running water, the Niobrara, pours down between the green hills. There are the graves of my fathers. There again we will pitch our tepees and build our fires" (quoted in Treuer 2019, 125). Chief Standing Bear had carried the bones of his son with him on his journey back home because he had promised his son that he would bury him alongside his ancestors.

Chief Joseph's speech received widespread media coverage and was published in its entirety in the *North American Review*, and when Judge Elmer Scipio Dundy rendered his decision in *Standing Bear v. Crook*, he noted that "an Indian is a 'person' within the meaning of the law" and ordered that the Ponca people be released to resettle in their ancestral lands. These successful appeals, unfortunately, were exceptions at the time of settler colonialism and in what seemed a muddle of doctrines, laws, and acts regarding Native people—the history of which set the context of the "Wall of Forgotten Natives" and the current challenge of homelessness among Native people.

The Doctrine of Discovery and Settler Colonialism

The Doctrine of Discovery provided a foundation for conquering Native people and seizing their lands. Although the more familiar Manifest Destiny was the nineteenth-century imperialist belief that settlers were destined by God to expand across North America and spread capitalism throughout the continent, from the mid-fifteenth to the mid-twentieth centuries the Doctrine of Discovery provided a broader foundation for discovering, exploring, conquering, and dominating these lands. The 1494 Treaty of Tordesillas between Spain and Portugal had clarified the Doctrine of Discovery to mean that only non-Christian lands could be seized, a decision that supported the conquest of Native people throughout North America. Much later, Chief Justice John Marshall in *Johnson v. McIntosh* (1823) concluded that, under the Doctrine of Discovery, Native people could live on the land but not own it—a stipulation that proved unfortunate for Natives when non-Native people sought to own these lands. Not until 2005, in *City of Sherrill v. Oneida Nation of Indians*, did the courts conclude, "We cannot accept that the Doctrine of Discovery was ever a true authority for the forced takings of lands and the enslavement or extermination of peoples." In the meantime, however, many Native nations were forced from their ancestral lands—and the very terms "Destiny" and "Discovery" were used to justify these actions.

Early on, such justifications and beliefs firmly supported settler colonialism. According to Dunbar-Ortiz (2014), this form of colonialism required "violence or the threat of violence to attain its goals" (8). Spanish settlers in early New Mexico, for example, killed more than eight hundred Acoma Pueblo Natives and enslaved the rest, cutting off the right foot of every male Native over the age of twenty-five to prevent their escape. And so,

> European colonists shoved aside a large network of small and large [Native] nations whose governments, commerce, arts and sciences, agriculture, technologies, theologies, philosophies, and institutions were intricately developed, nations that maintained sophisticated relations with one another and with the environments that supported them. (Dunbar-Ortiz 2014, 46)

Native people were certainly not inexperienced and naive; in fact they were quite advanced and sophisticated, but they were stigmatized, marginalized, and determined to be "lesser," if not expendable. Therefore, according to Goffman's (1963) and Link and Phelan's (2001) causes and components of stigmatization, we must add an economic "motive" regarding Native people—they simply got in the way of profit from the land that colonists sought to occupy. As a result, many of the federations of Native nations and their civilizations were destroyed. At the time of Columbus, for example, it is estimated that in North America there were between five and eight million Native people; by 1890, the Native population was about 250,000 people (Perdue and Green 2010, 16).

The Indian Removal Act (1830) and the Indian Appropriation Act (1871)

Overall, federal and state laws and acts regarding Native people and their lands contributed to stigmatization and eventual trauma even though these governments later tried to appease and rectify the results of these laws and acts. Initially, Article 1, Section 8, of the US Constitution declared that

Congress had the power "to regulate Commerce with Foreign Nations and among the several States, and with Indian Tribes," a power that made relations with Native people a federal matter as long as the government recognized the sovereignty of Native nations. Under this constitutional stipulation, the federal government could negotiate treaties with Native nations, even though those treaties were often violated by the government and substantially disadvantaged Native people. The Indian Removal Act of 1830, for example, certainly proved to be a disservice to Native people. As a result of the Removal Act, from 1838 to 1839 the Cherokee Nation was forced to move from their land east of the Mississippi River into so-called Indian Territory, territory primarily encompassing Oklahoma. During this six-month "Trail of Tears" relocation, 4,000 of the 14,000 Cherokees were forcibly removed, and many died along the way. During this same period, 26 Native nations were similarly removed from their lands. Under these circumstances, as Treuer (2019) concluded, removal from Native lands to a new home "was a chaotic mess, but it was a homeland of sorts and seemed, at first, more secure than the ones many tribes left behind. It didn't last" (83).

Indeed, it did not last. In 1871, the Indian Appropriation Act, the encompassing name of several acts passed by the US Congress, stipulated that the federal government need no longer treat a Native community "as an independent nation, tribe, or power with whom the United States may contract a treaty," but instead Native people would become wards of the federal government. This stipulation made it easier for the government to take away Native lands, in that the government could now make laws affecting Native nations without negotiations or consent. Although the sovereign status of those nations that already had treaties was reaffirmed, many of these existing treaties were eventually breached. Finally, the federal government seemed to retain the ward status of Native people in such legislation as the Major Crimes Act of 1885, which listed seven crimes, including murder, that when committed by a Native against another Native were "so heinous they could not be trusted to tribal jurisprudence" (quoted in Treuer 2019, 247). Government oversight of Native nations became a "give-then-take" relationship, and the assimilation and so-called civilization of Native people were ultimately linked to individual land acquisition.

The General Allotment Act (Dawes Act) (1887)

In the preamble of the Code of Indian Offenses (1883), Henry Teller, Secretary of the Interior, concluded, "When an Indian acquires property, with a disposition to retain the same, free of tribal or individual interference, he has made a step forward in the road to civilization" (quoted in Treuer 2019, 155). There was a distinction between mutually occupying property, such as ancestral land, and individually owning that land, such as private real estate. Then, the 1885 National Indian Defense Association pointed out that given the abuses in the Indian services, Natives still lacked the essential conditions to be considered civilized Americans. Native people seemed to be required to assimilate in terms of their relationship with the land—if they wished to be recognized and treated as citizens, they had to find their way to private ownership and the development and cultivation of a small allotted plot of land. This stipulation was more formally affirmed in the General Allotment Act of 1887 (called the Dawes Act), which awarded each Native head of household 160 acres, each single person or orphan 80 acres, and everyone under 18 years of age 40 acres. The federal government became the trustee for these homesteads for 25 years. The Native "owners" of these homesteads, however, were still considered noncitizens and could not sell their land; moreover, the government could sell any surplus Native land to non-Natives.

Overall, according to Thomas Morgan, Commissioner of Indian Affairs in 1890, the General Allotment or Dawes Act was meant to eventually incorporate Natives "into the national life, and deal with them not as nations or tribes or bands, but as individual citizens." Merrill Gates, who later headed the Board of Indian Commissioners, agreed with not only this goal but also the means: "We must make the Indian more intelligently selfish" through acquiring individual property to "break up the tribe as a social unit," to "encourage private enterprise and farming," and, of course, to "provide a land base for white settlement" (quoted in Treuer 2019, 113–14). Along with the Dawes Act, the 1889 Nelson Act tried unsuccessfully to move all Ojibwe bands to the White Earth Reservation to free up the forests in Northern Minnesota for timber companies; the 1898 Curtis Act abolished tribal governments, treaty lands, and communal holdings; and the 1906 Burke Act amended the Dawes Act to allow Natives to own land if they would pay taxes on that land. New land acquisition and cultivation endorsed the eventual goal of citizenship for Native people but carried with it a great many stipulations and so continued to marginalize Native nations and stigmatize Native people.

The Indian Reorganization Act (Wheeler-Howard Bill) (1934) and the Termination Act (1953)

It was not until 1934 that the Indian Reorganization Act, proposed as the Wheeler-Howard Bill and supported by John Collier, the Commissioner of Indian Affairs, ended further allotment of Native territories to non-Natives, although already allotted land was not restored to Natives. This act called for the Dawes Act to be overturned, created the Bureau of Indian Affairs (BIA), and asked Native people to initiate reformation of their governments. On the one hand, these reformed governments were required to consist of three branches created by popular elections and democratic principles instead of ancestral hierarchies and values. On the other hand, this reformation, Collier believed, could restore Native sovereignty, reduce losses of Native lands, and create economic self-sufficiency. Any acceptance of this type of government was voluntary, and by 1936, 177 Native communities voted for acceptance while 77 voted to not accept. For those who voted for acceptance, BIA attorneys offered to draft the new constitution. The large Navajo Nation declined, however, and the Red Lake Band of Ojibwe already had an acceptable hybrid government. Thus, Collier received praise from some contemporaries and historians for his "Indian New Deal," while others pointed out the continuing termination of Native identity, autonomy, and agency.

Indeed, the Termination Act of 1953, enacted fewer than twenty years after the Indian Reorganization Act, seemed to both affirm and negate the efforts of the Reorganization Act. The states were given greater entry into Native lands, but that entry was again based on the Native community having an acceptable government. Also, the Termination Act (consisting of House Concurrent Resolution 108 and Public Law 280) freed the Native nations and communities from federal supervision and control, but it also curtailed federal protection and payments guaranteed by prior treaties and other agreements. The act granted six states the right and responsibility to prosecute all criminal offenses and civil disputes within their borders; other states could opt in later. Minnesota was included in the initial list of six states, and these states could regulate and levy taxes, administer schools, oversee health care, and grant licenses for hunting and fishing on Native lands. The result of the Termination Act, however, according to Dunbar-Ortiz (2014), was the following:

> Despite the piecemeal eating away of Indigenous landholdings and sovereignty and federal trust responsibility based on treaties, the US government had no constitutional or other legal authority to deprive federally recognized Native nations of their inherent sovereignty or territorial boundaries. It could only make it nearly impossible for them to exercise that sovereignty, or alternatively, eliminate Indigenous identity entirely through assimilation, a form of *genocide*. (emphasis added, 174)

Thus, Public Law 280, an initial version of the Termination Act, was tested in court decisions such as *Bryan v. Itasca County, Minnesota* (1976).

In the *Bryan* decision, the US Supreme Court reversed a prior decision of the Minnesota Supreme Court and in doing so found that the state and county had no authority to levy a tax on petitioner Russell Bryan's personal property. Bryan was an enrolled member of the Minnesota Chippewa Tribe and resided on the Leech Lake Reservation. Given that Bryan was a Native resident of a reservation and was living on that reservation, and because that community had a "tribal law-and-order organization that functions in a reasonably satisfactory manner," the state could not assess personal property tax on his mobile home. In this decision, the Court interpreted Public Law 280 in favor of Native sovereignty. Overall, the Indian Reorganization Act and the Termination Act led to a mixture of gains and losses for Native nations—and most often dealt with the control and management of as well as the profit from the land.

The Indian Relocation Act (1956) and Aftermath

Then, in 1956, came the Indian Relocation Act (Public Law 959)—a robust attempt at Native assimilation by encouraging Native people to move from their homelands and reservations. With BIA funding, any Native individual or family could relocate to designated urban industrial areas, where the BIA promised to make housing as well as job training and placement available. The Act was designed to encourage Native people to assimilate into the general population of these urban areas, in some ways a significant step beyond land ownership and cultivation. Investigative reporter Alexia Fernández Campbell, writing for *The Atlantic* in 2016, for example, interpreted the Relocation Act as not just enabling Native people to join a supposedly more secure urban work force but also crippling reservation life: "Though the act didn't force people to leave their reservations, it made it hard for families to stay by dissolving federal recognition of most tribes, and ending funding for reservations' schools, hospitals, and basic services—along with the jobs they created." Similarly, Grace Sage, in Martinez, Sage, and Ono (2016), characterized the Relocation Act as "a policy that turned out to be the most forcible federal attempt to extinguish tribal communities and guarantee assimilation of American Indians to Western values, Western beliefs, and Western economics and laws" (31). As a result, the number of Natives living in urban areas rose from 8 percent to 64 percent by 2000 (U.S. National Archives and Records Administration 2016). However, the number of Native people experiencing unemployment and homelessness also rose.

Minneapolis was one of the first cities chosen for the relocation program, and as a result, Natives from 11 reservations in Minnesota were encouraged to leave their homelands to enter the urban workforce. Writing for *The Guardian*, journalist Jenni Monet (2018) called the Relocation Act a "termination" policy influenced by earlier efforts to assimilate Natives, "a form of cultural genocide on tribes and their citizens." However, Minneapolis did become the headquarters of the American Indian Movement (AIM) and the home of organizations such as the Minneapolis American Indian Center, the Native American Community Clinic, the Native American Community

Development Institute, the Minneapolis Indian Women's Resource Center; the location of schools such as the Anishinaabe Academy; and home of the Metro Urban Indian Directors, which monitored the "Wall of Forgotten Natives" encampment. Moreover, the Little Earth community in the city's Phillips neighborhood and near the "Wall," became the heart of the Native community in Minneapolis, a community not only characterized by close cultural ties but also plagued by poverty and crime.

Reactions to Relocation and Assimilation

The federal courts continued to interpret the sometimes conflicting and always complicated laws and acts passed by Congress to govern Native people and their land, particularly regarding past treaties. In *Williams v. Lee* (1959), for example, the US Supreme Court held that a non-Native owner of a general store on the Navajo Reservation could not bring a state action against a Navaho man and his wife to collect payment for goods sold to them on credit. The Court decided that such a motion "would infringe on the right of Indians to govern themselves, which right was recognized by Congress in the Treaty in 1868 with the Navajos, and has never been taken away." Also, in *Minnesota et al. v. Mille Lacs Band of Chippewa Indians* (1999), the US Court of Appeals for the Eighth Circuit interpreted an 1837 treaty with several Chippewa bands. The intent of the treaty was "to ensure the security and tranquility of the white settlements in an extensive and valuable district of this Territory [of Minnesota]" by removing the Chippewa from all lands within the territory. However, the Court found that although the Chippewas had ceded their lands in Wisconsin and Minnesota to the federal government, they did not give up their usufructuary rights (the rights to use and enjoy the property) to hunt, fish, and gather on that land.

Indeed, these laws, acts, and court decisions seemed at first designed to move Native people from their ancestral homes into reservations—by treaty or by violence—and then into urban areas—by relocation and assimilation. It is a wonder that so many Native people survived those interventions and that there are now more than 500 federally recognized Native communities and nations, 310 federally recognized reservations, and nearly three million Native people living in the United States (Dunbar-Ortiz 2014, 10–11). The goal for Native people, however, still seems to be assimilation into a dominant culture that values real estate and private ownership, with the exception of low-income housing and rentals. The goal of Native people seems to be freedom, autonomy, sovereignty, exercise of cultural values and ceremonies, and communal decision making and living. And, Native people want a voice in all decisions about their identity, homes, and land. In 2018, for example, Sam Strong was the tribal secretary of the Red Lake Band of

Chippewa, whose members represented a quarter of the population at the "Wall of Forgotten Natives" encampment. Strong noted that his father was a "relocation Indian" who became a cable repairman in Minneapolis. Given his father's background, Strong shared, "We talk a lot about historical trauma. In this particular context, there's a population of Natives down there at that Wall that don't have faith in the system. The system hasn't ever really worked for them" (quoted in Monet 2018). For Sam and his father, relocation represented not just personal assimilation but also ethnocide. In her *Guardian* article, Monet (2018) concluded that "the legacy of the attempted erasure is raw." Moreover, the Metropolitan Urban Indian Directors or MUID (2018) stated on the "Wall" encampment website that, despite the fact that Native people were "resourceful, resilient, and committed to our community, families, and our cultures and traditions," they faced disproportionate challenges with homelessness, mental and physical health struggles, chemical dependency, and "vulnerability to exploitation and violence," all of which are "byproducts of the generations of trauma experienced by our relatives." The voices of the "Wall" encampment residents offer further insight into this stigmatization, the spatial segregation that the encampment challenged, and the stories of progress and yet conflict.

SIGNIFICANCE OF THE "WALL OF FORGOTTEN NATIVES" ENCAMPMENT

Homelessness among Native people is noteworthy and concerning—and the causes tied to systemic oppression and stigmatization—but the traumatic effects of this homelessness are primarily linked to spatial segregation—boundaries around land and space. According to an estimate offered in a blog published by the Urban Institute, 1 in 200 Native people are homeless in so-called Indian Country or land occupied by Native nations, in contrast to 1 in 1,000 people in the US population overall. Such homelessness, however, may be somewhat inconspicuous and therefore affect many more in Native communities than these statistics reflect because of activities such as "doubling up." As one person interviewed for the Urban Institute blog defined doubling up, "People go from one family member's home to another. Everyone's homeless around here, but they just stay with family members and extended families until they get kicked out" (quoted in Bless 2017). Moreover, in urban areas, as reported by the National Alliance to End Homelessness (2020d), about 17,966 people experiencing homelessness identify as Native, even though the alliance indicated that it was difficult for the US Census Bureau and homelessness service systems to count Native people accurately. In southwestern cities such as Albuquerque, New Mexico, we do know that

Native people make up about 5 percent of the general population but between 10 to 15 percent of the homeless population (Varma 2018).

Within this context, the "Wall of Forgotten Natives" tent encampment grew in Minneapolis in 2018. The "Wall" encampment was located near the intersection of Franklin Avenue East and Hiawatha Avenue/Highway 55, known as the Franklin/Hiawatha corridor. The encampment existed on land owned by the Minnesota Department of Transportation (MnDOT) but near the Little Earth low-income housing development, a development occupied primarily by Native people on the land owned by the Red Lake Band of Chippewa, one group of Ojibwe people in Minnesota. Analysis of the "Wall" encampment reveals the nuances of White claims to and Native disenfranchisement from land and space, the stigmatization of Native people to spatially segregate them, and the contestation between and among internal and external forces affecting these marginalized people.

Throughout this case study, I depend on the blog created by Camille Gage to follow daily life within the "Wall" encampment as well as my personal correspondence (2020) and interview (2021) with her. A Twin Cities freelance communications/planner and although non-Native herself, Gage has worked with many nonprofit organizations in the Native community. She was hired to create the blog and to serve as an observer or chronicler of everyday life in the encampment—in particular, she was a conduit to MUID, the network of Native-led organizations in the Twin Cities, and later related to the many service providers who ensured that the "Wall" residents were fed and sheltered. Gage initially took this role when she was in discussion with Patina Park of the Minnesota Indian Women's Resource Center about doing some communications work for their capital campaign and when Minneapolis Mayor Jacob Frey called on Park and other Native leaders to join a meeting about the growing Minneapolis tent encampment. Park asked Gage to work with her on that effort, needing someone "to be boots on the ground—visiting, assessing, seeing what various Native-led organizations might bring to the issue of the encampment" (Gage 2020). Thus, the catalyst for Gage's blog was the concern about the tent encampment by several Native organizations, and although the blog might have reflected the characteristics of a community blog for these organizations and the "Wall" residents, at times it also assumed features of a personal blog in the extent of Gage's experiential knowledge.

Although public concern and media attention regarding the encampment arose mainly in 2018, the "Wall" encampment had been in existence for quite a while—and it was "totally organic" in its development and growth according to Gage (2021). MnDOT periodically dismantled the camp—swept it away—but it always seemed to come back. The encampment grew dramatically, however, about the time that Mayor Frey proposed the creation of a new temporary shelter for "Wall" residents and mentioned the use of housing trailers rather than tents, an attractive alternative for people currently living in crowded emergency homeless shelters who then moved to the "Wall" encampment in anticipation of better shelter (see, for example, Sepic and Nesterak 2018). Also, Frey and others wanted to connect the encampment to service providers, such as drug and alcohol counselors, and so MnDOT suspended their sweeps. At Park's and Gage's first visit to the encampment, there were about sixty tents in the encampment, and after that visit, Gage realized that "we needed to control the narrative" about the encampment or "it would default to 'just a lot of Native drug addicts'—people that society at large find easy to write off." Instead, Gage wanted to resist this stigmatization and to "humanize the situation through story telling—to offer a deeper understanding and a way for people to find and show compassion to those who are struggling. To not just look away." In her blog, Gage would provide the "eyes and ears" of daily life in the encampment through narrative—to record what she witnessed and, at times, what she personally experienced. Finally, the Native community wanted to control information about and reactions to the encampment rather than having the media do so, and Gage's blog became a "trusted source of information for camp members" as well as for those media (Gage 2020). Thus, Gage's blog often bore the responsibility for creating *communitas* among the "Wall" residents, for informing MUID and other Native organizations, and for presenting a common face to those watching and worrying about the encampment.

Initially, the space that the "Wall" residents occupied meant little to the broader Minneapolis socioeconomic society, but on that land, residents performed Native ceremonies, such as burning sage (smudging) and conducting talking circles, just as their ancestors did. Minneapolis itself is on what was originally Dakota Land in Mni Sota Makoce ("the land where the water reflects the sky"), and the "Wall" encampment itself was in the heart of the Twin Cities' urban Native population, according to some estimates "the most concentrated urban American Indian population in the United States" (Roper 2016). Not only did Native people make up a disproportionate number of people experiencing homelessness in Minneapolis (about 16 percent), but also their challenges included chemical and alcohol dependency, mental and physical health struggles, and "vulnerability to exploitation and violence," all of which were "byproducts of generations of trauma experienced by our relatives," according to MUID (2018). In the midst of these challenges, MUID concluded, "This land continues to be sacred land for many of the Urban Native population." The encampment served as a reminder of what was lost when Native land was stolen and what might be reaffirmed in the encampment community—if indeed stigmatization could be avoided from the outside community.

Rhetorical and Material Significance of the "Wall" Encampment

From the perspective of material rhetoric, again the analysis designed to illuminate messages and meanings conveyed by material things and by the corporal entities occupying certain spaces, the "Wall" encampment served as a text or texture to represent, by its very presence, homelessness. That material rhetoric was created by the residents in a community within a specific space and contained physical structures and bodily entities as well as discourse about the challenges of urban Native life. The "Wall" residents could occupy space and set up tents and other structures, create their own community rules, preserve their belongings with some stability, and celebrate their voices, all in contrast to the lack of identity and agency they might have felt spending the nights in homeless shelters, doubling up with relatives, waiting for a low-income apartment, or living on the city streets. As rhetorician Amy Propen (2012) noted, not only physical and visual structures but also multimodal representations of those structures and residents, such as Gage's blog and the media photos and maps of the "Wall," allow us to understand how material rhetoric includes embodiment—or, according to visual rhetoric scholars Greg Dickinson and Casey Malone Maugh (2004), material rhetoric allows us "to locate our bodies in relation to other bodies in the world" (272). Thus, the very structure and appearance of the "Wall" encampment had the potential to represent the cultural loneliness of Native people experiencing homelessness, to demonstrate the problem of homelessness to the more privileged or housed communities, and to convey to all how Minneapolis had failed to address successfully the plight of these Native people.

Of course, despite the obvious presence and texture of the "Wall," Native people overall are stigmatized and marginalized to justify discrimination and to diminish their *ethos*. History Professor Theda Perdue and American studies Professor Michael Green (2010) identified that "the Indian as savage" served as rhetorical trope to deny Natives "the ability to change, thereby relegating them to the past and condemning them to extinction." In turn, when Natives assimilated successfully, they found their cultural authenticity questioned. In contrast, according to Perdue and Green, "If an Indian does not wear long hair and turquoise jewelry, seek visions, respect nature, and dance to a beating drum, can the person be a real Indian? Is an Indian who lives in a city, has a college degree, and practices a profession authentic?" (117). In both ways, Native identity seemed the purview of empowered others rather than Native people themselves. Thus stigmatized, Native people might also self-stigmatize, blaming themselves, rather than historical violence and current economic and political systems, for their situation. They may "pass" as Thistle did when he claimed to be Italian, or they may numb their emotional reactions to loss of identity and homelessness through substance abuse, as Thistle also noted:

"Drugs helped me forget everything I didn't want to think about and made me feel good about myself" (191). In particular, alcoholism and more recently drug abuse both constitute and ease the stigma faced by Native people. As Dunbar-Ortiz (2014) concluded, initially substance abuse was encouraged to curtail Native resistance to removal from their lands: "Alcohol was an item in the tool kit of colonists who made it readily and cheaply available" (84). Moreover, Perdue and Green (2010) described how many Seneca people turned to alcohol as they lost their land and were dislocated, regardless of the efforts of Tenskwataws and Tenumseh among the Shawnee who urged their followers to give up drinking and "return to their traditional tools, clothes, and religion" (49; see also Lurie 1971). Given their history, stigmatization of Native people is complex—or again what Link and Phelan (2001) called "the full execution of disapproval, rejection, exclusion, and discrimination" of the marginalized other (367).

The material existence of the "Wall" tent encampment, however, did become a potential source of renewed physical and spiritual identity for some of the two hundred residents who lived in the encampment. As Rai (2016) concluded, "shared meanings and rhetorical forces inhabit and emerge from our spaces and bodies" and that to have force, "rhetoric must be consequential and have a strong affective capacity—which is to say that it must have a potential for producing social effects, like changing minds, maintaining status quo, producing emotional responsibilities, or mobilizing civic action" (6). Material conditions, such as in the "Wall" encampment, have the potential to catalyze, transport, constrain, and constitute rhetorical forces that, in turn, "shape materialities" and become a "means of persuasion available in a social space" (14). The very number of "Wall" residents and their tents made their material and bodily occupation of the land not only visible but also inescapable to a great many Minneapolis citizens and policy makers. As Joy Friedman from the Minnesota Indian Women's Resource Center said, "This isn't a pond anymore. It's like the dam broke and it's turned into an ocean" (quoted in Du 2018). Thus, Friedman, blogger Gage, the Twin Cities and national print media, and Native organizations such as MUID watched carefully to see if the "Wall" encampment reached its rhetorical potential for empowerment or became just a problem to be solved.

Social and Print Media Coverage of the "Wall" Encampment

Minneapolis residents could follow the extensive print and electronic media coverage about the increasing number of tents erected in the "Wall" encampment and the health and safety concerns within the space. Indeed, print media coverage of the encampment was broad, including sources such as *News from Indian County* (Hobot 2018), the Associated Press (2018) via

NBC national news, and *The Guardian* (2018) both US- and UK-based. Residents could also personally witness the activities of the encampment in the heart of the Phillips neighborhood and alongside a freeway sound barrier.

But social media became an important source of information for those living in and monitoring the encampment, particularly Gage's blog. Overall, use of social media has grown common among Native people; as Treuer (2019) stated, "Social Media helps connect us" (443). Moreover, according to Martinez, Sage, and Ono (2016), social media and digital technologies now "allow tribal members to connect to their homelands and families to reinforce a sense of collective identity" in a form of "digital transnationalism" that supports relationships over geographical distances (xviii). For the Montana Little Shell Tribe of Chippewa Indians, for example, who until January 2020 was not recognized by the federal government, the eventual celebration of the Little Shell Restoration Act, Section 2870 of the National Defense Authorization Act, took place primarily via their Facebook page (Montana Little Shell 2020). Moreover, their fight for recognition and federal benefits was documented by the YouTube video *"The Whole Country Was . . . One Robe"* (Vrooman 2013). In turn, the Tribal Alliance of Sovereign Indian Nations (2021) maintains a website regarding Native sovereignty as does the National Congress of American Indians (2021), which provides updates on tribal governance and has reviewed some of the 120 court decisions since the 1950s that have dealt with Native affairs, rights, and sovereignty.

News of the "Wall of Forgotten Natives" encampment so spread via social and print media as well as Native organizations that AIM cofounder Clyde Bellecourt, a member of the White Earth Nation, visited the "Wall" encampment in December 2018. He noted, "The Great Spirit is the one that moves us to come together as people, as family" (quoted in Serres 2019c). Quite often in her blog, Gage wrote that the "Wall" could become a place where Native "relatives" rested and that within the encampment community the "immediate needs of unsheltered relatives" should be served (12.7.2018). Optimistically, Sam Strong predicated that the encampment itself, including the use of social media, "had already spurred change simply by forcing officials to address homelessness head-on" (quoted in Adler and Serres 2018). And yet, even though some of the "Wall" residents felt that they had established an acceptable, albeit temporary, home, many still suffered from spiritual homelessness and intergenerational trauma, the result of their ancestral history of ethnocide and genocide.

Spiritual Homelessness and Intergenerational Trauma

On the "Wall of Forgotten Natives" website, MUID (2018) described the land and space upon which the encampment grew as follows: "The water, trees, and all living things growing out of the ground carry with them the spirit of the original Dakota inhabitants because this ground is literally saturated with the DNA of our Indigenous ancestors," ancestors who "lived here for millennium before Minneapolis even became a City." Given that strong relationship with the spirit world, Native ancestors, and the land, MUID leaders seemed to recognize that the encampment residents might suffer not only from spiritual homelessness but also from intergenerational trauma. Blogger Gage noted the "invisible traumas" that might plague the "Wall" encampment residents and how the intergenerational trauma of these residents often took away their voices and their ability to articulate their needs (10.11.2018).

Therefore, when Gage launched her blog on September 7, 2018, she wrote, "Homeless people often struggle to find a voice within the system that makes so many decisions that affect their lives and wellbeing. They are often denied dignified means to assert their humanity." She felt it essential that blog entries be created as much as possible from the encampment residents' "own words," which included affirmations, promises, requests, and even resistance to outside policy makers monitoring the encampment, as she addressed those policy makers in the following blog entry:

> We know that your goal is to create more affordable housing. That would take years to meet the gap. In the meantime, the entire community benefits when people have emergency shelter. It is a public health crisis and very costly to have people living in public. We will do our part to improve our living situation but need emergency shelter to provide a safe place to sleep and address daily activities of functioning. (9.7.2018)

In the meantime, the "Wall" residents, according to Gage, would try to live as a family and community: "The old adage is apt because it's true: it does take a village to care for our youth and seniors, our sick and struggling. The same is true for the unsheltered people at the Franklin Hiawatha encampment" (10.25.2018). In turn, Sargent Grant Snyder, the Minneapolis Police Department's liaison to the city's homeless and vulnerable adult population, affirmed in Gage's blog that all of the "Wall" encampment residents "desperately want to end the suffering of those affected by homelessness and historical trauma" (emphasis in original, quoted in 12.16.2018). Thus, the "Wall of Forgotten Natives" encampment reflected the past and current struggles of Native people not only in recognition of their history but also in the encampment's very name.

The challenges to the Native people who sought refuge in the "Wall" encampment stemmed from trauma, not only from economic hardship and homelessness but also from separation from original families, lands, communities, and cultures, what geographer Julia Christensen (2013) defined as "spiritual homelessness." In Christensen's five-year ethnographic study of Native people who were homeless in the Northwest territories of Canada, spiritual homelessness came from "the profound sense of rootlessness that may come about when a relationship to place, both collectively and individually formed, becomes fragmented or fractured." For those whom she studied, homelessness was "indelibly tied to collective experiences such as colonisation [sic], sociocultural change and intergenerational trauma." "Home," concluded Christensen, although experienced differently by the many Native groups, was generally tied to the land, cultural identity, community, and generations of family (809). For many US and Canadian Native people, "home" became a trope for such qualities—and the loss of home became the cause of spiritual trauma.

Moreover, according to Porter's (2012) research on land and spirituality in Native cultures, these cultures "tend to include the seen and the unseen and build upon rather than segregate the sacred" (3). Native spirituality, a stance that reflects the values and behaviors rather than involvement in religious institutions, includes

> certain cosmological approaches, the idea of pervasive supernatural force, respect for dreams and visions, for song and dance, varying understanding of the afterlife, respect for ancestors, a sense of kinship with all things including the animate and inanimate and specific reverence for certain symbols and materials such as tobacco and medicine bundles. (4)

Porter found that Native people often tended to see land as sacred space "invested with meaning through lived experience and as something defined by its construction rather than its borders"; land was honored and held collectively rather than individually in bordered sections (5). On that land, Native people worked to create kin-based social organizations, the purpose of which was to ensure that the community survived and experienced only a minimal level of internal conflict. The central idea of these community relationships is still reciprocity, and no crime against the community is greater than "selfishness, no attitude more antisocial than arrogance, no behavior more loathsome than argumentativeness" (Perdue and Green 2010, 12–13). Therefore, quite often in her blog, Gage noted that the "Wall" community must build strong relationships, independent of the outside world, to address spiritual homelessness and intergenerational trauma.

Family social science scholars Laurelle Myhra and Elizabeth Wieling (2014) defined such intergenerational trauma as the result of "an assault on one cultural group by another that disrupts natural functioning, thereby creating vulnerabilities that may place individuals, families, communities, societies, and future generations at risk" (290; see also Stamm, Stamm, Hudnall, and Higson-Smith 2010). Ultimately, the actions of the European colonists, including the federal and state laws, treaties, and acts reviewed at the beginning of this chapter, served as the main cause for the intergenerational trauma of Native people. Dislocation, starvation, stress, disease, and genocide were the result of colonial conquest. The cultural trauma experienced by Native people included not only the political disappointment of broken treaties but also family disruptions, such as when Native children were forced to attend boarding schools or placed in foster families. Placing Native children in boarding school beginning in the 1870s constituted a deliberate "attempt to break a people," the results of which are still being felt today (Treuer 2019, 142). The Carlisle Indian Industrial School in Pennsylvania, for example, followed the motto of founder Captain Richard Henry Pratt that one must "Kill the Indian, and Save the Man." Native children were expected to assimilate into Western culture by losing their Native identity, language, and culture. Also, the violence and sexual assault that they experienced within the boarding schools was often the catalyst for domestic violence within their own homes for generations to come. As a result of intergenerational trauma, according to Myhra and Wieling (2014), an assaulted cultural group may experience "individual and community viewpoints that are permeated with fear, a sense of vulnerability, disillusionment, and distrust" (290). And, because of such internalized oppression, Native people may realize "suicide, family dysfunction, and community, institutional, and tribal violence," which lead to the "intergenerational patterns of learned helplessness" experienced today (290). Thus, this intergenerational trauma may be compounded by sexual and physical abuse, self-stigmatization and cultural racism, neglect, and family violence, which in turn can result in compromised mental and physical health, substance abuse, poverty—and, of course, homelessness.

Spiritual homelessness and intergenerational trauma can also reinforce the dichotomies and stigmatization of normal versus abnormal, housed versus homeless, and citizen versus other—and it can contribute to mental instability and loss of hope. As one former resident of the "Wall" encampment commented in a video interview, he grew up in "multiple homes, it was foster homes. Stuff like that. So home was never a real statement. There was nothing I could call home," and when asked about seeking counseling for such emotional issues, he responded, "I don't really tap into any of my emotions" ("Getting Deep" March 27, 2019). The "Wall" encampment, however, had the potential to represent not only ancestral connections but also present need, not only past injustices but also future redemption. However, as Jason Wasserman, a scholar in biomedical sciences, and Jeffrey Clair (2010), a scholar in sociology, cautioned their readers regarding homelessness, "It seems that rather than cling to our implicit sense that we can fix the problem, implying in the process that we could not possibly be the problem, we must in politics, service programs, social science, and throughout the public square, learn first to be friends to those who are homeless . . . [or] friends of the truth" (emphasis in original, 217). It is not enough to provide shelter for Native people struggling with homelessness; it is essential to realize the extent of their spiritual homelessness and intergenerational trauma as well as address their current situations. Listening to the voices of the homeless through social media, such as the blog created by Gage, provides one means to do so.

THE "WALL OF FORGOTTEN NATIVES" AS A CONTESTED SPACE

Overall, for many Native people, intergenerational trauma and spiritual homelessness compound the economic, psychological, and physical trauma suffered by people experiencing homelessness in general. Separated from ancestral lands, cast into a society in which profitable real estate became the norm, and having experienced loss of community and kinship relationships, all could lead to a feeling of helplessness and hopelessness among urban Native people. The "Wall of Forgotten Natives" encampment not only grew as a temporary remedy to the gap in affordable housing but also as a community in which Native traditions and connections might flourish, even on "marginal" space as defined by Snow and Mulcathy (2001). However, the "Wall" was located in urban space that seemed to have no immediate economic or social value but had the potential to be prime space if MnDOT sold the land to developers. Moreover, those observing the encampment internally and externally became suspicious of the "Wall" residents, who might bring crime and public health problems to the surrounding private homes.

The "Wall" encampment was fortunate in having articulate and involved organizations. In a timeline, linked to Gage's blog, several such organizations gave the encampment credibility. Moreover, on August 21, 2018, a group of Native leaders met with Mayor Frey, the city coordinator, and the deputy commissioner of the Minneapolis Department of Health. The Native representatives came from the Minneapolis American Indian Center, the Native American Community Development Institute, the Division of Indian Work, the Minnesota Indian Women's Resources Center, and the American Indian Community Development Corporation. At the meeting, MUID was recognized as the community advisory body for deliberations and decisions regarding the encampment as based on a Memorandum of Understanding (MOU) that MUID had with the City of Minneapolis. This MOU established a framework for the city's engagement with the Native community. Thus, a great many people and organizations monitored the encampment until an alternative place could be established.

Growing Pains

Like most such tent encampments created by people experiencing homelessness, the "Wall" experienced growing pains as the number of residents and tents increased and as the community became aware of how the land and space were being used. According to Gage, there was an "incredible outpouring of support from the community—that thousands of hot meals prepared and shared" (Gage 2020). The American Indian Community Development Corporation (AICDC) provided information on a range of services to the "Wall" residents, such as drug and alcohol counseling, and set up a hygienic service area where residents could take showers. Another "Wall" supporter, the Minneapolis Public Works, assisted in removing trash from the encampment, and in her blog, Gage urged "Wall" residents themselves to pick up trash, titling one blog entry "Trash, Trash, Trash and Did I Mention TRASH?" Much of this trash, Gage noted, came from clothing and food donations that were not used or preserved and ended up being thrown away. By late October 2018, given the increasing response to the media attention to the encampment, the "Wall" was "drowning in a sea of donations," including perishable food. In just over a week, Gage blogged that the encampment received twenty-five cases of quarts of heavy cream, six cases of potato salad, "case upon case" of romaine lettuce, "cases and cases of brown speckled bananas," and thousands of hamburger buns—all without a place to refrigerate and store the food (10.23.2018). Gage's blog not only asked residents to care for the environment but also encouraged sponsors to donate refrigeration units—all to help create *communitas* or a shared social media community in a reasonable and manageable physical environment.

The residents of the "Wall" encampment also worked with local police and other first responders to limit crime and avoid negative attention from their neighbors. Sergeant Snyder, for example, monitored potential threats within the encampment, such as reports of "groups of people going from tent to tent looking for single women," which indicated a threat of sex trafficking (quoted in Serres and Jany 2018). Snyder recognized, "In a lot of ways it's really a small city, and with that it's brought city-sized problems." And so, after a fire at the "Wall" encampment, Gage alerted her blog readers that the Minneapolis Fire Chief was so concerned about the safety of the residents that he donated a warming tent where residents could warm up without depending on hazardous space heaters in their individual tents. Various volunteer groups brought cooked meals to the encampment, and two groups did the laundry of the residents, an "incredible gift," as Gage noted in her blog. But she also commented: "It's difficult to witness so much raw need in a country where a small percentage of people have so very, very much. Some days the heart is heavy because of the staggering inequality" (9.24.2018). Initially, then, the "Wall" encampment seemed well-run even though the perceived contrast to housed citizens in the neighborhoods outside the encampment might be extreme.

Public Health Concerns

Increasingly, public health agencies became alarmed by such things as the number of used needles in the area surrounding the encampment. Here again, homelessness as a trope reinforced the image of "just a lot of Native drug addicts" that Gage had feared. Additionally, as one physician who volunteered to examine and recommend treatment to the residents of the "Wall" encampment concluded, "These are Third World conditions" (quoted in Serres 2018f). Several residents developed MRSA (methicillin-resistant Staphylococcus aureus), which could lead to sepsis, pneumonia, bloodstream infections, and death. Other residents tested positive for hepatitis C, scabies, and sexually transmitted diseases. Then James Cross, founder of the Natives Against Heroin, said, "This is a public health emergency. Nearly everyone here is sick—some of them seriously—and no one is getting treated" (quoted in Serres 2018f). In her blog, Gage described for her readers, including residents as well as Native organizations, the growing pains in the tent encampment, and she implored the residents to take care of their temporary but essential home as well as their own health.

Inevitably, there were deaths among the "Wall" residents as there are among people experiencing homelessness elsewhere. Gage reported in her blog first a number of near deaths in the encampment—in just 36 hours, for example, there were two overdoses from opioid drugs by residents who were revived by Narcan injections. In the same entry, however, Gage offered news of the death of a twenty-six-year-old camp resident, Alissa Rose Skipintheday, from an asthma attack. As Gage blogged, "Alissa's spirit fire no longer burns at the center of camp, but the presence of loss still remains" (9.12.2018). The spirit fire, a ritual in Native communities, is believed to guide a person's spirit as he or she joins ancestors after death. Just days later, the media reported a second death in the encampment, that of twenty-year-old Wade Redmond. Although the cause of Redmond's death was unclear, his mother shared that he had "struggled with a number of issues" including his sexual identity and that the "Wall" encampment "draws many people who do have homes but may struggle with mental illness, drug addiction and other issues in their lives" (quoted in Miller 2018). Then, a third death, a mother of eight children, was caused by an apparent overdose, as was a fourth death of a twenty-three-year-old woman who had recently moved to the encampment. With this last reported death, the *Star Tribune*, the largest newspaper in Minnesota, concluded,

> Her death is expected to renew concerns about safety at the sprawling homeless encampment near the Little Earth housing project, which since the summer has become the temporary home of approximately 200 men, women and children. Despite an intensive outreach effort by local health agencies and American Indian nonprofits, heroin and methamphetamine use is common at the camp, and overdoses have become an almost daily occurrence, outreach workers have said. (Serres 2018d)

Substance abuse, in the eyes of many, caused not only death but also jeopardized the encampment residents' freedom and autonomy within a bonded community—and threatened to confirm the stigma attached to the "Wall" residents.

Substance Abuse and Addiction

The stance taken by MUID regarding the "Wall" encampment, however, was to accept people where they were and to cast no judgment, including on their use of drugs and alcohol. As expressed in her opening entry to her "Wall" blog, Gage's goal was to capture the voices of the encampment residents as well as those voices of Native organizations and of policy makers. She included, for example, a statement signed by current encampment residents that any shelter that might house the "Wall" residents in the future must be "a safe haven . . . *without a sobriety requirement* and funded to provide compassionate, culturally sensitive staff" (emphasis added, quoted in 9.7.2018). A few days later, Gage reported the principles that future housing recommendations should follow, as agreed upon during a September 7, 2018, meeting with Mayor Frey as well as representatives of MUID, Natives Against Heroin, the Red Lake and Leech Lake Community, the Shakopee Mdewakanton Sioux Community, and various city, county, and state agencies. The group agreed that no "widespread dispersal of residents from the encampment" should happen before transition plans were firmly in place. Moreover, the location where residents might go next must include the following principle according to the group: "*Drug use at a shelter site has a particular and significant impact on women and children; therefore, care should be taken to be aware of and address this concern in any plan*" (emphasis added, 9.10.2018). The initial call for a no-sobriety requirement and the later thoughts on drug use may have seemed initially in conflict, particularly given the autonomy and freedom that attracted some encampment residents and the self-governing practices still being worked out at the "Wall"—but these two statements conveyed the difficulties of dealing with substance abuse and addiction and the nuances of maintaining personal freedoms.

Debates over whether homeless shelters should be free of drugs and alcohol are not unusual. Rose Lamatt (2011), for example, in her memoir about staying in a women's shelter, asked, "Should there be different sections for [the] homeless? Those with addictions, and those just 'homeless'?" (171). One of the organizations that continued to monitor the "Wall" encampment, however, was Natives Against Heroin, and the group's approach to substance use within the encampment was not as nuanced as were those approaches quoted in Gage's blog. Moreover, this organization's actions eventually contributed to the encampment becoming contested space among the residents and supporting organizations.

Natives Against Heroin

Natives Against Heroin (NAH) is a grassroots organization based in Duluth, Minnesota, whose founder, James Allen Cross, identifies as a spiritual healer and activist. At the age of four, Cross and his twin brother were taken from their Anishinaabe and Dakota parents and adopted by White parents. Cross often told the story of his family troubles, his twenty-two-year incarceration in prison, his subsequent recovery from drug abuse, and his worry about his brother who was not successful in his own recovery. Cross became an outreach worker for the White Earth Nation's Minneapolis drug treatment program, whose meetings began with the traditional Native smudging ceremony. Then Cross founded NAH in 2015, first as a talking circle and then as an activist organization. As Cross characterized NAH, "You know, we don't just talk about it, we do action" (quoted in Walsh 2018). Subsequently, NAH members patrolled the "Wall" encampment first with the purpose of administering Narcan to overdose victims and then to monitoring and eventually banishing suspected drug dealers. As Cross commented to the print media about the encampment, "We've gotta show who's in control. Otherwise, it would be chaos out here" (quoted in Serres 2018e). When Cross's goals went beyond monitoring of the encampment and as he reflected on his own street work against substance abuse, he expressed in a video interview, "We are strong people from the land. We have got to continue to help these people so we can rise up as a nation" ("Group Leading the Way" November 10, 2019; see also Collins 2016). NAH's actions within the "Wall" encampment were represented as being tied to Native identity in relationship to the land and in response to the relocation and stigmatization of Native people, people whose resolve would be weakened by substance abuse.

Scholars have long explored the substance abuse problems among Native people, first focusing on alcoholism and then on opioids. Psychiatrists Wesley Kaspros and Robert Rosenheck (1998), for example, found that Native veterans reported more alcohol abuse, more hospitalizations for alcohol dependence, and more days of "recent alcohol intoxication than members of other ethnic groups" (345). According to Martinez, Sage, and Ono (2016), "American Indians tend to start drinking at earlier ages, consume more both in quantity and frequency, and have more alcohol-related life consequences than any other group" (46). Specifically, Susan Logo and Margaret Mortensen Vaughan (2003), scholars and activists involved in Native cultures, found that homeless Natives used alcohol and drugs "to become comfortable or brave enough to panhandle, to handle harsh circumstances such as cold weather, to self-medicate for mental or physical stress, for recreation, or as a tool for metaphysical insights or spirituality" (66). Moreover, substance abuse and its causes and effects are often discussed in detail by Natives experiencing homelessness. One such Native, for example, stated in his video interview how he feared dementia from alcoholism: "It hasn't hit me yet—one day I will just wake up and start talking to myself" ("Homeless Alcoholic— Wolf" April 14, 2012). And Thistle (2019) described in his memoir the physical and psychological effects of his own withdrawal from crack cocaine: "[T]he ever-increasing psychosis of withdrawal from crack broke me into shards of shame and pity and guilt that burned under my forehead like napalm with gasoline and lit by a blowtorch" (250). In the "Wall of Forgotten Natives" encampment, drug and alcohol abuse became an internal aspect of conflict, particularly as exercised by NAH and as reflected upon by the Native organizations that constituted MUID. This conflict was fought with rhetorical strategies as well as with physical assault.

Intragroup Conflict

Gage's blog entries, media coverage of the "Wall of Forgotten Natives" tent encampment, and statements from MUID and NAH differed about whether to curtail substance abuse and whether to rely on exile or banishment to do so. Generally, stigmatization of people experiencing homelessness might not include a recognition of such intragroup conflict. People experiencing homelessness are imagined in conflict with the housed or so-called normal community, rather than with each other, but conflicts based on differing principles and protocols exist among the people experiencing homelessness—particularly regarding substance abuse as in the case of the "Wall" encampment.

As Wasserman and Clair (2010) reminded their readers, "Homelessness is not purely an economic disadvantage, but also a stigmatized social identity that is given meaning according to its conceptual distance from the 'norm'" (2). Stigmatization depends on othering individuals according to a supposed common characteristic, such as homelessness—hence, homelessness becomes a trope for a great many assumed features. Just as Ratcliffe (2000) explained, failure to examine the social and cultural origins of a trope as well as the power hierarchies involved in those origins "blinds and blindsides people by offering them socially constructed concepts, such as race and gender, presented as The Truth" (105). One of those "Truths" involved substance abuse—both as a cause for and a feature of homelessness. This trope was harshly extended to Native people; again, for Thistle's childhood friends, "Indian" was a trope for drunkenness. More recently, researchers Robin Tipps, Gregory Buzzard, and John McDougall (2018) reported in *The Journal of Law, Medicine & Ethics* that the overdose mortality rates in Minneapolis among Natives were "strikingly high" (426) and that tribal nations used banishment to address substance abuse problems in their communities. However, these scholars cautioned, "Banishment is not a healing or restorative practice; it does nothing to address the drug use disorder that the banished person or others may be experiencing" (432). Additionally, banishment does very little to diminish the supply of drugs coming into Native territories, particularly in less remote areas. The "Wall" encampment was not at all a remote area, and so drugs were readily available, but even given all the good that NAH did in administering Narcan to people suffering overdoses, NAH also promoted banishment from the encampment to control substance abuse. NAH also helped residents participate in chemical health assessments ("Rule 25") and make contact with treatment centers, but in terms of the "Wall" encampment, NAH insisted that the drug dealers leave, an ineffective way to address the problem and a violation of the goal openly accepting all people to reside in the encampment. Thus, in the "Wall" encampment, NAH assumed the role of protectors as Wasserman and Clair (2010) defined them—those who deal with threat and conflict in homeless encampments and interject themselves on behalf of others. In this case, that interjection was not altogether welcome.

"Wall" residents soon began to complain about NAH's aggressive tactics based on that protector role. At first, Gage had praised NAH's contributions in relationship with those of other organizations, such as MUID. Also, when Peggy Flanagan, then candidate for Minnesota lieutenant governor, toured the encampment, she was accompanied by both Robert Lilligren from MUID and James Cross from NAH. Early in her blog, Gage thanked NAH for its continued work and leadership (9.12.2018). By December 7, 2018, however, Gage posted a blog entry titled "The Challenges of Collaboration," in which she wrote to clarify local media coverage of the NAH's activities in the encampment. NAH frequently complained that MUID-affiliated agencies and the Minneapolis Police Department were "not doing enough at the camp," and NAH spread rumors that MUID-affiliated agencies were withholding donations from the encampment. NAH's aggression included obscenities that "were hurled at female and Two Spirit staff and volunteers" and actions that meant other staff members were "literally run out of the camp." Gage herself clarified hearsay that was circulated within the encampment about her own interaction with NAH: "I can state that I was the object of such an attack and that my experience with this is first hand" (12.7.2018). This clarification might have moved blogger Gage from reporter to framer, a role defined by Humphreys (2016) as "strategically referring to a social issue, practice, or group to heighten some of its attributes and downplay other aspects" (248). Gage did include a statement that NAH leadership "has now adopted a pro-prietary view of the encampment" in that they "believe they had the power to decide who enters the camp, who brings food and donations to campers, and even what campers can remain in the encampment." This blog entry was somewhat unusual for Gage as she worked to maintain her stance as trusted reporter and conduit. Moreover, she conveyed a statement from MUID issued that day:

> We are in an era where Native people and the organizations that serve them have been striving to work in more collaborative ways. In doing so, MUID seeks to build on the example of Standing Rock to throw off the mantle of colonization and return to more Indigenous ways of being together. These ways reflect that all Native people have roles in the community, and to respect the roles that each person and organization plays. (12.7.2018)

In the same blog entry, Gage reported that NAH was destroying the tents of those whom they believed were drug sellers or undercover police. But again, she included MUID's plea: "Let us ALL join together in service to the immediate needs of the unsheltered relatives at the encampment. May we work together in a good way, with mutual respect and dignity shown to all who come to help with positive intent and an open heart" (12.7.2018). Gage affirmed her *ethos* as trustworthy reporter by sharing her observations and experiences as well as providing a link to the stance of MUID, in essence letting MUID confirm the problematic role that NAH had taken.

Reflections on the Dispute

In conjunction with Gage's blog, MUID condemned NAH's use of threats and intimidation "in attempts to disrupt service delivery and organizing efforts" and their "spread" of inaccurate information, particularly regarding a proposed navigation center that was designed to eventually provide safer and more secure shelter to those "Wall" residents who wanted it (quoted in Serres 2018c). Perhaps the most disturbing complaint against NAH was the group's supposed encouragement of "racial divides" among the encampment residents and NAH's employment of violence "to deter people from delivering support to those living at the camp." Thus, MUID announced that it could "no longer support the current actions and tactics of NAH," actions and tactics that had divided the community and which were "creating distrust, suspicion and fear" that are not "Indigenous values" (12.7.2018; see also Park and Lilligren 2018). Because of their attempt to banish those selling drugs within the "Wall" encampment, NAH itself was exiled from the "Wall" encampment, and Gage's blog chronicled this result. Overall, NAH's actions threatened not only the principles of acceptance within the encampment but also a sense of agency or choice among its residents, both of which proved more important to the Native organizations than the stigmatization that had plagued them.

The traditional media coverage of the conflict between NAH and MUID and Native organizations was less sanguine and philosophical than were Gage's blog and MUID's social media posts. The quotes from NAH and its detractors or supporters as captured by the print media provided evidence that the "Wall" encampment was becoming a contested space:

- From MUID—"We can't do our work if people are harassing us";
- From NAH—"If people are fearful, that's on them, because they don't understand our ways and this lifestyle";
- From one resident whose tent was labeled "UNDER COVER PIG"—"Someone sees that written on your tent, and you're likely to get a bullet through your heart";
- From an outreach navigator with the Indian Women's Resource Center—"It's crazy that we've become the enemy. The problem is, I can't get donations over there—not without putting other people at risk";
- And, finally, from NAH volunteers—"Shut it down!" they shouted as they "ripped out tents they said belonged to drug dealers and threw their belongings in a giant pile, near the center of the camp, according to the videos that members of the group posted on Facebook" (quoted in Serres 2018b).

What began as intragroup conflict was displayed in such discourse as open warfare, the catalyst for a public meeting held on December 8, 2019.

At this meeting, more than two hundred people gathered to discuss the upcoming move of "Wall" encampment residents to a future navigation center as well as how the encampment might be devolving and how people working in the camp were being mistreated. As Mayor Frey told the group assembled at the American Indian Center, "What I don't want is a showdown between our Native American brothers and sisters." Native leaders from Red Lake, Leech Lake, White Earth, and Fond du Lac attended the meeting, and Clyde Bellecourt reminded the group, "The women and children are the ones that suffer the most because we are divided and can't get our act together" (quoted in Adler and Serres 2018). In turn, Kevin DuPuis, from the Fond du Lake Band of Lake Superior Chippewa, said that if the group could not get organized and eliminate conflict, "We will become our own worst enemy, like always. We have the ability to choose our own destiny." DuPuis continued with a story about the unfortunate results of such conflicts: "I think everybody here has heard of the crab syndrome, right? Whenever a crab gets to the top of the bucket, the other crabs pull it down. It's no different. So I'm here for that simple reason: find a resolution to what's happening down here as best as we possibly can" (quoted in Du 2018). Native groups resolved to solve their own problems, based on their cultural values and beliefs. Finally, to address the problems stemming from and conflicts regarding substance abuse, Frey announced that future residents of a navigation center would not be tested for drugs upon admittance, but they could not use drugs in the center.

NAH members, however, would not accept this compromise. Cross was reported to have pounded the table and shouted, "We're out here in the cold, rain, snow, providing resources for our community. And if nobody [else] was out there, guess what? There would have been more deaths, more ODs, more sexual assaults" (quoted in Du 2018). In the midst of these discussions, NAH members left the meeting "in apparent anger" (Adler and Serres 2018). A month earlier, Cross himself had been served with a warrant for dealing heroin based on his entering "a variety of tents for brief stops"; one of those tents belonged to a known heroin dealer, and Cross was accused of allowing the dealers whom he "controls" to stay in the "Wall" encampment (FOX 9 News 2018; District Court 2018). No arrest was issued based on the warrant, but the "Wall" encampment was surrounded by a cloud of conflict and suspicion—played out in the space itself, featured in the media, and reported in Gage's blog.

The case study of the "Wall of Forgotten Natives" homeless encampment offers a unique opportunity to understand how space is discursively and materially created—a product of discourse, a reflection of power and hierarchy, a kind of text or texture that conveys the complexity of community and culture, and, overall, a social construction. Certainly, the "Wall" encampment must be contextualized within the history of conquest, assimilation, ethnocide, and genocide of Native people in North America. Although the US federal government participated in treaties, acts, and laws to address Native nations, their main goal was to take ownership of the land populated and cultivated by Native people—and to convince Native people of the value of private real estate and to dissolve Native nations and kinship communities. The very names of the federal acts and laws represent this goal of sustaining White colonialists and settlers and controlling Native nations: "Removal," "Appropriation," "Allotment," "Reorganization," and "Relocation."

The "Wall" encampment is representative of the stigmatization of Native people experiencing homelessness. And, the voices of those Native people experiencing homelessness and seeking to create their own communities, out of practical necessity as well as the need for autonomy and agency, can be heard within social media such as Camille Gage's blog. Gage not only created the "Wall of Forgotten Natives" blog and reported on the encampment activities, but she maintained, as much as possible, neutrality in order to capture and convey the voices of encampment residents themselves—to exercise rhetorical listening. Gage went on to become the Digital Communication coordinator of WiiDooKoDaaDiiWag ("They Help Each Other"), an organization that focuses on Native voices and grassroots solutions to "the issues facing the Indigenous community, especially the challenge of creating culturally appropriate and affordable housing, shelter and supportive services." The Bush Foundation supported this project along with the Native American Community Development Institute and MUID. In 2019, Gage wrote this organization's blog.

Overall, analysis of the past actions of the federal and state governments against Native people as well as the spiritual homelessness and the trauma they experienced increases our understanding of Native people experiencing homelessness. My analysis included how the health and safety of "Wall" residents were compromised within the encampment environment itself, how encampment residents sought to maintain their personal and cultural identities, and how addiction and substance abuse inevitably became issues. Moreover, an illustration of intragroup conflict among people experiencing homelessness illuminates the hard-fought value of voice and agency among those experiencing homelessness. In the fourth chapter in this book, I return to those "Wall" residents who moved to the navigation center created to address their homelessness. Overall, in this chapter and in the next one, I focus on the spatial segregation of certain stigmatized groups as a way to contain and control them, to marginalize them, and to exclude them from the benefits that the housed and empowered enjoy. These measures seem a deliberate way to maintain and increase the value of the land owned by the socioeconomically advantaged and to blame those without such advantages for their own problems.

Chapter Two

"Not in My Neighborhood" or Even in My City

Legal Restrictions in Private and Public Spaces

In 2015, Canadian blogger "Lawrence" (B4) wrote an entry just after the Supreme Court of British Columbia struck down the city of Abbotsford's bylaw that prohibited sleeping in public, being in a city park overnight, and even erecting a temporary shelter, such as a tent, without a permit. The Chief Justice of the Supreme Court, according to Lawrence, told the city that "homelessness was not something to be treated like a crime" and that "there were clearly not enough shelter beds for them [people experiencing homelessness] to sleep in—and people needed their sleep!" Lawrence maintained his blog throughout his homelessness, once using a laptop he found while dumpster diving. For several years, he used his blog to illuminate how city ordinances and bylaws marginalized and discriminated against people experiencing homelessness in order to spatially segregate them. In this particular blog entry, Lawrence went on to critique the newly defunct Abbotsford bylaw: "The [Supreme Court] ruling was most definitely a loss for Abbotsford and its years spent treating homeless people like poop and foot-dragging on the issue of shelters." Lawrence then reflected on how Abbotsford's attempt to outlaw such activities in public space stemmed from the universal stigma attached to people experiencing homelessness. When the Abbotsford law was overturned, Lawrence commented, "Hopefully the biggest loser of all was the old bigoted idea that still seems to have some currency in places like Abbotsford, that marginalized groups are less deserving of human considerations and that the majority can treat such groups as criminals or even animals, just because they are marginalized" (10.22.2015).

Like Lawrence, California blogger "Patrick" (B3) used social media to expose the power of what he called "negative" myths, referring in essence to the rhetorical trope of homelessness that includes the supposition that "homeless people are lazy." These tropes might appear in newspaper articles, internet discussion groups, and political forums: "For example," wrote Patrick, "it is easy to sway a city council, or police department, if nothing but negatives are declared concerning the homeless, especially when there is no one around to counter these statements" (6.8.2015). Again, various bloggers as well as memoir writers have used their voices to report on the challenges of homelessness and to deconstruct the tropes about homelessness. They also expose the political stances and social misunderstandings that affect the survival, health, and safety of people experiencing homelessness, and they encourage their readers to question the stigma that sets up visible as well as invisible spatial boundaries to separate the housed from the homeless. As Michael Gaulden (2017) began his memoir about his escape from homelessness, "Allow this memoir to serve as a window into my soul. This is my true story. Feel my grief, feel my hunger, and feel my sorrow—but then, feel my success" (7). To understand homelessness, we must listen to the voices of Lawrence, Patrick, Gaulden, and others, and we must question the attempted exclusion of people experiencing homelessness from our neighborhoods and even from our cities.

In this chapter I extend the analysis in chapter one, moving *from* how land was taken from Native people for its value *to* how space became a tool to restrict and segregate racial, religious, and ethnic minorities by way of state and city ordinances as well as the practices of real estate developers and mortgage brokers in urban settings. Again, the impulse to spatially segregate people experiencing homelessness often leads to marking or classification of space—whether it be the pleasure, refuse, and function spaces identified by Wright (1992) or the prime, marginal, and transitional spaces named by Snow and Mulcathy (2001). As Wright added, certain actions and events constitute the *exclusion* of people experiencing homelessness "from particular areas, discourses, narratives, and any given means of communication" while they also suffered *repression* actions and events to "forcibly remove, punish, or harass" them for "occupying space or communication in ways not sanctioned by authority" (183). Again, these spaces are dynamic, but they are also subject to political, economic, social, and, as I show in this chapter, legal attempts to solidify the spatial categories themselves.

Initially, the perspective of eugenics was used to stigmatize minority groups and to exclude them from urban neighborhoods occupied by empowered White majorities. Based on this perspective, spatial boundaries were maintained through racial zoning, redlining, and restrictive covenants, which led to the spatial segregation of Black families such as in the Five Points area in Denver, Colorado, a primary case study in this chapter. The population of Five Points grew during the Great Migration of Blacks to the North to escape Southern Jim Crow laws and expanded once again during the housing crisis after World War II in which Blacks, in particular, were prohibited from renting and owning homes in other areas of Denver. I developed Five Points as a case study example not only because, as a Denver native, I was familiar with this area, but also because, despite these spatial restrictions, the community uniquely flourished at one point only to be diminished again by gentrification. Overall, from before the 1920s through today, various racial, ethnic, and religious groups are often confronted by limited housing and resulting homelessness in cities across the United States, from Baltimore to Denver and Los Angeles.

More recently, city ordinances have been used to exclude so-called dangerous others from neighborhoods and entire communities. And, according to geographer Don Mitchell (2003), other local ordinances were created "to control behavior and space such that homeless people cannot do what they must do in order to survive without breaking laws. Survival itself is criminalized" (163). Social media and personal memoirs again illuminate how people experiencing homelessness are affected by and react to the enforcement of these "quality-of-life" laws that forbid activities such as camping on public land, loitering and drinking in public spaces, urinating and defecating in public, and sleeping or even sitting on sidewalks during certain hours or for specified lengths of time—the survival activities that Lawrence, Patrick, Gaulden, and others identify.

THE FIVE POINTS NEIGHBORHOOD OF DENVER

Five Points was named in 1881 for a five-way intersection in the heart of Denver, formed where Welton Street, East 26th Avenue, Washington Street, and 27th Street meet. The name also proved useful because the streetcar signs could not accommodate all those street names for the one stop at the intersection. By 1890, Denver had become the third largest city in the West, and a great proportion of Black workers found employment in Denver by laying track for the railroad companies. Close to these railroad yards and subsequent industrial plants, Five Points became the heart of the Black community in Denver (see, for example, Denver Public Library 2020; Five Points Business Improvement District; Hansen 2007; Jones 2018; Mauck 2001; Stephens, Larson, and the Black American West Museum 2008).

When Black workers and their families moved to Five Points, the population of the community shifted from European immigrants, including the many wealthy and professional German, Irish, and Jewish peoples who then moved to newer and better housing farther from the downtown area. In particular, upper-class Whites moved to Capitol Hill and into the new mansions there, as Black individuals and families stayed closer to the railroad yards along the South Platte River. Then, in the 1910s and 1920s during the Great Migration from southern states when new Black residents moved to Denver and settled in Five Points, the White population began to create discriminatory housing policies and spatial boundaries to keep the Black population confined to Five Points. Thus, a *Colorado Encyclopedia* entry on "Five Points" noted, "By 1929, about 5,500 of Denver's black residents (more than 75 percent) were concentrated in the neighborhood." Such deliberate actions spatially segregated Black individuals and families from more prosperous and desirable neighborhoods in Denver.

As a cultural, educational, and business community, however, Five Points eventually flourished. In 1881, for example, the first Black newspaper in Denver, *The Denver Weekly Star*, was published. Whittier Elementary School served the predominately Black community on the edge of Five Points that was named after the abolitionist John Greenleaf Whittier. Businesses such as Crescent Flour Mills, the Colorado Iron Works, and the Denver Fire Clay Company appreciated the proximity of Five Points to the railroad yards. Also, according to historian Laura Mauck (2001), at this time Welton Street housed "the largest black business community in the west" (72). In 1868, Denver's first public park, Curtis Park, was established in Five Points, and the second public park, Fuller Park, was created in the Whittier neighborhood. Then Camp Nizhoni, organized by the Phillis Wheatley Colored YWCA on Welton Street, allowed Black girls who were excluded from other camps to enjoy the mountains near Lincoln Hills, an all-Black mountain resort community founded in the 1910s. Subsequently, the Glenarm YMCA was built in 1924, became the "unofficial town hall of Five Points," and offered everything from a swimming pool and gymnasium to dormitories and a branch of the Denver Public Library (Denver Public Library 2020). The first Black dentist in Denver, Dr. Clarence Holmes, opened his practice on Welton Street and helped found the Colorado-Wyoming branch of the National Association for the Advancement of Colored People (NAACP). Another doctor, Justina Ford, treated Black, Korean, Japanese, Latino, Hispanic, and White patients during her fifty years in Five Points, reflecting the racial and ethnic diversity that Five Points enjoyed. In 1984, Dr. Ford's former home and office became the Black American West Museum. Finally, the Black Zion Baptist Church has remained in Five Points, and Juneteenth and the Five Points Jazz Festivals are still celebrated in the neighborhood.

Specifically, at such establishments as the Rossonian Hotel, the Two-Tap Room, Casino Cabaret, Lil's, and Benny Hooper's Ex-Serviceman's Club, jazz musicians entertained the Five Points community, and thus the area became known as the "Harlem of the West." Because these musicians could not stay in the segregated Denver hotels as they continued on their national tours, Five Points residents offered them shelter. In return, musicians such as Duke Ellington, Count Basie, Lionel Hampton, Billie Holliday, Ella Fitzgerald, Miles Davis, and Nat King Cole played after hours in Five Points jazz establishments. According to Mark Hanna Wilkins's 1945 review of the "Racial Situation in Denver," when orchestras visited Denver, their Black sponsors would rent the Rainbow Ballroom for one night, and although White patrons could attend as spectators, they could not dance even if they selected companions "from their own group." In turn, one of Denver's leading entertainment centers, Elitch Gardens, would admit Black spectators, but they were not permitted to dance. Within this segregated environment, Wilkins recalled a story of one White couple's attempt to dance at the Rainbow Ballroom while Lionel Hampton and his orchestra were playing for Black dancers: "The white girl reported that a Negro girl kicked her rather severely on the legs when she attempted to dance." Despite how Five Points flourished culturally in these early days, the community still reflected the perspectives and discriminatory measures that created residential and spatial segregation in Denver and other major US cities—segregation that contributed to homelessness among racial minorities. One such perspective came from the eugenics movement.

INFLUENCE OF THE EUGENICS MOVEMENT ON SPATIAL SEGREGATION

From the 1920s to beyond the end of WWII, spatial boundaries and racial restrictions reflected eugenics beliefs and practices that were supposedly designed to improve the genetic quality of the human populations in the United States and other countries by marginalizing and segregating the so-called undesirables. In *Buck v. Bell* (1927), for example, the Supreme Court set the precedent that states could legally sterilize inmates of public institutions to prevent those considered genetically defective from reproducing. In the *Buck* decision, the Court held that Carrie Buck, the so-called feeble-minded daughter and granddaughter of similarly affected women, could be sterilized under the 1924 Virginia Eugenic Sterilization Act and that such sterilization laws did not violate the Due Process Clause of the Fourteenth Amendment. In his majority decision, Justice Oliver Wendell Holmes offered the now infamous statement, "Instead of waiting to execute degenerate offspring for crime, or let them starve for their imbecility, society can prevent those who are manifestly unfit from continuing their kind. . . . Three generations of imbeciles are enough." Holmes's opinion became fuel for the argument that certain ethnic and racial groups were not only inferior but also undesirable in neighborhoods and cities—and marginalized people became unwelcome in private spaces even though they might become homeless as a result. The overall fear was that such so-called undesirables would bring crime into public spaces and lower the value of private spaces.

Although *Buck v. Bell* itself was never overturned, by the 1970s most states had repealed such sterilization laws. However, as Antero Pietila (2010) offered in his book *Not in My Neighborhood*, at one time 239 cities set spatial boundaries "according to white-supremacist eugenic assumptions that ranked nationalities according to race, religion, and pseudoscientific stereotypes" (vii). As Pietila discovered, Homer Hoyt, the 1934 Federal Housing Administration's chief economist, "saw ethnicity as a key to predicting [housing] value" (62). To use Hoyt's language, he ranked English, Germans, Irish, and Scandinavians as the most desirable homeowners and neighbors, and Russian Jews, Negroes, and Mexicans as the least desirable. According to Pietila, "Hoyt's list looked suspiciously like the hierarchical rankings that eugenicists had been publishing about various ethnic groups for decades" (63). In turn, the Chicago School of Sociology created a system of concentric circles reflecting these hierarchical rankings, radiating from the center of the city and reflecting the constant movement of higher economic groups to the suburbs, leaving behind lower socioeconomic groups who were marginalized by their race, ethnicity, and religion to occupy space considered undesirable.

This marginalization was not only based on eugenics thinking but was also linked to White supremacist groups such as the Ku Klux Klan (KKK), the hate group that targeted Black people among other minorities, protested interracial mingling, and promoted nativism (see, for example, Largent 2002 for such activities in Oregon; Rhomberg 1998 for California). As Mauck (2001) noted, in the 1920s the Colorado branch of the KKK was second only to Indiana in number of members. Even the former Denver Mayor Benjamin Stapleton, after whom Denver's first major airport was named, was a high-ranking KKK member in the 1940s. However, to alert the Denver Black community to the KKK's activities, Dr. Joseph Henry Peter Westbrook passed as a White man to infiltrate the KKK. And, in response to this oppressive atmosphere, the Cosmopolitan Club, an interracial organization, promoted interracial and interfaith understanding and protested discrimination. Despite these last two efforts to curtail racial segregation, commentator Wilkins (1945) alluded to Horace Greeley's recommendation, "Go west, young man, and grow up with the country," when he concluded that Black migration to Denver was a mixed bag: "The Negro who 'goes west' to Denver will find relief from some of the sordid conditions of the South, but he will not escape the 'long arm of racial prejudice.'" This impression was confirmed decades later by Ronald Stephens, La Wanna Larson, and the Black American West Museum in Five

Points (2008): "Racial segregation was pervasive in Denver. So too was the Ku Klux Klan. . . . The average Klan member worried about the peace of this community and the honor of his daughter" (9). Thus, the eugenics perspective dominated such thinking in the years before and immediately after WWII.

As early as 1927, however, Black students and their parents from Morey Junior High School near the Five Points community and Manual High School in the Whittier neighborhood turned to the law to address racial inequality in the schools. This group successfully sued Jessie H. Newlon, the Superintendent of Public Instruction of the City and County of Denver, for establishing a system that separated school social functions based on race. But later on, in *Keyes et al. v. School District No. 1* (1973) in which when petitioners sought school desegregation of the affluent Park Hill area in Denver, the US Supreme Court decided that although the Park Hill schools needed to provide equal facilities for all races, an overall policy of deseg-regation was not needed in all Denver area schools. Today, as David Rusk (2003) discovered, Denver public schools continued to be "somewhat more segregated than its peer communities and the average of the 100 largest metro areas" (8). Overall, eugenics thinking about racial identity was one of the factors contributing to housing discrimination, which contributed in turn to marginalization of certain groups and homelessness among these groups.

Racial segregation measures in housing, for which such eugenics thinking served as a catalyst, remained for over a century in many neighborhoods in Denver and across the United States. That continuous approach was captured by T. B. Benson in 1915 as he analyzed whether the Fourteenth Amendment to the Constitution, as interpreted by the Supreme Court in *Plessy v. Ferguson* (1896), enforced absolute equality of the Black and White races, including access to housing. According to Benson (1915), the *Plessy* decision did not mean that "distinctions based on color" should be abolished, particularly when "a commingling of the two races [was accomplished] upon terms unsatisfactory to either" (335). Moreover, concluded Benson, it was a false assumption that the only way for Black families to improve their condition was to move into a neighborhood of mainly White residents: "To admit the soundness of this assumption would be to ascribe to the negro [sic] race a lack of capacity for self development, a want of self respect and of thrift, and a degree of dependence on the White race which, it seems, the history, past and current, of that people does not sustain" (335–36). The Black race would flourish, thought Benson and others, in spatially segregated neighborhoods.

The perspectives that Benson offered, as well as the racial segregation jus-tified by eugenics, led to the promotion of housing restrictions that emerged at the end of the nineteenth century and that remain, to some extent, today. Furthermore, as the National Alliance to End Homelessness (2020b) con-cluded, "disproportionality in homelessness," among Blacks in particular, "is a by-product of systemic inequity" or "the lingering effects of racism [that] continue to perpetuate disparities in critical areas that impact rates of homelessness" (see also National Alliance to End Homelessness 2020a and 2020d). These housing restrictions were exposed and legally challenged with limited results, and they negatively affected generations of Black people to come. Moreover, they were as effective as the federal acts regarding Native lands in terms of controlling who could freely occupy and manage urban neighborhoods and, at times, entire cities.

HOUSING RESTRICTIONS IN URBAN SPACES

Racial zoning, redlining, and restrictive deed covenants are all measures used to spatially segregate people by housing availability. These measures were based initially on eugenics and then for decades on the assumption not only that minority renters and homeowners would accept crowded and rundown housing but also that any move on their part to prime spaces would turn those neighborhoods into dangerous and undesirable spaces. Specifically, if minority residents moved into White and more privileged socioeconomic neighborhoods, they would destroy property values and bring crime into the area. As sociologist Kevin Gotham (2000) described the cultivation and development of such housing restrictions, they were "an exercise in the racialization of urban space that linked race and culturally specific behavior to place of residence in the city" (617). Thus, racial zoning, redlining, and restrictive deed covenants were created to ease the prospect of neighborhood decline, and control and categorization of space became tools to restrict and segregate the stigmatized other.

In a way, a minority racial identity became a trope for destructive behavior in private spaces, from individual houses to neighborhoods. Moreover, according to Gotham (2000), the association of "black behavior and culture with deteriorating neighborhoods and the creation and maintenance of the color-line in housing became the raison d'etre of the real estate industry" (617). In the 1960s, at the same time that the Denver chapter of the Congress on Racial Equality (CORE) was established to protest unjust treatment throughout urban space, Black residents sought to leave Five Points. But by then, as historian Moya Hansen (2007) noted, the reputation of Five Points "as a dangerous neighborhood was well established." Exiting Five Points became very difficult—and housing restrictions and spatial boundaries made such exits almost impossible. These housing restrictions were also supported by court decisions; by interpretations of the Fifth, Thirteenth, and Fourteenth Constitutional Amendments; by professional real estate organizations, mortgage lenders, and bankers; and by individual homeowners and their neighborhood associations. Conflict over such housing segregation reflected both sides of the "rights consciousness" issue as described by historian Jeffrey Gonda (2015): Black individuals and families "asserted that the ability to purchase a decent home free from discrimination was a vital and human right," while White homeowners "countered by insisting upon a set of property and contractual rights that entitled them to protect their homes and by extension the financial and social stability of the neighborhoods where they lived" (7). In such conflicts, the increasing acquisition and commercial value of private urban spaces served as a catalyst for strict racial differences and social identities.

Such restrictions, according to Richard Rothstein (2017), not only reflected racial discrimination but also stemmed from *de jure* segregation or segregation initiated and maintained by law and public policy, including the practices of the Federal Housing Administration (FHA). This *de jure* segregation set the stage for homelessness among Black and other minority individuals and families. As public policy expert Joy Moses (2020) concluded, most recently 40 percent of Black people experiencing homelessness are families with children, while only 22 percent of homeless White people have families: "If the representation of families within black homelessness resembled these other groups, the black rate of homelessness would drop from 55 to 42 people per 10,000." Overall, racial zoning, redlining, and restrictive covenants were housing discrimination measures that contributed to this state of homelessness, again peaking during the Great Migration and at the end of WWII.

Racial Zoning and Redlining

Racial zoning ordinances regulated where Black people, in particular, were allowed to live in urban areas, mainly because these areas were private rather than public spaces. In other words, some housing ordinances may have been created by public officials, but private homeowners often welcomed and enforced these ordinances. Originally these ordinances were justified by officials, such as Milton Dashiel, the attorney who drafted Baltimore's zoning ordinance in 1910 according to racial bias and stigmatization: "Ordinarily, the negro [sic] loves to gather to himself, for he is very gregarious and sociable in his nature. But those who have risen somewhat about their fellows appear to have an intense desire to . . . get as close to the company of white people as circumstances will permit them" (quoted in Rothstein 2017, 44). Twelve years later, as Rothstein (2017) noted, the 1922 Atlanta City Planning Commission divided the city into an "R-1 white district" and an "R-2 colored district," because "race zoning is essential in the interest of the public peace, order and security and will promote the welfare and prosperity of both the white and colored race" (46). Moreover, in St. Louis, Missouri, zoning ordinances allowed land for future industrial development, rather than private housing, "if it was in or adjacent to neighborhoods with substantial African American populations" (49). Thus, zoning ordinances were based on racial segregation and the impulse to divide and categorize land and space, and the authors of such ordinances justified their effects according to racial prejudice and stigmatization. These ordinances, in essence, protected prime and private space, and racial zoning laws employed three specific strategies: (1) They reserved spaces for single-family homes that could be afforded by White middle-class families and made it difficult, if not impossible, for Blacks to live there; (2) they successfully evaded any legal prohibition on racially explicit zoning established by the courts; and (3) they protected White neighborhoods from, according to Rothstein (2017), "deterioration by ensuring that few industrial or environmentally unsafe businesses could locate in them." Thereby, the ordinances created "urban African American slums" where industries would locate, to the determinant of private housing for minorities (57). Although the Supreme Court overturned the racial zoning ordinance of Louisville, Kentucky, in *Buchanan v. Warley* (1917) and determined that racial zoning laws interfered with the rights of property owners to sell to whomever they pleased, a great many states ignored the *Buchanan* decision for decades.

Then, in the late 1940s, a housing shortage in urban areas threatened to cause returning World War II veterans to become homeless. In 1945, for example, after my father left the Army Air Corps, my parents, my older brother, and I lived in a converted garage in Denver until we found available housing. According to Kristin Jones (2018), at this time WWII veterans "elbowed for space, and rents skyrocketed," and consequently Black families found it almost impossible to leave segregated areas such as Five Points. Although Black veterans believed that they had earned the same rights as other citizens, they found the housing market closed to them. Gonda (2015) determined that at the end of WWII, while returning soldiers and their families waited for access to newly built homes, one in five Black families "doubled up," while only seven percent of White families did (31). George Brown, a Black *Denver Post* reporter, confirmed this situation in 1951:

> Jim Crow has the Negro going and coming. He will not let the Negro buy outside the restricted zone, and he creates barriers to prevent many from buying within. I tried to buy a house inside the boundaries and I couldn't get adequate financing from any bank because they said the house was in an "area which is deteriorating and becoming blighted." (Quoted in Jones 2018)

Finally, Terri Gentry, a volunteer docent with the Black American West Museum, recalled that such measures perpetuated segregation of "the have versus the have not." Gentry's great-grandfather was head of the first Black family to move to Marion Street in Denver, but because of racial zoning he "had to walk up the alley to his house. He couldn't walk up the street" (quoted in Porter 2019). White returning veterans faced a tight housing market, but Black veterans often faced a closed one.

Eventually such racial zoning contributed to redlining, a more subtle but extremely effective measure of spatial segregation and one not as susceptible to examination in the courts. Rather than based on city ordinances, redlining was supported by real estate brokers, federal agencies, banks, and mortgage lenders who refused to make loans or give mortgages to Blacks and other marginalized groups—or they extracted unusually severe interest terms and fees from these groups. Maps of urban areas, such as those 239 cities monitored by the Home Owner's Loan Corporation (HOLC), were marked by color—for example, green, yellow, and red. The safest neighborhoods were marked in green, where homeowners were considered so financially secure that they could obtain fully insured and amortized mortgages from the FHA and Veterans Administration. These mortgages allowed them to pay off some principal as well as interest each month and therefore they could look forward to owning their homes once the loan was paid off. In contrast, as Pietila (2010) noted, "Red, the universal color of alarm, smeared neighborhoods deemed to be 'hazardous' and 'dangerous,' where banks had stopped issuing mortgages altogether or charged exorbitant fees and interest rates" (61–62). According to Rothstein (2017), "A neighborhood earned a red color if African Americans lived in it, even if it was a solid middle-class neighborhood of single-family homes," thus contributing to the creation of not only exclusive White suburbs but also "urban African American slums" (64, 57). On the redlining map, yellow indicated transitional spaces, ones that could become prime or could remain marginal spaces.

Racial zoning and redlining were not only supported by lending institutions but also by White supremacist groups. Terri Gentry in a video interview about Five Points, for example, recalled when George Morrison, a Black man, bought a house on Gilpin Street in Denver outside of the red zone, the KKK was allegedly to have burned the house down—three times (Porter 2019). Also, Mauck (2001) noted that crosses were burned in front of Dr. Clarence Holmes's dental office. Throughout the 1930s to the 1960s, Five Points activists pushed for the redlined area to be enlarged in Denver, and as Gentry noted, the Colored American Loan & Realty Company located on Welton Street helped Black families finance housing. Later such spatial segregation became more covert and perhaps more effective when restrictive deed covenants took the place of redlining and racial zoning. These deed covenants not only continued to restrict marginalized people who sought safe and secure housing but often operated under the sanction of the law.

Restrictive Deed Covenants

Most deeds contain covenants as to what the homeowners and landlords might do with their property and the conditions for paying back any loan on those properties. In May 1947, for example, my parents signed a Deed of Trust for 631 South Eliot Street in the Mountain View Park area of west Denver. The home had just been built, and the deed, drawn up by the mortgage company, contained 12 covenants, such as the new owner "should not commit or permit waste; and shall maintain the property in as good condition as at present, reasonable wear and tear excepted." Racial restrictive covenants were similar in wording but quite different in content and were very prevalent in the 1940s. These covenants also became a common device used by property owners and neighborhood associations to prohibit homeowners from selling or renting their properties to marginalized and stigmatized groups. The impetus for restrictive covenants, according to Gotham (2000), was the idea that "racial separation for residences was necessary to maintain property values, real estate profits and neighborhood stability" (623). Moreover, these covenants were initially created by protected private actions rather than legal application and enforcement, and therefore they were almost untouchable.

A typical racially restrictive covenant, such as one recorded in June 1949 for Burns, LeFant, Nielsen, and Dyatt, who owned the Burns Brentwood subdivision in Denver, read as follows: "Only persons of the Caucasian race shall own, use or occupy any dwelling or residence erected upon said lots or tracts; provided, however, that occupancy by persons of another race who are employed as domestic servants by the occupying owner or occupying tenant shall not constitute a violation of the protective covenant" (document linked in Jones 2018). Such covenants often excluded Hebrews (Jews), Ethiopians (African ancestry), Malays (Filipinos), and Asiatics (anyone from the Asian continent), according to public policy researcher Catherine Silva (2016). But as Gonda (2015) noted, a great many restrictive covenants were primarily a form of spatial segregation against Blacks, because the "combined effect of deeply restricted access to new homes and heightened levels of overcrowding forced African Americans into the oldest and most inadequate segments of America's urban housing stock and greatly overtaxed the capacities of these homes" (31). As a result, Black individuals and families were eager to move to other neighborhoods. Finally, according to Gotham (2000), prominent real estate firms and builders as well as organizations such as the Kansas City (MO) Real Estate Board used the restrictive deed covenant "as the primary mechanism for creating segregated living spaces," based on the belief that "racial separation of residences was necessary to maintain property values, real estate profits and neighborhood stability" (623). But in some cases, most important to such real estate entities, homeowners, and neighborhood associations, was that restrictive deed covenants avoided most legal challenges.

The Courts Permit Spatial Segregation

In a rather complicated court decision, the Supreme Court of Colorado in *Chandler v. Zeigler* (1930) determined that the Fifth, Thirteenth, and Fourteenth Amendments did not prohibit private individuals from "entering into contracts respecting the control and disposition of their own property," contracts such as restrictive deed covenants. The Zeiglers complained to the Court that they had relied on the verbal assurance of Chandler, a real estate dealer who had bought and sold small tracts or lots, that all the lots in Kelton Heights, Jefferson County, Colorado, were restricted to White owners. Because of Chandler's promise, the Zeiglers bought and built upon Lot 13. Later they discovered that Lot 14 had been bought and was occupied by a Japanese family, whom the Zeiglers claimed were noisy and generally annoying. Specifically, the Zeiglers argued before the Court that the house built upon Lot 14 obstructed the Zeiglers' view, that the nearby children shot off fireworks around their house, and that trash was piled up outside of the house on Lot 14.

On the one hand, the Supreme Court of Colorado was willing to remand the complaint to a lower court but only if the Zeiglers wanted to ask for a new trial for specific damages to their property, where the Court cautioned that Chandler could be held liable for his false representation regarding all the Kelton Heights lots. On the other hand, the Court noted that the restrictions that Chandler initially represented to the Zeiglers would have been easily upheld had they been recorded in the written deeds to the Kelton Heights lots rather than based on a verbal promise. Had the restrictions been recorded in writing, the Zeiglers could have prevailed based solely on the race of the family on Lot 14, given that such restrictive covenants, according to the Court, were *private agreements*. Without this final stipulation, and if restrictive deed covenants were reviewed and upheld by state rather than federal courts in the future, the covenants could be found to violate the Due Process and/ or Equal Protection Clauses of the Fourteenth Amendment. The Fourteenth Amendment specified that *no state* could "abridge the privileges or immunities of citizens of the United States; nor shall any State deprive any person of life, liberty, or property, without due process of law; nor deny to any person within its jurisdiction the equal protection of the laws." For the time being, racial covenants written into deeds could indeed prevent certain marginalized groups from moving into all-White neighborhoods. In other words, although racial zoning and redlining had successfully been challenged in the courts, for the time being restrictive racial deed covenants prevailed unless state courts chose to enforce them by ordering Black families to vacate homes purchased in White neighborhoods—an action that state courts seldom took.

Eighteen years later, the US Supreme Court in *Shelley v. Kraemer* (1948) affirmed that if state governments did participate in such segregation measures, restrictive covenants would indeed violate the Fourteenth Amendment, a decision that annoyed the empowered majority in most states and a route that state courts still could avoid. However, this court decision became noteworthy because one of the four plaintiffs who initiated the *Shelley* case directly raised the question of how to determine racial identity in enforcing housing segregation. When plaintiff James Hurd purchased a home in Washington, DC, White homeowners objected that a restrictive covenant prevented the previous owner from selling to Hurd, who was thought to be Black. However, Hurd had been listed in the prior census as a "mulatto" and at other times identified as a "Mohawk Indian." He did admit that he had found the presence of a racially restrictive covenant that could have prevented him from purchasing his new house, but Hurd claimed, "I didn't know I was of negro [sic] blood" (quoted in Gonda 2015, 40). The *Shelley* Court avoided considering just how to tell racial identity—it was assumed that physical appearance would prevail. However, the NAACP in their continuing opposition to racial segregation used Hurd's statements in *Shelley* as a centerpiece for their legal position regarding systemic racism. And, it was not until the 1970s that the courts ruled that such restrictive deed covenants violated the Fair Housing Act and that the very recording of such deeds did constitute state action in violation of the Fourteenth Amendment (see Rothstein 2017; *Mayers v. Ridley* 1972).

Gentrification and Homelessness

At the end of the twentieth century, many residents in the Five Points neighborhood faced being uprooted or even forced into homelessness because of gentrification. Recently, *The Denver Post* newspaper (Rufino 2017) noted that the Five Points area was deemed one of the "fastest-gentrification areas in the country between 2000 and 2010" and that the White population in the Five Points community jumped 27 percent during that period. Gentrification, or the process of renovating a house or an established neighborhood, usually takes place in a downtown area of a major city, and these renovations conform more to the preferences of higher socioeconomic groups than to those of residents currently living in the area. Higher socioeconomic groups might be attracted to the history and architecture of the area or its proximity to their work downtown, or they might assume that the value of a renovated house in an "improved" neighborhood would increase because of their efforts. *The Denver Post* cautioned, however, that it was becoming more difficult to keep long-time Five Points residents from being involuntarily displaced and in some cases made homeless. Albus Brooks, the city council president who represented Five Points, noted the government was establishing protections for long-term residents more slowly than gentrification itself was taking place: "That's why you see the anger" (quoted in Rubino 2017). The long-term residents of Five Points were once again facing spatial segregation and possible homelessness.

As a result of this gentrification, in 2017 Five Points had the highest median two-bedroom rent in the city of Denver—$2,130 per month (Svaldi 2017). This statistic is informative and alarming when considered in the context of homelessness in Denver during this time. Metro Denver Homeless Initiative volunteers, for example, counted people experiencing homelessness on one day in January 2019 and found 5,755 homeless, an increase from similar counts in both 2017 and 2018 (Butzer 2019). Also, in 2018 Black individuals made up a disproportionately large segment of that population in the seven-county Denver metro area (Minor 2018). When in 2020 Denver Mayor Michael Hancock, however, proposed a possible location for a temporary, sanctioned homeless camp in the Five Points neighborhood, the idea was scrapped because of the pushback from the new and wealthier residents there (Chavira 2020).

In essence, gentrification is another spatial segregation measure in terms of housing and homelessness, along with racial zoning, redlining, and restrictive deed covenants, all pertaining to what would be considered private space or prime land whose value could be affected by the racial, ethnic, and religious identity of the residents. According to Jones (2018), "Exclusion is the thread that ties segregation to gentrification. Gentrification, operating in coalition with discriminatory lending practices and income inequality, has managed to offer a different way than Jim Crow of excluding people of color from building wealth through homeownership." Moreover, bloggers who have experienced homelessness share this insight. "George" (B9), for example, who maintained his blog from 2005 to 2017, focused on the problems that gentrification caused low-income renters. When property values increased to the level where people could not afford the rents, wrote George, landlords eagerly evicted tenants and then sold these properties for a high profit. George concluded that "increased property value leads to gentrified areas, squeezing those in poverty into smaller geographic areas," so much so that "the problem with homelessness in a gentrified city is that it doesn't fit—anywhere. . . . There is simply nowhere to go" (10.13.2015). Therefore, racial zoning, redlining, and restrictive deed covenants, along with gentrification, work directly or indirectly to spatially segregate marginalized and stigmatized others who are perceived to threaten the value of the urban space.

RESIDENCY RESTRICTIONS REGARDING
THE "DANGEROUS" STRANGER

Another case study illustrates that in urban space people experiencing home-lessness can be marginalized by yet another type of spatial segregation—legal ordinances designed to exclude entire groups from some communities, not so much to maintain the value of land but primarily to create a shared sense of safety among the housed. Residency restrictions designated in city and state ordinances so limit the housing options of convicted sex offenders who have served their prison sentences that this group is extremely vulnerable to homelessness and subsequent recidivism. Usually all convicted sex offend-ers have undergone treatment while in prison, are carefully and continuously monitored when released on parole, and, contrary to public perception, gener-ally have a very low rate of recidivism. But without stable housing, this group becomes desperate and thus much more likely to reoffend—defeating the very purpose of ordinances that exclude these so-called dangerous strangers from neighborhoods and cities.

A 2017 study in California determined that there were 6,329 homeless sex offenders on the California Justice Department's sex-offender registry (Editorial Board). Also, Miami, Florida, police reported that more than a quarter of all convicted sex offenders living in the county were homeless (Kornfield 2019). In most places, landlords are not required to rent to a convicted sex offender, and generally federal law prohibits anyone on state sex-offender registries from admission to public housing. Because many of these offenders have a hard time finding private housing, they often end up in homeless shelters, halfway houses, or tent encampments. Sadly, homeless sex offenders have been known to purposely reoffend in order to go back to the security of prison. Florida sex offender Raphael Marquez, for example, asked a judge to send him back to prison because the only "legal and affordable" housing option he could find "was a rat-infested overpass in Broward County next to a park filled with 100 other sex offenders" (quoted in James 2009). Thus, when assessing the stigma attached to this group of prior offenders and the ways in which their reentry into public spaces is so severely limited, we once again see how boundaries are set to control access to space and to exclude the marginalized other. In particular, feminist theorist Sara Ahmed (2000) noted a powerful impulse to exclude from society "the dangerous stranger," such as the convicted sex offender:

> Strangers are not simply those who are not known in this dwelling, but those who are, in their very proximity, already recognised [sic] as not belonging, as being out of place. Such a recognition of those who are out of place allows both

the demarcation and enforcement of the boundaries of "this place," as where "we" dwell. (21–22)

Such exclusion may mean that the stranger, marginalized and homeless, becomes dangerous indeed.

Restricted Spaces in a Community

What further complicates spatial segregation of convicted sex offenders is that offenders who have completed their prison sentences, again often including therapeutic treatment, must still meet strict parole rules, including securing acceptable housing in a timely way—and because of city ordinances, that housing must not be located in certain areas of a community. Those restricted spaces are meant to protect what Ahmed (2000) called "the vulnerable body" in society, the "one who is most at risk"—and so the child "becomes a figure of vulnerability, the purified body that is more endangered by the contaminating desires of strangers" (34). Level III sex offenders, those considered most at risk to reoffend, are listed on sex-offender registries so that society can mark them as dangerous strangers and follow their movements regardless of their individual criminal history, particularly excluding them from spaces where children might congregate even though their history of offenses might not include children.

"Sam," for example, a convicted sex offender who testified on February 28, 2019, at the "Residency Restrictions: Wise or Unwise?" symposium at Mitchell Hamline School of Law in St. Paul, Minnesota, described to the audience the restrictions that he faced in his community. (Note that I have anonymized the prior offenders who spoke at this symposium.) According to Sam, "The 2,000-foot rule seems to be the first choice of restrictions," describing the rule that a sex offender cannot have a temporary or permanent residence within two thousand feet of any school, licensed daycare center, or park or playground, and cannot loiter in a place where children regularly gather. In some cases, city clerks provide official maps showing these prohibited areas, reminiscent of the redlining maps used to exclude minorities from obtaining insured and amortized mortgages from lenders. The US District Court for the Southern District of Iowa found, however, the two-thousand-foot restriction completely banned prior sex offenders from living in many small towns and cities in the state, such as Lone Tree, North Liberty, Oxford, Shueyville, Solon, Swisher, and Tiffen. This Court also found that maps displaying these two-thousand-foot restricted circles in Des Moines, Iowa, left open for the sex offenders "only industrial areas or some of the city's newest and more expensive neighborhoods," neighborhoods that a just released convicted sex offender could not afford (White 2008, 164; *Doe v. Miller* 2004).

Any convicted sex offender who violated these city ordinances, however, was subject to a misdemeanor and a violation of parole that might mean a return to prison. In Sam's case, he discovered that he had only twelve to thirteen blocks where he could live in the Minnesota community he wished to join. Moreover, he had to find housing quickly or return to prison because he was still on parole—ironically, Sam found it easier to find employment than a place to live.

Similarly, "Luke," who testified along with Sam at the Mitchell Hamline symposium, concluded, "Sex offenders cannot go home." Luke resided in a halfway house, while "John," who testified with Luke and Sam, was living in a Salvation Army homeless shelter. At least twenty states have enacted such ordinances and effectively limit sex offenders to just a few, or even no, areas to reside in a community. As Kari White (2008) suggested, such restrictions are a form of "modern-day banishment" or, as defined within the legal system, as "expulsion in fact" of a person from a community (174), reminiscent of the banishment of drug sellers suggested by the Natives Against Heroin in the "Wall of Forgotten Natives" encampment. In turn, Asmara Tekle (2009) revealed that sex-offender restrictive deed covenants have joined "a long line of prior 'who' covenants, those grounded in personal and largely immutable characteristics and often unsubstantiated fear" (1826). Sex-offender deed covenants concern not the use or sale of land, as they did with racially restricted covenants, but instead focus on protecting who seems the most vulnerable in that community.

Also, the sex-offender restrictive deed covenant is specifically designed to protect the children of a community or neighborhood, based on the commonly mistaken belief that the stranger rather than the family member or friend is more likely to abuse a child. Indeed, as Tekle concluded, the basis of such deed covenants was that one population could "terrorize another" and the best solution was to create "sex-offender free communities" (1819). A covenant for Milwaukee Ridge in Lubbock, Texas, for example, reads, "No registered sex-offender . . . shall own or reside on any part of any Lot in the Addition. . . . The failure to comply with this restriction may, at the Association's option, subject the Owner to a fine of $1000.00 per day for each day that such Owner fails to comply with this restriction." If a background check reveals that the resident or property owner has a criminal history for sexual misconduct, regardless of sex-offender registration criteria, the housing contract will be "rejected by the Association and shall not be accepted by the owner/seller" (quoted in Tekle 2009, 1819). Quite recently, the law has been challenged to decide whether to uphold the validity of deed covenants and city ordinances that restrict sex offenders from residing in a community. In *Mulligan v. Panther Valley Property Owners Association* (2001), for example, the New Jersey Superior Court recognized that Level III sex offenders were not a protected class and therefore that arguments based on constitutional protections could not invalidate a sex-offender restrictive covenant written into a deed. The Court did caution communities about excluding certain groups:

> Common interest communities fill a particular need in the housing market but they also pose unique problems for those who remain outside their gates, whether voluntarily or by economic necessity. The understandable desire of individuals to protect themselves and their families from some of the ravages of modern society and thus reside within such communities should not become a vehicle to ensure that those problems remain the burden of those least able to afford a viable solution.

The Court recognized that communities might indeed fear those who reflected these "ravages" of society, such as convicted sex offenders, but did not suggest any viable solution to accommodate those prior offenders who wished to live in a community.

Overall, given that the convicted sex offender has received treatment and is usually carefully monitored, these ordinances and restrictions reflect a somewhat irrational fear, reflective of the stigma assigned to the marginalized other. One city council member, for example, proclaimed in a debate over such restrictions in West St. Paul, Minnesota, "Nobody wants anybody who's nasty living next to them" (quoted in Adler 2018). In contrast, "Owen," who testified with Sam, John, and Luke at the Mitchel Hamline symposium and had been civilly committed to and eventually discharged from the Minnesota Sex Offender Program (MSOP), admitted that he committed "terrible crimes" but confirmed that he worked hard in his treatment programs to control internally any impulses to reoffend. When Owen tried to transfer between communities to more easily find stable housing, he was not allowed to do so because of county ordinances. He reflected that there "might be a terrified public, but sex offenders are terrified of being rejected" by their community, their employers, and their neighbors—of being threatened, as Owen experienced from one neighbor, or because of homelessness as a result of being excluded from the support systems that would help them reintegrate into any such community. Such city ordinances create spatial segregation and resulting homelessness similar to that instigated by racial zoning, redlining, and deed covenants, and they are based on stigmatization and marginalization—all based on a feeling of vulnerability by those who are actually empowered.

Profiles of Convicted Sex Offenders

Although the impulse might be to essentialize all sex offenders, they are indeed diverse, so much so that the stigma imposed upon them is easily challenged. Placed within the context of who is likely to commit a sex offense, who is likely to appear on a sex-offender registry, how often convicted sex offenders reoffend, how many offend and/or reoffend against children, and what factors may contribute to such recidivism, subsequent space and housing restrictions for convicted sex offenders seem emotionally and stigmatically driven rather than based on statistics or logic.

The majority of sexual assaults, for example, are committed by White men, but Black men are more likely to receive harsher sentences than White sex offenders (see, for example, Wheeler and George 2004). Also, Black men are placed more often than White offenders on sex-offender registries at the state and national level. In states such as Oregon and Minnesota, which place on the register those sex offenders considered at the highest risk, Blacks are 7 to 10 times more likely to appear on such registration sites (see, for example, Ackerman and Sacks 2018; *Race & Justice News* 2016). In terms of how often sex offenders reoffend, the 2017 Sex Offender Management Assessment and Planning Initiative (SOMAPI) found that recidivism rates of sex offenders ranged from 5 percent after 3 years to 24 percent after 15 years. Moreover, Roger Przybyiski (2015) found that sex offenders are far more likely to reoffend for a non-sexual crime than for a sexual crime and that sex offenders have a lower overall recidivism rate than most other non-sex offenders, although the highest recidivism rates of sex offenders are found among those who offend against boys. Finally, those who do offend against children often gain access to their victims through marriage, occupation, or the neighborhood in which they live rather than in front of a school or in a park or in a place where children gather, places where convicted sex offenders are banned by city ordinances (see, for example, Duwe, Donnay, and Tewksbury 2008).

Most significantly to my research, criminologists and social workers Jill Levenson, Alissa Ackerman, Kelly Socia, and Andrea Harris (2013) found that residency restrictions may create "unintended consequences including transience, homelessness, and housing instability—outcomes that may carry significant public safety implications" (320; see also Levenson 2008; Levenson, Zgoba, and Tewskbury 2007). When one community passes such restrictions, a "domino effect" may result when "neighboring towns pass similar ordinances in order to prevent exiled sex offenders from migrating to their communities" (Levenson, Ackerman, Socia, and Harris 2013, 320; see also Socia 2012). Thus, these restrictions may be so based on misconceptions about sex offenders that they create instability for those offenders who actively try to avoid reoffending. As Dr. Michael Thompson, a forensic psychologist and spokesperson for the Minnesota Association for the Treatment of Sexual Abusers (MnATSA), concluded, a "lack of stable, permanent housing increased the likelihood that sex offenders will reoffend and abscond from community-based correctional supervision. Stability protects the community against sexual reoffense" (quoted in Serres 2020c). And so, the conflict between providing housing stability to counter recidivism among convicted sex offenders and the impulse of the community to protect its most vulnerable citizens has recently moved into the courtroom—as evidenced in the following court decisions.

Legal Challenges to Sex-Offender Housing Restrictions

In 2007, the Minnesota Department of Corrections traced the patterns of 224 recidivists released from prison between 1990 and 2002 who were then reincarcerated for a sex crime prior to 2006. The goal was to see whether the 224 cases were affected by residency restrictions. In particular, four criteria were used: (1) The offender gaining direct contact with the victim rather than through an acquaintance or relative; (2) the contact having been made within at least one mile of the offender's residence; (3) the first contact location having been near a school, park, daycare center, and such; and (4) the victim having been under the age of eighteen at the time of the offence. The department found that not one of the 224 sex offenses would likely have been deterred by residency restrictions in city ordinances. Thus, the department concluded, "Rather than lowering sexual recidivism, housing restrictions may work against this goal by fostering conditions that exacerbate sex offenders' reintegration into society." In turn, Richard Weinberger (2017), representing MnATSA, found that there was no correlation between residency requirements and sex offenses against children but that the number of offenders unaccounted for doubled after such restrictions went into effect. From these perspectives, residency restrictions seem futile and deleterious. Moreover, three legal challenges to such city ordinances in Minnesota cities challenged the impulse to marginalize that so-called dangerous stranger in order to protect a community.

The first legal challenge involved Ordinance No. 2019-05, which amended Chapter 130 of the Dayton Code of Ordinances (City of Dayton 2019) to exclude Level II and III sex offenders from establishing a temporary or permanent residence or loitering within two thousand feet of not only parks and playgrounds, schools and daycares, and places of worship but also amusement parks, indoor and outdoor ice skating facilities, public or commercial swimming pools, golf courses, bowling alleys, gymnastic and dance academies, and even seasonal pumpkin patches and apple orchards. Moreover, such offenders could not come within one thousand feet of any public school bus stop. All these measures, according to justifications in the ordinance, were designed to curtail the "extreme threat to the health, safety, and welfare of the citizens" of Dayton that "sexual offenders and sexual predators" present. In December 2018, however, three convicted sex offenders who were civilly committed and then provisionally discharged from the Minnesota Sex Offender Program (MSOP) challenged the Dayton ordinances in the District Court, Fourth Judicial District (*Braylock, Breland, and Mathews v. the City of Dayton* 2018). Sex offenders committed to MSOP are considered too dangerous to be released into the community immediately after serving their prison sentences, but after they complete a treatment program, they may appeal for review by both a Special Review Board and a Judicial Appeal Panel for provisional discharge—discharge that usually includes GPS monitoring, continued therapy, and residence in a group home. Braylock, Breland, and Mathews were provisionally discharged to a group home, the River Road House, but they complained to the Court that the Dayton city ordinance would deny them the ability to live in this group home because of its proximity to some of the restricted spaces in the city. The District Court decided that although there were approximately eighty-eight such local residency restrictions throughout Minnesota, in its present form the city of Dayton's ordinance was in conflict with state law that allowed such provisional discharge from MSOP and therefore was void and invalid. In response, the city deleted a number of prohibited areas from the ordinance, including ice skating facilities, golf courses, bowling alleys, and pumpkin patches and apple orchards, and allowed for the three complainants to reside in River Road House.

The second legal challenge to such ordinances came in January 2018 when Thomas Wayne Evenstad sued the City of West St. Paul, claiming that the city's ordinance, which restricted convicted sex offenders from residing within 1,200 feet of schools, daycare centers, and group homes, violated the Ex Post Facto Clause of the Constitution, one that forbids the application of retroactive laws and ordinances created after "the fact" of a violation, such as the initial sexual offense by Evenstad (*Evenstad v. City of West St. Paul* 2018). The justification for the ordinance was similar to that offered by the city of Dayton:

> Repeat predatory offenders, predatory offenders who use physical violence and predatory offenders who prey on children and vulnerable individuals are predators who present a threat to public safety. . . . It is the intent of this chapter . . . to promote, protect and improve the health, safety and welfare of the citizens of the city by creating areas around locations where children and vulnerable individuals regularly congregate wherein certain predatory offenders are prohibited from establishing a primary or secondary address. (City of West St. Paul Ordinance 2020)

Based on a map provided by the city, Evenstad illustrated to the Court that he was spatially segregated from 95 percent of the residential areas in West St. Paul. Even though the Court resolved that such ordinances did not violate the Ex Post Facto Clause, the Court did find the West St. Paul ordinance overly broad, particularly because the ordinance did not distinguish among offenders with low, moderate, or high risks of recidivism and because all group homes were located in restricted areas. As a result, Evenstad settled with West St. Paul for $85,000 in damages, and the city revised its ordinance to apply only to Level II and III sex offenders whose crimes included children (Ferroro 2018a; Ferroro 2018b).

Finally, three convicted sex offenders made similar arguments but achieved less success in *John Doe 1, John Doe 2, and John Doe 3 v. City of Apple Valley* (2020). Apple Valley created an ordinance that forbade convicted sex offenders from living within 1,500 feet of schools, parks, playgrounds, churches, and daycare centers, thus excluding such offenders from more than 90 percent of all residential properties, just 5 percent lower than the percentage of restricted areas marked on the map of West St. Paul. One of the "John Doe" plaintiffs had been convicted of possession of child pornography, and after he served his sentence and was released, he and his wife put their life savings into a down payment on a house in Apple Valley. Soon after buying the house, the man was told by the Apple Valley Police Department that he would be charged with violating the city ordinance regarding convicted sex offenders if he did not move out. In turn, his attorney argued, "Establishing a stable home for oneself and one's family is something that everyone should be entitled to do" (Serres 2020c; see also City of Apple Valley Ordinance 2020). The District Court again rejected the argument that the ordinance violated the Ex Post Facto Clause but decided that the Does were so unlikely to succeed in their suit that their motion for a preliminary injunction against enforcement of the ordinance was denied. In part, the Court relied on *Doe v. Miller* (2005), an Iowa case in which a court supported the two-thousand-foot residency restriction for convicted sex offenders in Des Moines. Thus, the Court found that Apple Valley's ordinance was not only consistent with protecting the health and safety of children but also was not unconstitutionally punitive to sex offenders "simply because it lacks a close or perfect fit with the nonpunitive aims it seeks to advance." In other words, the ordinance might not protect the community in the way imagined, but it was close enough in effort to remain in effect.

Overall, housing and gathering restrictions are designed to spatially segregate convicted sex offenders; are based on often unsubstantiated fears that such offenders will reoffend, particularly against children; and are often marked or categorized on city maps, just was redlining. These restrictions may address Level II and III offenders, those likely or most likely to reoffend, but they fail to recognize offenders' individual criminal histories, such as whether their initial victims were children and whether they are strangers to or relatives of their victims. Although the courts have generally found that the ordinances do not violate constitutional rights, they may conflict with state laws and are certainly overly broad in not allowing convicted offenders to live in group homes or by including some rather obscure public spaces such as pumpkin patches and apple orchards. Most important, these restrictions expressed in such city ordinances may render convicted sex offenders homeless—and therefore more likely to reoffend. These city ordinances not only may be used to spatially segregate people likely to experience homelessness but also may create homelessness itself.

MEASURES TO CRIMINALIZE HOMELESSNESS

Community ordinances may also target people experiencing homelessness by criminalizing their activities and by excluding their very presence from urban public spaces. Certainly, those experiencing homelessness frequently express their dismay about this criminalization of homelessness in their social media and memoirs. As Gnawa (2016) shared in his memoir about homelessness, "Imagine yourself being a homeless [person] who had to spend his or her days outdoors or in public places and was denied access to a public restroom at a hotel nearby or at Mac Donald [sic] down the street. And, you can't urinate or defecate outside for fear of being arrested by the police if you were caught" (10). In turn, through their observations of Santa Cruz, California's municipal ordinances, scholars in psychology Erin Toolis and Phillip Hammack (2015b) affirmed that homeless people were contained, displaced, and excluded from public space, even regarding these fundamental needs:

> Consequently, attempts of displaced groups to meet their basic needs in public—seeking shelter, bathing, and disposing of waste—are not seen as symptomatic of deep underlying social injustice but as a result of deviant behaviors that threaten that local economy, defile the aesthetic and order of the street, and disrupt the enjoyment of the consumer experience. (370)

Public space, according to Toolis and Hammack (2015b) "is governed by material and symbolic boundaries separating 'insiders' from 'outsiders,' which are negotiated through discourse and institutionalized through public policies," an aspect of so-called social justice or the relationship among space, law, and social expectations (368). Again, as a result, those experiencing homelessness are often prohibited from sitting, standing, panhandling, sleeping, loitering, or littering in public spaces. If people experiencing homelessness enter private spaces, they can be arrested for trespassing; in public parks, they may be fined or jailed for creating a nuisance or for staying beyond closing time. And in shelters, they are expected to obey a number of rules, such as leaving by dawn, signing up for a bed or a shower, refraining from substance abuse, smoking only outside, and taking all possessions with them each day when the shelter closes. Moreover, in these spaces, people experiencing homelessness may be exposed to the harshest elements and to social rejection.

Within the context of criminalizing people experiencing homelessness, bloggers, memoir writers such as Gwana, and video interviewees and storytellers are very aware of how they are stigmatized and restricted in public spaces. As they describe their experiences with ordinances that govern their public actions, they reveal that they try to abide by those ordinances, or they admit that they are complicit in violating them. They laugh at how often they disobey the ordinances, or they rant against the restrictions. Finally, they admit how problems, such as substance abuse, prevent them from obeying these ordinances, or they justify such disobedience by the need to numb the discomfort of homelessness itself by way of alcohol or drugs. Most important to my study, people experiencing homelessness use social media and memoirs to help their readers understand their situation and question their exclusion from public space. They do so by personalizing their entries, interviews, and memories, often through the descriptions and narratives that give them *ethos* and voice—and may link their readers to sources that support these personal accounts.

Blogger Patrick, for example, warned his readers that across the country "in just about every medium to large size city, there is a movement underway—a somewhat secretive movement—a plan for getting rid of the homeless" (6.22.2015). Patrick described the participants within this movement: the large businesses that create "downtown partnerships" and that have the financial and political power in their cities. These downtown partnerships, according to Patrick, share a common belief that "the existence of homeless people is detrimental to making profits" because they repel customers (6.22.2015). One effort of this partnership was confirmed by anthropologist Marina Peterson (2006) in her exploration of the creation of privatized public space in the entertainment center California Plaza, space that celebrated elite and corporate consumption and excluded people experiencing homelessness. As Peterson concluded, "The homeless, recognizable as such by virtue of being unbathed or poorly clothed, make class differences visible, and thus cannot be part of a consenting harmonious public" or sought-after consumers who are welcomed in those privatized public spaces (378). And, one way to exclude the "unbathed and poorly clothed" from such spaces is to criminalize a great many aspects of homelessness, aspects with which bloggers and memoir writers are familiar.

And so, in his memoir Todd Murphy (2018) listed on over fifty pages all the rules and laws that restricted or punished people experiencing homelessness: disorderly conduct and resisting arrest (37), peddling without a license and sidewalk sleeping (49), public intoxication (71), trespassing (94), soliciting (109), begging (109), obstructing the sidewalk (109), littering (168), creating a public nuisance (168), and public lewdness, including urinating and defecating in public (189). Murphy's goal was to alert his readers to such forbidden actions so they could avoid them if at all possible. In turn, blogger Lawrence offered a long entry in which he analyzed the difficulties that people experiencing homelessness have with just one such restricted activity, finding a place to urinate. He concluded that, on one hand, most people experiencing homelessness, particularly women, prefer "a degree of privacy when compelled to perform bodily functions that may leave them feeling exposed and vulnerable"; on the other hand, "peeing in public is not otherwise such a privacy concern for men" because men seek "hid[e]y-holes" behind bins and dumpsters "to do their business in" (4.12.2019). Lawrence organized this blog entry around his impression of how people might react differently to a sign he recently saw: "Please Stop Urinating in this Corner." Only a person dealing with homelessness would anticipate the full effect of this sign—and approach it with some humor as Lawrence did. In essence, both Murphy and Lawrence are concerned about how to survive homelessness on the most basic level given the number of restrictive city ordinances.

Moreover, memoir writer Murphy and blogger Lawrence have discovered just what law scholar Terry Skolnik (2016) did: "The law can be practically impossible for the homeless to obey in three contexts": (1) The law prohibits behaviors that homeless people "cannot avoid engaging in as part of their daily existence"; (2) the law "imposes narrow prohibitions against certain behavior which, individually, may each be possible to obey" but are so accumulative and comprehensive that all such laws cannot be followed; and (3) "quality of life offenses can regulate nearly every act that the homeless engage in" (743–44). According to Skolnik, people experiencing homelessness might avoid sleeping in public but may not be able to find a private place to urinate, and they might avoid panhandling but may have no private place to drink alcohol, and so on. Finally, so-called quality-of-life offenses pertain not to the ease and comfort that people experiencing homelessness seek but instead to the aesthetics, security, and homogeneity that the housed expect—supposedly it is their quality of life that is in jeopardy because of the actions of people experiencing homelessness.

Control and Protection of City Spaces

To achieve the goal of excluding people experiencing homelessness from much of urban public space and likewise to indicate to the socioeconomically advantaged where in the city it was safe and desirable to go, professor emeritus of property and urban law Robert Ellickson (1996) resorted to a customary way of addressing the problem: mapping and categorizing urban public spaces. According to Ellickson, the color red could signal the ordinary pedestrian to take "extreme caution" in entering this zone; yellow could indicate some caution should be taken; and green signaled "a promise of relative safety" (1220–21). Moreover, in red zones (about 5 percent of downtown spaces) "normal standards for conduct in public spaces would be significantly relaxed" and so, in this small amount of space, many sidewalk activities considered disorderly elsewhere would be permitted in a red zone. As Ellickson explained, "In these relatively rowdy [red] areas, a city might tolerate more noise, public drunkenness, soliciting by prostitutes, and so forth" (1221). The yellow zone (about 90 percent of the downtown public spaces) "would be a lively mixing bowl" where enough misbehavior would be curbed that most citizens would be willing to enter the space but where public decorum would still be maintained by forbidding activities such as chronic panhandling and "bench squatting" by people experiencing homelessness. Finally, the green zone (about 5 percent of the downtown) would contain "unusually pleasant environmental conditions" for the elderly, families with young children, and "bench sitters reading poetry" (1221–22). Unlike the bloggers and memoir writers who expressed some humor about such divisions, Ellickson seemed quite serious about his proposal and such proposals are enacted in certain urban spaces.

Certainly, the distinct boundaries set by Ellickson's zoning scheme leaned toward banishment of people experiencing homelessness from any place but the red zone and perhaps, at some times and in many ways, the yellow zone—a sort of transitional space, to use Snow and Mulcathy's (2001) terms again. In turn, law scholar Randall Amster (2008) pointed out that one strand of homeless stigma includes "invocations of disorder, illegality, and immorality," and leads to the "processes of regulation, criminalization, and enforcement." The other strand includes "the disease and decay image, which leads to processes of sanitation, sterilization, and quarantine." But both strands, according to Amster, aspire to the same ends of "exclusion, eradication, and erasure" (81). Again, banishment itself is a measure that seems too extreme but in essence exists, most often under the guise of relocation. In 1956, for example, law scholar Caleb Foote revealed that banishment of unwanted persons from Philadelphia was still active although no statute allowed passing "the urban derelict . . . back and forth from one jurisdiction to another

(623). Then, six decades later, journalists Michael Brice-Saddler (2019) and Kevin Williams (2020) revealed how New York City was coercing its homeless residents to move into substandard housing in New Jersey, and how Middletown, Ohio, located between Dayton and Cincinnati, found itself a "dumping ground" for people experiencing homelessness from those two major cities. Banishment from entire cities might be forbidden by statute but exists in practice and represents an extreme example of criminalization and spatial segregation of homelessness.

Eviction

Somewhat comparable to banishment but used more frequently is eviction or exclusion from temporary or permanent housing, a legal action that often leads to homelessness. People may be evicted because of failure to pay rent or breaking the rules of a lease, such as exceeding the number of residents allowed in any one apartment or permitting a convicted felon to join the tenant. As sociologist Matthew Desmond (2016) found, however, the majority of poor renting families in the United States spend over half of their income on housing, and "at least one in four dedicates over 70 percent to paying the rent and keeping the lights on" (4). According to these statistics, a great many families are vulnerable to homelessness. After eviction, families often end up in homeless shelters, live in abandoned houses or on the street, double up with relatives and friends, take shelter in their cars and vans, and join tent encampments. Moreover, according to Desmond, being evicted "invites depression and illness, compels families to move into degrading housing in dangerous neighborhoods, uproots communities, and harms children." Overall, eviction "is implicated in the creation of poverty" (4)—and of homelessness. As memoir writer Liz Murray (2010) began her story of homelessness, "Daddy had fallen behind on the rent and gone to live in a men's shelter. . . . I found the entire contents of our apartment had been taken away in dumpsters, way before I ever got there" (163).

Similarly, bloggers may share with their readers how their homelessness started with an eviction. "James" (B1), for example, used his blog to rant about his latest eviction from a subsidized apartment and to defend his position when the sponsoring organization "decided to walk into his apartment without proper notice while I was sleeping." According to James, this action was against the law "plain and simple," even though James was behind in his rent and had been accused of performing illegal activities in his apartment, which he wrote, "IS A BUNCH OF CRAP" (emphasis in original, 10.13.2011). He did fail a drug test for marijuana but claimed that he had smoked it outside his apartment. In a less personal but equally dismayed reaction, blogger Lawrence reported that two people experiencing homelessness were evicted from their encampment "on a tiny patch of waste land alongside an unnamed foot and bike path." Lawrence's friend spoke to the operator of the front-end loader who was depositing boulders on the bed of gravel that had served as the couple's camp and was told that although the camp had been "tidy in appearance" and "well-made and maintained," a wall of inter-locking boulders would be placed there and in other encampment areas to deter people experiencing homelessness from living in the area (11.13.2018). Finally, and in contrast to James's anger and Lawrence's dismay, blogger "Dan" (B5) accepted with some humor his eviction from a public park. Dan had received a ticket for sleeping in public but shared that he had not slept in two nights and had little choice but to sleep in a park—he *had* to sleep. When a police officer reported that a woman in one of the apartments surrounding the park complained about noise, Dan joked with the officer and his blog readers that this complaint must mean that Dan "must have been snoring or something" (6.15.2009). Regardless of the nature of their responses, ranging from anger to humor, bloggers James, Lawrence, and Dan created described circumstances to alert their readers to the effects of strictly policing people experiencing homelessness.

Finally, to understand the comments of these memoir writers and bloggers, we must remember what Mitchell (1997) concluded:

> The anti-homeless laws being passed in city after city in the United States work in a pernicious way: by redefining what is acceptable behavior in public space, by in effect annihilating the spaces in which the homeless must live, these laws seek simply to annihilate homeless people themselves, all in the name of recre-ating the city as a playground for a seemingly global capital which is ever ready to do an even better job of the annihilation of space. (305)

Increasingly, the only space that people experiencing homelessness can enter safely is public space, which is becoming more and more monitored and restricted, but where the homeless may be forced to do some very private things. The annihilation of open space, according to Mitchell, is "unavoid-ably (if still only potentially) the annihilation of *people*" (emphasis in origi-nal, 312). Finally, city ordinances and state laws may be challenged as overly restrictive, but the impulse to create them still remains strong.

The Broken-Windows Theory

One often highly regarded theory supporting the impulse to restrict the homeless in urban public spaces and the consequent need to protect the city's "innocent" or "legitimate" residents is the "broken-windows theory," a theory that not only incorporates the rhetorical trope assigned to homelessness but also uses the criminalization of homelessness as a strategy. In an article for the 1982 issue of *The Atlantic* magazine, social scientists George Kelling and James Wilson described how one of them walked the streets of Newark, New Jersey, along with foot-patrol officers to see how these officers maintained order in their community. During this walk, the police officers had shared the broken-windows theory as promoted by social psychologists at the time—if a window in a building was broken and not repaired, all of the rest of the windows would soon be broken The authors concluded that applying the broken-windows theory could safeguard neighborhoods. Thus, a broken window became a metaphor or a rhetorical trope that signaled no one cared about the building, or as Rai (2016) called it, "any sign of negligence, indifference, or social decay that can be read in an environment" (153). Likewise, if disorderly behavior went unchecked, serious street crime would flourish and the neighborhood would be destroyed. And so, law enforcement protected individuals and communities by arresting not just criminal gangs but also so-called criminal individuals, the "single drunk or a single vagrant," categories that included people experiencing homelessness.

Rai (2016) suggested that the broken-windows theory was as much a theory and a "practice of spatial rhetorics [sic]" as it was one of crime fighting, because "both focus on how symbolic, rhetorical focuses become enmeshed in the spaces of everyday life" (161). Rai recognized that the broken-windows theory was "underscored" by four assumptions—(1) "that the environment communicates messages about a neighborhood's susceptibility to crime"; (2) "that strong, healthy neighborhoods demonstrate control over criminal behaviors by 'fixing broken windows'"; (3) "that social divisions between insiders and outsiders, upright citizens and deviants, should be enforced by the built environment"; and (4) "that crime is best addressed through everyday practices of concerned citizens" (153; see also Herbert and Brown 2006). Therefore, physical aspects of a public space were indicative not only of the care taken to maintain that space but also who might be welcomed into or should be excluded from that space. More specifically, in regard to people experiencing homelessness, Kelling and Wilson (1982) offered, "The unchecked panhandler is, in effect, the first broken window." Behavior by people experiencing homelessness was thus linked to the criminal behavior by way of the broken-windows theory—even though Mitchell (2003) warned that such behaviors might not be by choice, and even though Amster (2008) asked "what caused the windows to break in the first place" (103). Finally, under this theory, homelessness as a trope for criminality was reinforced. Blogger "Ralph" (B7), however, confronted this trope: "There are laws against being homeless. There are laws against sleeping in public, in your car, on the beach, anywhere in the public view. It is the only law that I know that prohibits a behavior that is involuntary" (10.19.2004). Systemic neglect of those experiencing homelessness as well as the failure to provide all such people with support and shelter might just lead to those broken windows. And certainly, spatial segregation might confine those homeless populations to neighborhoods where more broken than repaired windows existed.

Crimes by and against People Experiencing Homelessness

The concern about homelessness and crime remains apparent, even as activists, scholars, memoir writers, and social media users have assessed the differences between crimes by and crimes against people experiencing homelessness. One perspective on crimes committed by people experiencing homelessness hearkens back to housing restrictions placed on convicted sex offenders. According to the National Law Center on Homelessness & Poverty (2019b), the odds of someone from the general population experiencing homelessness in any given year are 1 to 200, but the odds of those released from prison becoming homeless are 1 in 11 (40). Scholars and advocates Stephen Metraux, Caterina Roman, and Richard Cho (2017) concluded that "a tenth of the population coming into prisons have recently been homeless, and at least the same percentage of those who leave prisons end up homeless, for at least some period of time" (72). Finally, law scholar Valerie Schneider (2018) described how homelessness in general can lead to a criminal record, not just a minor record but often a more serious one: "Homelessness is often a direct path to arrests for crimes both consequential and minor. Without housing, individuals are more likely to engage in crimes of survival, such as burglary, and are also more likely to seek money through illegal means, such as the drug trade" (432). People experiencing homelessness have committed crimes and have been victims of crimes, given their difficulties and vulnerabilities on the streets and in shelters and encampments.

And again, their very existence may be criminalized. Blogger Dan, for example, shared with his readers his experience of being given a ticket for panhandling too close to "a bank machine" and then later a ticket for panhandling "near a transit vehicle." With this second offence, Dan asked his readers, "How am I gonna [sic] be on the side walk and not be near a street car? If you can figure that out, you could probably win the Nobel Prize" (4.23.2008). Memoir writer Nicole Lowe (2016) shared with her readers the story of her first engagement in petty theft: "Sam, Mariah, and I were all decent thieves and acquired most of our belongings—journals, beads, crystals, pens, books, jewelry, and clothes—by way of the five-finger discount" (171). Similarly, Maria Fabian (2013) described in her memoir how as a high school student she stole gum, chips, candy, and sodas from the corner store and then sold these items during class: "I never saw myself as a criminal. . . . I was a business lady and business was good" (48). Finally, "Lovely" told the audience of her video interview that she had been in trouble and on probation most of her life. She reflected that when she aged out of foster care, where she had been since she was five years old, "I didn't know what to do" but reflected that she found it better on the streets than in jail ("Lovely" February 5, 2015). For the person experiencing homelessness, crime seemed a constant aspect of life, whether subject to arrest for being visible in public spaces or for actually engaging in petty crime.

Some bloggers, memoir writers, and video interviewees, however, did confess that they committed major crimes while being homeless, although these crimes were few and far between and were usually connected to substance abuse and drug selling. Blogger "Norman" (B10), who spent some time in prison, shared with his readers that he sold drugs: "I didn't care, I was forever telling myself I was smarter then [sic] the police and they would never get me. I was making a lot of money doing this. . . . I wasn't doing crime to support a habit, I was doing crime for the excitement of it, which is just as addictive in it's [sic] own way" ("My Life Journey 2"). Also, blogger Dan was arrested because he "punched the boyfriend of a woman" and then was arrested again when he forgot his court date for the assault (10.23.2006). However, the majority of the homeless bloggers, memoir writers, and video interviewees that I studied seemed to be victims or potential victims, instead of perpetrators. Murphy-Scott (2019), for example, told the story of getting "jumped" and being admitted to the hospital for a cracked rib (3.5.2017). Unfortunately, he sold the pills that the medical staff gave to him for the pain. Blogger "Elaine" (B12), who described her 10 years on the road in her blog, was hitchhiking when a truck driver tried to sexually assault her: "The only way I could ride with him was by sleeping with him in his sleeper. I told him to go bore somebody else. But inside I wanted to pound him to pulp" (3.13.2005). Along with these stories of individual assault, bloggers and memoir writers take a broader view of violence against people experiencing homelessness. Murphy (2018), for example, described how "small violent gangs of 'bum bashers' could be merciless" and took "special pleasure in opening your backpack and scattering your things all over. . . . There are groups of drunken young men in their twenties who, like high school bullies, got their thrills from tormenting the defenseless" (13). And, Norman concluded in one blog entry, "As part of my life on the street, violence has always played a significant role in my daily way of life, either through having to defend myself from other violent streeties [sic] or watching people have violence used against them for a variety of reasons" (7.18.2004). These "streeties," as Norman called them, were addicted to various substances and would "fly off the handle at the merest slight, imagined or real, so violence becomes part of your every day [sic] life . . . and you never know whether or not you are going to need to fight or if you can talk the other person down."

Indeed, the National Coalition for the Homeless (2014) noted that, during a fifteen-year period, 1,437 reported acts of violence had been committed against people experiencing homelessness, including 375 victims who lost their lives as the result of the attacks—and most of the perpetrators were teen-age boys, the "streeties" whom Norman feared.

Murphy-Scott, Elaine, Murphy, Norman, and others experiencing home-lessness recognized to various degrees how they were victimized while home-less, and their descriptions and stories about their lives on the street offered their readers perspectives that countered the broken-windows theory. They did not break that first window—or subsequent ones. Norman, for example, used his blog to start "my journey to a better life," even though he shared with his readers that because of the violence he had experienced he was "encoun-tering difficulties in putting my life into perspective for want of a better way of explaining things." He feared "moving into society" as someone who had never been taught that violence "was not the answer and that hurting people is wrong and there are other ways of dealing with the problem" (7.18.2004). However, Norman not only confessed to those violent aspects of his life but also shared his growing perspective on leaving the streets and drugs behind for a permanent home. Without listening to the "voices" of these bloggers and memoir writers, we miss the nuances of violence and crime while homeless, and we might accept blindly the broken-windows theory.

Addiction and Homelessness

Drug and alcohol abuse are also part of the homeless life, hard to escape yet easy to start—and that start is understandable given the challenges and trau-mas of homelessness as I explored in chapter one regarding Native people. According to the Addiction Center (2020), a referral service that offers information about treatment practitioners and facilities throughout the United States, homelessness and addiction go "hand in hand" in that 38 percent of people experiencing homelessness are alcohol dependent and 28 percent are dependent on other chemicals. Although the center states that substance abuse may contribute to homelessness, it makes the following quite clear: "Often times, addiction is the result of homelessness. The difficult conditions of liv-ing on the street, having to find food, struggling with ill-health, and being constantly away from loved ones create a highly stressful state of being." Moreover, individuals experiencing homelessness "may additionally develop psychiatric conditions in response to the harsh lifestyle of feeling threatened by violence, starvation, and lack of shelter and love," conditions that self-medication might ease. Such struggles with addiction contribute to crime by and against the homeless.

Blogger Lawrence made clear that "nothing contributes as much to the misery and social harms of homelessness as street drugs do" and that "whatever led these men and women to start taking street drugs in the first place—the high, the pain relief, the peace of mind, the need to forget painful memories, or plain, old boredom—the drugs always end up taking more than they give" (10.13.2014). And so, according to blogger "John" (B2), addictions are an "escape from reality," although only in the short term and with long-term aftereffects (3.9.2010). In fact, concluded blogger Lawrence, some addicts only occupy stable housing intermittently, "preferring to still sleep on the streets where the money they need to buy drugs can be found and where the friends they like to do the drugs with are also to be found" (10.13.2014). Thus, one striking and poignant aspect in the social media used by Lawrence and others are the overt confessions and insights regarding their substance abuse. Indeed, breaking the patterns of addiction are so difficult among the homeless that blogger George offered a complex but potentially effective solution: "I think we need a 'campus' of addictive care that provides safe injection/consumption areas, a drop-in center with an outdoor courtyard, a shelter/housing area with a meal plan, and [a] team of health care and community care workers." The campus that George imagined would "prescribe clean and regulated cocaine and heroin through an onsite doctor, and develop a drug management plan with each user," a plan covered by health care or free to drug users, and abstinence would be encouraged but not required (10.14.2006). Housing seemed a minor concern in light of the treatment services that George imagined, perhaps because autonomy and agency remained critical to people experiencing both homelessness and addiction. Systemic changes required for such services are difficult and must involve the cooperation and support of people such as George.

One systemic change, the Safer City Initiative (SCI) in the "Skid Row" area of downtown Los Angeles, failed because it was linked to criminalization of homelessness rather than the cooperation that George recommended. SCI had incorporated what was called "therapeutic policing," or as sociologist Stuart (2016) critiqued it, "a paternalistic brand of spatial, behavioral, and moral discipline designed to 'cure' those at the bottom of the social hierarchy of the individual pathologies deemed responsible for their abject circumstances" (6). SCI was a plan to force withdrawal and abstinence by emphasizing personal responsibility for substance abuse, a perspective that often homeless individuals such as George already had but might not be able to employ. More specifically, as part of SCI, the local police cooperated with the three Los Angeles homeless shelters in a program called Homeless Alternatives to Living on the Street (HALO). People who received fines for breaking one of the many quality-of-life laws that criminalized homelessness were given the option of "working off" their fines by enrolling in a drug rehabilitation program. Around the same time, a similar effort to force the homeless off the streets and into shelters eliminated food giveaways "to literally starve Skid Row residents into rehabilitation settings" (117; for restrictions on food giveaways in other cities, see Dolan and Carr 2015; The National Law Center on Homelessness & Poverty and The National Coalition for the Homeless 2009, 2017). According to Stuart (2016), the SCI program operated with a "normative geography," which "delineates what is normal, just, and appropriate within a given location," an effort designed to move a location from a "rabble zone" to a "recovery zone" (82, 84), or from a marginal space to a transitional space. The SCI program, Stuart found, "obfuscates and marginalizes the role of structural causes" of homelessness (106). As a result, many people experiencing homelessness left the Skid Row area for other locations in the city, dropped out of the rehabilitation programs without permission and disappeared, or selected to serve time in jail in lieu of entering the program. They resisted such monitoring and shepherding. Thus, attempts to address substance abuse among people experiencing homelessness as well as to curtail the violence that they encounter are likely to fail unless systemic changes are made to provide safe and affordable housing, to ease the trauma of homelessness, and to rethink the impulse to criminalize homelessness and to spatially segregate those without stable housing.

In this chapter, I revealed how ordinances and spatial boundaries have served as tools to exclude so-called undesirable racial, ethnic, and religious minorities from more desirable spaces in cities and neighborhoods. Housing restrictions, such as racial zoning, redlining, and deed covenants, were designed to protect the property of empowered homeowners, to the detriment of those marginalized groups who wished to find better housing, safer neighborhoods, and more inclusive schools for their children. Although federal courts have found that constitutional rights were violated should the state courts support such housing segregation, private agreements in the form of deed covenants were difficult to overturn. The Five Points district of Denver serves as an example of how racial minorities were contained and confined by way of these housing restrictions and then negatively affected again should their community be gentrified.

In turn, city and community acts and ordinances, such as the ones created in three cities in Minnesota, attempted to ease the somewhat distorted safety concerns of housed residents by excluding released convicted sex offenders from living and "loitering" too close to where children, in particular, might congregate. However, such ordinances contributed to homelessness among such offenders, an unstable condition that encouraged recidivism and failed to address the specifics of the past transgressions as well as therapeutic progress made by the majority of these offenders. Finally, so-called quality-of-life laws attempt to banish people experiencing homelessness and diminish their sense of agency and self-worth—and make it, in essence, illegal to be home-less. The failure of this enforcement is particularly revealing when memoir writers, bloggers, and video interviewees explain how crimes, by and against them, are ongoing parts of their world. Overall, in this chapter I argue spatial segregation contributes and creates homelessness as I analyze specific case studies that reveal the challenges in addressing the homelessness crisis. In the next chapter, I turn again to rhetorical analysis, particularly the home as a trope for safety and loving support as perceived among two groups who might find themselves homeless: female victims of domestic violence and unaccompanied youth.

Chapter Three

This Space Called Home

Women and Youth Facing Homelessness

In September 2010, single mother and blogger "Clare" (B6) expressed her concern about her older child as the family faced homelessness: "I worry because my teen always looks at other relatives and sees that their life is better than ours. Then she gets angry inside" (9.9.2010). Because Clare had little family support or no financial resources when she lost her job, she and her two children resorted to living in a used camper van. Embarrassed by the van, Clare's older daughter asked her mother to drop her off down the street from her school so her classmates would not realize she did not have a "normal" home. Clare concluded in her blog that for this teenager "the damage has been done. She suffers from depression because her world fell apart when we became homeless" (9.7.2010). In these blog entries, Clare not only revealed intergenerational trauma of homelessness, but she also asserted that her older child's struggles revolved around lacking what she perceived others had—a socially acceptable and secure home. In turn, memoir writers Nicole Lowe (2016) and Janice Erlbaum (2006) described their own experiences with homelessness after they fled their childhood homes. Lowe's family were members of what could be considered a cult, and she told her readers, "Home was not a shelter to me. It was an icy pond and I was at the bottom with a chain clamped around my ankle" (14). Erlbaum fled from her childhood home because of "the chaos and violence" of her mother's most recent marriage (248). Erlbaum sought self-reliance and autonomy in leaving her home, but in doing so, she "was deprived of a lot: normalcy, privacy, and security. I bore the stigma of being 'homeless' . . . of being a 'bad girl'" (248). Throughout their narratives, Clare, Lowe, and Erlbaum encountered home as a trope, a metaphor for stability, safety, and security, even though their actual homes brought insecurity, embarrassment, and even violence.

According to Ratcliffe (2000), a rhetorical trope generally "fosters stasis by resisting and denying differences" (98) and presents socially constructed concepts as "The Truth" (105). There lies the persuasive and sometimes destructive power of a trope. Ratcliffe focused on whiteness as an enduring trope, but the same analysis can be applied to the homeless and the homed (or the housed). Homelessness is a state rejected by society, and the home is a goal and achievement for the so-called legitimate citizen. The home as a trope is, as Ratcliffe would say, "embodied in all of us (albeit differently) via our socialization" (96). Lowe and Erlbaum did conclude their memoirs with cautious optimism and insight on how to find stability, safety, and security, or a newly imagined or acquired home—but to do so, they needed to resist the socially constructed trope or modify its associations. Again, as Aune (1983) called this process, they had to "transume" or convert the trope to make it their own (339). At the end of Lowe's memoir, Salt Lake City became her home after she earned a college and law degree, married and had children, and, at the time she finished her memoir, was Assistant Attorney General for the state of Utah and the program director of the Homeless Youth Legal Clinic. And yet, the past and present for Lowe, the trauma of homelessness and the relief of being homed, remained for her "side by side, sometimes hand in hand, and at other times staring at one another through a looking glass" (305). To Lowe, these images seemed both reflective and contrastive, both permanent and momentary. In turn, Erlbaum confirmed the wisdom of fleeing her family home, even if she had to leave "behind people I love in order to get out." She predicted, however, that she would eventually "find a new home. And I know, wherever that home is, being there will be the most significant experience of my life" (249). Indeed, at the end of her memoir, Erlbaum described the apartment she rented where she could do the following: "Make some soup. Roll a joint. Take a bath. Double-check the locked door, keeping me safe inside" (252). Although alone, Erlbaum celebrated the safety and freedom that this home seemed to provide.

In this chapter, I review historical and theoretical perspectives of the home as a trope, one created in the early history of England and the United States, one inherited by those who have more recently acquired and maintained a socially accepted and admired home, and one contested by people experiencing homelessness who are excluded from this idealized and metaphorical space. In my analysis, I adopt the perspectives of scholars such as Chávez (2011), who noted that to illuminate and challenge an established trope, activists not only must interpret "external rhetorical messages that are created about them," but they also must "invent rhetorical strategies to publicly challenge oppressive rhetoric or create new imaginaries for the groups and the issues they represent and desire to bring into coalition" (3). To a certain extent, Clare, Lowe, and Erlbaum take on the role of activists in exposing the features that might make a home unsafe and undesirable, despite the social and emotional "truths" we assign to the home as a trope. Of course, homes occupy spaces and become actual, realized, or even imagined places, and so geographer Doreen Massey (2005) reminded her readers that space is "always open, always contested, and always changing," but place, such as a house or home, "has a specificity in our experience" (quoted in Dickinson 2020, 301). Home not only as a trope but also, as often an actual place, is a powerful and persuasive rhetorical image for those experiencing homelessness, an image that has the potential to comprise their sense of agency.

Using these perspectives, I focus on two particularly vulnerable groups of people experiencing homelessness: (1) female victims of domestic violence and (2) young people without stable housing. I selected these two groups because of the statistics that make these groups prominent in the homeless crisis and because their related stories reveal not only the links between homelessness, domestic violence, and the trauma experienced by both women and children but also the need to redefine or flee the space called home. Specifically, when children view domestic violence (whether sexual, physical, emotional, psychological, or financial) as did Erlbaum, and when they and their mothers suffer such violence as did Lowe, children may leave the home for the streets and experience not only homelessness but also additional violence on those streets. Thus, according to sociologists Jana Jasinski, Jennifer Wesely, James Wright, and Elizabeth Mustaine (2010), "Certainly, a substantial portion of homeless women have been victimized by childhood sexual abuse, and some researchers argue that childhood victimization is directly related to homelessness among adult women" (6; see also Wenzel, Leake, and Gelberb 2001). As a result of this intergenerational trauma, these adults and youth suffer from "low self-esteem, inability to maintain 'normal' or 'healthy' relationships, an equation . . . between violence and love or attention, a tendency to seek out abusive relationships, lack of trust, inability to recognize the warning signs of abusive relationships, depression, and substance abuse" (7). In this chapter, I focus on how women decide whether to flee or stay in the home to escape violence and abuse, and how youth may leave their families for alternative shelter.

According to the National Domestic Violence Hotline (NDVH) (2020), more women experience sexual abuse than do men (29 versus 10 percent), and more women have been injured as a result of intimate partner violence than have men (14.8 versus 4 percent). In the case of female victims of domestic violence, Ellen Malos and Gill Hague (1997), both from the Department of Social Policy and Planning at the University of Bristol, found "in addition to the violence they have experienced, the loss of home is in itself an element in the complex nature of the trauma that women in a violent relationship suffer" (397; see also Administration for Children & Families 2016; Ayesh 2020; Wilder Research 2014). In Fargo, North Dakota, for example, 44 percent of homeless women reported that they "stayed in an abusive relationship at some point in the past two years because they did not have other housing options" (Wilder Research Center 2004). Finally, in my analysis of women experiencing domestic violence and facing homelessness, I use the term victim throughout, rather than victim-survivor or survivor, for a number of reasons. For one, the law requires the existence of a victim before an offender can be arrested and prosecuted for domestic violence or before a person suffering domestic violence can obtain a restraining order against an abuser. Also, the term survivor, according to sociologist Jennifer Dunn (2010), may shift the responsibility to abused persons themselves and away from "the social structures and forces that they must overcome" (20). Finally, given the ongoing incidents of domestic homicide, not all victims live to be survivors. Thus, in an earlier study, I concluded, "Only by first being a victim might the individual then become a survivor and perhaps an activist" (Schuster 2019, 18).

In the case of youth experiencing homelessness or unstable housing, according to the US Interagency Council on Homelessness (2018), families with children represent one-third of all people experiencing homelessness on any given night, and these families are comprised most often by single women with one or two children. Moreover, John Coates and Sue McKenzie-Mohr (2010), scholars in the field of social work, found that young people may face the trauma of chronic poverty, family instability, parental substance abuse, mental illness, social isolation, and physical and sexual abuse. They might be forced to leave after divulging a pregnancy or identifying as lesbian, gay, bisexual, transgender, or queer or questioning (LGBTQ+). And, they may encounter sex trafficking once they leave their homes (see, for example, Olson 2020). As a result of such continuing trauma, such young people may experience a loss of trust, fail to development healthy relationships, and develop diminished self-worth. According to the National Law Center on Homelessness and Poverty (2019a), each year about 4.2 million youth and young adults experience homelessness, and 700,000 of them are minors without a parent or guardian.

The challenges that might cause victims of domestic violence and youth to leave home are complicated by systemic racism, classism, and gender discrimination, all aspects of intersectionality, which according to Anne Roschelle (2019), a sociologist and scholar of women's, gender, and sexuality studies, "shape social structures" but are also "themselves social structures . . . [or] shifting categories of oppression" (10). The perspective of intersectionality reminds us not only to see the complications that cause homelessness but also to acknowledge that individuals do not react uniformly to such social structural constraints.

Within this chapter, I again use social media and memoirs as sources of data and analysis, but I enhance these sources with (1) an in-depth study of the Supreme Court decision *Town of Castle Rock, Colorado v. Gonzales* (2005), which showed the legal responses and limitations of excluding a domestic abuser from the household; and (2) three personal interviews. These three interviews were with (1) Katherine Meerse, the Executive Director of Avenues for Youth, which supports youth ages sixteen to twenty-four in two locations in Hennepin County, Minnesota, by "providing a stable home, building trusting relations, and navigating the youth's education, career, health and wellness and housing goals" (avenuesforyouth.org); (2) Ryan Berg, Program Manager of ConneQT, affiliated with Avenues for Youth and a community-based response to LGBTQ+ youth experiencing homelessness, which provides safe and culturally responsive housing in a Host Home in the youth's own community; and (3) Mason Persons, an advocate for youth experiencing homelessness and a former resident with ConneQT Host Homes.

PRIVACY AND SAFETY IN A SPACE CALLED HOME

Scholars have attempted to categorize individuals and groups experiencing homelessness, most likely to get a sense of the causes and effects of homelessness and to recommend solutions. Jasinski et al. (2010), for example, divided the people who became homeless into three groups, those who are (1) "transitionally homeless for short periods before transitioning back into a stable housing situation and might never be homeless again"; (2) "episodically homeless or more in and out of homelessness with each episode lasting a short time, usually recurring episodes of shelter use"; and (3) "chronically homeless who stay homeless for extended periods of time, years or decades" (43–44; see also Vasilogambros 2018). Sociologist Anne Roschelle (2019) might add yet another category: A "hard-core group of chronically homeless families" as most likely "single-mother families, with children under the age of six . . . women [who have] had prolonged exposure to physical and sexual violence. Many of the mothers suffered from depression, had significant health problems, and struggled with drug and alcohol addiction" (47). The children in all of these families, concluded Roschelle, have serious physical and developmental difficulties as well as emotional and behavioral problems. In turn, the US Department of Housing and Urban Development (HUD) (2020) placed youth experiencing homelessness into four categories: (1) "throwaway youth," or youth who have been asked, told or forced to leave home; (2) "runaway youth," or youth who have left home without permission and stay away for one or more nights; (3) "street youth," or youth who have spent some time living outside or in the rough without a caregiver; and (4) "systems youth," or youth who have aged out of foster care or exited the juvenile justice system. As with the categorizations of space, these distinctions reflect the impulse to identify those experiencing homelessness in order to administer to them.

Although most likely the two groups I analyze in this chapter would fall into Jasinski et al.'s second category or all of HUD's four categories, I argue for a more nuanced view of people experiencing homelessness. Some of the young people who take advantage of Avenues for Youth, for example, found themselves in alternative shelters because their families could not support them in times of unemployment, particularly during the 2020–2021 COVID-19 pandemic, but they and their families often hoped for reunification. Memoir writer Liz Murray (2010) reminded her readers that she chose to leave for what she perceived as a better life, regardless of the outcome: "I just needed to have life around me—the pulse and vibration of people out in the world doing things. I traded school for this. I traded my home for this" (112). These categorizations represent the situations that might create or sustain homelessness, but individual stories add so much more. As I analyze next, the space we call home evolved from a private space in Western culture, and our perceptions of home are affected by the degree of agency of the inhabitants in that home.

The Home as a Trope

The ideal home might be conceived as a private, contained, concrete, and stable place, and one that can support the agency and freedom of its inhabitants. To adapt Blair's (1999) final question in analyzing material rhetoric—how a space as text "acts on people?"—a physical home not only exists but also is created by our expectations and assumptions about it and our restrictions within it. In the broadest sense, the home become a trope or a metaphorical idea, seen as static but in actuality ever dynamic not only throughout history but also at any given moment in a lifetime. Or, according to novelist James Baldwin (1956), "Perhaps home is not a place but simply an irrevocable condition" (121; also quoted in Berg 2015). Moreover, for many decades the home was thought to constitute a firm division between private and public space, between security and chaos, and between safety and danger, again a division more metaphorical than literal. And so, as law professor Jeannie Suk (2009) reminded us, home once "evoked the intimate freedom of private interior space," but now home can be "the place of unique potential for terror and vulnerability" (1–2).

The goal of having a private and supportive space remains important, however, as when memoir writer Erlbaum (2006) described her disappointment with her friend Jimmy when he rejected her proposal that they marry and create a home together. In light of Erlbaum's persistent homelessness, Jimmy's indifferent response caused her to question their entire relationship: "How did he manage to walk to the fridge and get the milk and pour it into glasses and stand there in front of me, offering me milk and cookies his mother baked for him, and not die of shame" (82). Clearly, Jimmy was much loved by his parents, and his home was a place that he would not leave for Erlbaum. Later, she returned temporarily to her own family home, even though living with her irresponsible mother was "more like having a thirty-nine-year-old roommate" (150). As with Erlbaum, the desire for a private space is a strong one, regardless of the instability and even violence that might characterize such a space. Thus, Suellen Murray (2008), a global, urban, and social studies scholar in Australia, concluded that for some women who suffered domestic violence "the sense of belonging, particularly to family and place, was a barrier that stopped them from ever leaving, despite the violence" (65). Even a very brief review of the early assumptions about and controversies regarding the home reveals a space that has been long problematic for many women and children.

According to historian Elizabeth Pleck (2004), during the colonial period in the United States, the home promoted the concept of the "Family Ideal" and supported "distinct ideas about family privacy, conjugal and parental rights, and family stability" (7). To achieve this family ideal, the husband and the wife were one person in the law, and as concluded Sir William Blackstone, "the very being or legal existence of the woman is suspended during the marriage" (quoted in Bell and Offen 1983, 33; see also Dubois and Dumenil 2018). Therefore, the wife gave up her property upon marriage, and the husband controlled and disciplined the wife and children so that marriage and family could be preserved at all costs. A cultural myth remains that this discipline was governed by the "rule of thumb," indicating the maximum width of a stick that could be used by the husband to beat his wife. Regardless of the validity of that rule, Blackstone (1765–1770) explained that the law did allow moderate beatings of wives by husbands. Additionally, the concept of coverture meant the wife indeed had no separate existence and remained in the home to attend to her reproductive and household duties. Overall, political scientist Carisa Showden (2011) defined coverture as "the commonly accepted views about men's duties to keep their wives in line with the rights of chastisement, that scope which varied by state, and women's responsibilities for maintaining the tranquility of the home, moderating men's baser instinct, and providing their children with a father who lived at home" (44). Thus, according to Marcus (1994), "violence against women in the home was the readily available and normativity endorsed accompaniment of coverture" (17), and women learned to "keep in their culturally and socially designated 'place' by the threat or imposition of physical injury" (32). The ideal family and home was often not ideal for women and their children.

Even before domestic violence was defined as such, it was a private family affair, beyond the scrutiny and intervention of the state, and the voices of women who might be abused either inside or outside of the home were discredited. In 1642, for example, Massachusetts defined sexual assault as an act that "forcibly and without consent ravished any maid or woman that is lawfully married or contracted" (quoted in Reddington 2009, 319), so only those women who were underage, virginal, engaged, or married might successfully claim sexual assault. Other single women were suspect. Moreover, complaints made by the assaulted woman were suspicious, as Lord Chief Justice Matthew Hale charged juries in sexual assault cases in the seventeenth century: "[T]he testimony of the [sexual assault] victim requires more careful scrutiny by the jury than the testimony of the other witnesses in the trial" (quoted in Morris 1988, 155). For decades, the courts required corroboration of an eye witness and evidence of physical injury and resistance in sexual assault cases. Although these requirements were later modified and eventually dropped, long after these reforms a complaint might be pursued only if there were evidence of lack of consent. Similarly, until 1639, women were not allowed to sue for divorce and then only on the grounds of bigamy, adultery, desertion, and abuse. In addition, although by 1771 New York allowed women to have some say in what their husbands did with their assets, women were not allowed to own property in the state until the 1848 Married Women's Property Act and the 1860 Act Concerning the Rights and Liabilities of Husband and Wife were passed. The latter act acknowledged that mothers were joint guardians of their children and had some legal authority. However, the home as a trope restricted women's often thwarted attempts to gain agency—and to maintain safety.

Therefore, according to Suk (2009), the home has long been a "spatial metaphor of private refuge from crime—a crime-free zone," and its "sacredness and inviolability consist not only in the integrity of its boundary but also in the freedom from crime within" (20). Scholars such as geographer Molly Warrington (2001) have noted that early criminology research focused on violence in public spaces by dangerous strangers who might intrude into private spaces, while the home was "considered only as a space of violence insofar as it is vulnerable to incursions from a threatening external world" (368). Now we acknowledge that, on the one hand, women and children may seek refuge outside the home, even to the point of homelessness, if that dangerous person is a family member—for women that might be the husband, and for children that might be a parent. On the other hand, only recently might that woman seek an order for protection or restraining order to exclude that dangerous person from the home so she could remain there. Thus, as Jenni Southwell (2002), at the Domestic Violence Resource Centre in Victoria, Australia, expressed, "[F]amily violence disrupts and violates the sense of safety and belonging that are culturally associated with the home and to this extent robs its victim of such a space" (4). In these cases, the question of agency becomes essential but is complicated, and it involves a perception of choice, either eased or restricted, and it affects identity.

A Sense of Agency

Feminist philosopher Susan Hekman (1991) cautioned that a sense of agency is "a product of discursive forces" rather than an "individual capacity deriving from 'inner space'" (59–60). Such a definition reflects how a sense of agency might be imposed upon the individual rather than developed within. Hekman's perspective was extended by Koerber (2001), who proposed that our perspective of agency must be reconfigured because "the forms of power enacted over subjects in the modern world are so complex and diverse," and these subjects are "constructed by multiple discourses that often conflict with each other" (224). People who are subjected to and resist these multiple discourses must "create modes of resistance to those discourses out of the elements of the very discourses that shape them," according to Hekman (51). Thus, agency is highly related to the tropes that are imposed upon us as well as the tropes that we deconstruct, in the latter case perhaps using the very discourse that constructed those tropes.

People experiencing homelessness might weigh options such as spending the night on the streets or in a homeless shelter, joining an encampment or contacting relatives, dumpster diving or panhandling, or linking up with other homeless people or remaining separate. Of course, those options are limited if city ordinances forbid sleeping outside, if there is no space in the closest shelter, if the temperature is too extreme to spend the night outside, if nearby shelters accommodate only men or only women, and so people experiencing homelessness may lack a sense of agency over their situation. Moreover, those options are restricted by city ordinances, spatial boundaries and segregation, and the social perceptions of and discourse about homelessness as manifested by the homeless trope itself. Regardless of these kinds of limitations, people do tend to flourish most when they have a sense of agency over their lives—and that sense of agency is highly related to the development of a strong and positive identity. If that identity is sustained and supported, it may enable an individual to better resist stigma and recover from trauma. In turn, stigmatization affects both social and personal identity. Finally, identity within social media, as literary critic Katherine Hayles (2005) concluded, may be ever evolving (212). Blogging, for example, according to Jeff Rice (2021) may be "a way of generating identity," an identity that "we associate as having traits, characteristics, and features of meaning" (183). Overall, identity and agency are complex notions, and contribute to the traits essential for people tolerating or escaping homelessness—or as Showden (2011) said, not only "deliberating on choices" but also "having choices on which to deliberate" (ix).

In their interviews with youth experiencing homelessness, for example, Toolis and Hammack (2015a) revealed the psychological and material nuances of both identity and agency. They said of one youth, "Although homelessness was not expressed as a choice or a positive experience for Alejandro, he was able, through narrative, to redefine his identity on positive terms by constructing a story in which his hardship was necessary for growth" (55). In other words, Alejandro had no opportunity to be homed at the time, but he attributed his current strength to his ability to survive homelessness, and his personal identity was bolstered by this feeling of agency. A sense of agency was also manifested in Clare's blog entries when she acknowledged that some of her readers might wonder why she did not "just go out and live off some man as though that were the only option a woman had in getting a better life" when her personal experiences led her to other conclusions: "Having a man in your life does not guarantee your life will be any better" (3.24.2011). And memoir writer Lowe found that life on the streets of Salt Lake City brought a damaged sense of agency when she experienced a violent rape and later a lengthy abusive relationship. Lowe concluded, "Relationships and sex were a means to an end. Love had nothing to do with either. I wasn't sure that love was even real. It was something people talked about and desired, but it was impossible to hold onto. Relationships consisted of you benefitting me, and me benefitting you. When that ended, we ended" (78–79). Lowe made her choice, but her choices were limited.

On the one hand, in acknowledgment of these personal experiences, evolving identities, and often limited choices, advocates helping women who have experienced domestic violence are trained to maintain or enhance the victim's sense of agency by supporting her choices rather than by selecting one for her. In fact, the first shelter in the nation for women and their children escaping domestic violence, Women's Advocates in St. Paul, Minnesota, explains that it "*walks* with victims/survivors and our community to break the cycle of domestic violence," rather than persuading a victim to leave her abuser, to cooperate in a criminal complaint, to obtain an order for protection, or such (emphasis added, wadvocates.org; see also AlexandraHouse.org; Tubman. org). Affirming victim agency rather than trying to persuade a victim to escape from her abuser may challenge advocates, but as suggested by sociologists Jennifer Dunn and Melissa Powell-Williams (2007), an effective advocacy approach might be "conceptualizing agency as a continuum" to avoid dichotomizing agency and victimization (978). Anywhere along that continuum, the victim of domestic violence might choose a path. Thus, agency, according to Showden (2011), "can be—and frequently is—partial," because of both material and discursive norms, because of the structural existence of the home, and because the notion of the ideal home may be deceptive (6). Victim advocates are trained to listen to and provide resources that support victims' choices, such as safety plans and emergency shelter.

On the other hand, facing similar challenges as victim advocates but governed by mandatory arrest laws, law enforcement officers responding to a domestic violence incident must make an arrest if they find probable cause to believe that an offense has been committed, regardless of whether the victim cooperates or recants and of whether the offender is present at the time. Called "probable cause arrests for domestic violence" in Minnesota, a police officer may arrest a person without a warrant if the person is suspected of having committed nonfelony domestic abuse "even though the assault did not take place in the presence of a peace officer"; moreover, that officer is immune from civil liability for a contested arrest (Minnesota Statutes 2020, 629.341; see American Bar Association Commission on Domestic Violence 2018 for a complete list of other states with such mandatory arrest laws). In some cases, if both parties have been injured and if no one party's complaint seems more credible, both parties may be arrested, a practice often seen by both victim advocates and some legal scholars as problematic (see, for example, Bridgett 2020; Cambria 2006; Hirschel, Buzawa, Pattavina, and Farriani 2007). Finally, if an officer suspects that a victim might be in danger of being severely injured or killed by the abuser, that officer might administer what is called a Lethality Assessment Protocol or LAP, which can be used as a tool to persuade the victim to contact an advocate and perhaps move to a domestic violence shelter, to provide support for an order of protection, and/ or to use as evidence in prosecuting an abuser (see, for example, Propen and Schuster 2017). Overall, even given the goal of establishing and maintaining a victim's agency, law enforcement may be instrumental in a domestic violence victim's electing to leave her home—even if that means she and her children might face eventual homelessness—which complicates the victim's sense of agency.

Ideally, effective agency takes the form of not only altering one's circumstances in positive ways but also exercising the ability to challenge and change limitations. Such agency, according to Showden (2011), accounts for both "the critically reflective component composed of one's internal dispositions and individual intentions (autonomy)" and "the external impediments to, and resources available for, achieving one's goals (freedom, and its limitation)" (xi). Thus, in his memoir, youth counselor Ryan Berg (2015), who directs the ConneQT program in the Twin Cities, described starting a writing group among the young people experiencing homelessness with whom he worked in an LGBTQ+ group home in New York City. Such gender-expansive youth (or youth whose expressions of gender clash with the dominant societal notions of masculine men and feminine women) are victimized more by violence, frequently have substance abuse problems, may undertake risk-taking activities, and often feel isolated, rejected, and self-destructive. And so, in forming the writing group, Berg had hoped that by writing their stories these young people would gain a "greater sense of agency" (122). The group initially grumbled about the task of writing, which Berg attributed to typical teenager behavior, but their stories moved some of them to reflect upon their pasts and to recognize their future opportunities.

Finally, all youth experiencing homelessness may also use social media and memoirs to remind their readers that, without stable housing and because of trauma, a sense of agency is difficult to achieve. Blogger "George" (B9) who had been homeless since the age of fifteen, noted,

> Because you are so small when it [physical, mental, or sexual abuse] first happens, you learn to cope with abuse from a powerless position. . . . By the time you reach adulthood, you're left with a screwed up sense of what "choice" means, and a bitter view on the topic of justice. Because you've been lied to over and over again you cannot trust others, and thus you cannot trust yourself. (3.11.2007)

In George's case, he feared that he would have no choice but to become an abuser himself unless he undertook a "slow form of suicide," such as substance abuse, risk taking, or other destructive behavior (3.11.2007). As memoir writer Roy Juarez, Jr. (2018) confirmed, "Growing up as a homeless teenager can really strip you of an identity. You get lost in the streets of survival by becoming whoever and whatever others want you to be," even if "you try to hold on to your identity." Juarez concluded, "It becomes easy to throw your values out the window when you're hungry" (186). A sense of agency, as it informs or challenges personal and social identity, may be affected by multiple and powerful discourses, including stigmatization. A positive sense of agency, however, may provide an essential tool to overcome homelessness and/or reconstruct the home as a rhetorical trope.

Normative Competence

A sense of agency—including forming an identity, recognizing choices, or feeling empowered to make changes—can also be either promoted or restricted by what philosopher Paul Benson (1990) called normative competence or "an array of abilities to be aware of applicable normative standards, to appreciate those standards, and to bring them competently to bear on one's evaluations of open courses of actions" (54). Agency can be the ability not only to understand a situation but also to recall the norms of society, adhere to those normative principles in order to be accepted by a community (perhaps by passing), and yet retain a sort of contextualized agency. As Showden (2011) concluded, agency is both a capacity and a process, and such public or social identity not only "flattens out differences between us and others" but it can also flatten out "the complexity of our own sense of self" (27). Identity may be affected by the desire to be accepted in so-called normal material, social, and political conditions, such as home ownership, employment, financial stability, and even marriage and parenthood. Competency seems a desirable attribute, but the adjective "normative" may limit its advantages. Clinical psychologist Sean Kidd (2007), for example, found that youth experiencing homelessness may come from homes considered to "deviate from the ideals of the 'social norm' and therefore place the young person outside the cultural models of 'normalcy'" (291). Such perceived deviance and resulting lack of normative competence may invite stigma and negatively affect a sense of agency.

Also, groups experiencing homelessness may encourage, teach, and expect normative competence within their community. Applying a social scientific view of medicine, Colette Auerswald and Stephen Eyre (2002), for example, conducted interviews with 26 street youth in San Francisco, California, and found a set of five tenets that determined normative competence among these young people: (1) "Shared identity as an outsider, as having been rejected by the mainstream"; (2) common rejection of that mainstream culture; (3) common adversity among the homeless, including the belief the residents of a homeless group or community "will share even their last scrap of food"; (4) universal belief that "people who live on the street are free, liberated from the pressures of the rat race"; and (5) a common assumption that "basic needs would be met in the face of adversity and scarcity," a sort of "magical provision" of those basic needs (1505–6). Accepting these tenets not only marked normalized competence among certain youth experiencing homelessness but also rationalized "a transient lifestyle and persistent scarcity," a perhaps compromised sense of agency that was difficult for the youth to challenge and modify (1506). And certainly, this normalized competence was in direct contrast to that assumed by housed communities.

Finally, as with agency, such principles of normalized competence are fluid, depending greatly on individual experiences. Blogger and memoir writer Brianna Karp (2011), for example, in her *Girl's Guide to Homelessness*, reminded her readers, "As long as you're alive and healthy and physically/mentally capable of coming up with a plan and executing it, you will be OK. . . . There is *always* another avenue, another option, another choice, another route, another door to pursue if one is closed off to you (and often, that door is reopened later on—check back on it after trying a few other options first)" (emphasis in original, 2.26.2009). Normative competence may strengthen a sense of agency but could obstruct reintegration into the other societies. Therefore, this space called home, that ideal space designed to house the ideal family, serves as the trope that we inherited long ago and, in many ways, maintain today. Agency becomes hard to come by if choices are limited, and multiple discourses intervene and even conflict. Moreover, as I explore next, the very life of a victim of domestic violence may be threatened by a once loving partner—and that victim's choices are challenged by safety concerns, personal experience, and the potential of homelessness.

HOMELESSNESS AND DOMESTIC VIOLENCE

Scholars still disagree about how much domestic violence contributes to homelessness among women and their families. On the one hand, attorney Gretchen Mullins (1994) speculated, "Fifty percent of the homeless women and children in this country are fleeing domestic violence" because "abused women and their children must weigh living with the violence in their homes against the insecurity of living on the streets" (237). Similarly, Jasinski et al. (2010) concluded, "Approximately one homeless woman in four is homeless mainly because of her experience with violence" (157). On the other hand, Roschelle (2019) stated, "While there is a substantial body of scholarship on domestic violence, much less is known about the specific relationship between domestic violence and family homelessness" (40). Despite these various conclusions, those who have experienced homelessness as a result of domestic violence have affirmed the relationship between the two conditions in social media as well as published memoirs.

In the video interview "Homeless Woman Sleeping Rough," for example, the interviewee stressed the "extensive domestic violence" that she suffered and described the result of this abuse: "And, I became homeless. He doesn't know where I am. . . . I rely on the generosity of the public, that's how I survive" (10.26.2019). Moreover, "Dianna," interviewed in a story by Vicky Inoue (2016) for *Street Sheet*, an independent street newspaper dedicated to covering issues of homelessness and poverty, recalled how her "baby's dad tried to kill her, because I found out he had some other women and I was supporting them without knowing." Because of this attempted domestic homicide and resulting homelessness, Dianna remained on the street for 30 years, resorting to alcohol and drug abuse to numb her trauma. Over these years, stated Dianna, "I worried about how I'm gonna [sic] protect myself and where I'm gonna sleep, because there might be a man coming up and just grabbing me and doing bad things to me; I had all that done to me, it's hard." These stories add a personal face to the statistics about domestic violence and homelessness. Moreover, the essential choices that women who experience domestic violence have and the decisions that they make are complicated, in particular regarding their sense of agency—whether they choose to stay in the home with their abusers; to escape to friends, relatives, or a shelter; or to turn to the law to exclude the abuser from the home.

Staying with or Returning to the Abuser

Although the three choices listed above might seem distinct, at times they are not choices at all. On average, for example, it takes a victim of domestic violence seven times to leave her abuser and stay away for good, according to advocacy groups such as the National Domestic Violence Hotline (2021). Advocate Sarah Buel (1999) listed fifty different obstacles to leaving an abuser, such as believing the threats from the abuser should the victim leave, denying the severity of the abuse, fearing losing child custody or facing homelessness, accepting cultural and racial defenses articulated by either the victim or the abuser, and such. Moreover, according to Warrington (2001), a woman "suffering sustained domestic violence may be spatially and socially restricted" to the home, "rarely venturing outside the home environment except for specific timed or accompanied trips," and so the "fear of further attack may restrict her movements" (378). Indeed, the victim's isolation may deprive her of support and confidence, and she may rightly worry about what law professor Martha Mahoney (1991) identified as "separation assault" if she does attempt to leave her abuser (5).

Victims of domestic violence have blogged in great detail about how they were threatened by their abusers and yet remained with them. Blogger "Susie" (B15), for example, described in her entry "Can I Change Him?" the following dilemma: "Often the thought is if you love him enough he will stop abusing you. This thought usually occurs after the victim has suffered for awhile and they desperately want it to stop." This strategy may take the form of small gestures that often prove unsuccessful, and Susie explained how arbitrary and unpredictable such abuse might be. When she fixed dinner a certain way, for example, her abuser "exploded about there being too much grease in the meal and it resulted in various pieces of cutlery being thrown at me while he screamed at me." A few weeks later when she made that meal again, she related, "I obviously remembered the past incident and was trembling inside. I made sure that I really drained the meat grease this time, but in the end the meal turned out the way it had before. I felt sick with fear. I waited for my ex to explode once again, but . . . he told me it was the best meal ever and thanked me for supper." As a result, Susie concluded that she "had lost all control. He had it. He could decide how my day went. After years of such incidents I no longer knew what was right or wrong" (1.23.2014). Thus, victims of domestic violence may lose their sense of agency because they are forced by their abusers to relinquish control and because they face constant unpredictability.

Also, victims of domestic violence may undergo a period of grooming in which their abusers isolate them. Blogger "Jessica" (B14), for example, told how her abuser "reeled" her in: "There were red flags that I didn't see before any of the abuse. We were so happy that we didn't spend time with anyone else, I quickly quit going out and hanging out with friends." She blogged about what happened as a result of this isolation: "When he did start the abuse it was slow and subtle, we shared all of our past hurts with each other . . . so he knew exactly where to press to hurt me the most. . . . He would apologize but it would happen all over again time after time" (2.15.2020). In turn, victims may want the abuse to stop but the relationship to continue, as blogger "Nancy" (B13) explained. She related that she had once returned to her dormitory later than she expected and found her boyfriend furious with her: "That's when I started crying, then he was crying too, and we were all blubbering into the phone. I was totally stressed out, but we made up as always and I've never loved him more" (1.26.1996). After such grooming, victims of domestic violence often lose confidence in their ability to "handle" their abusers to avoid getting hurt and so conform to their wishes and remain with them—a constricting kind of love but a sort of normative competence.

Susie and Jessica eventually did leave their abusers, despite the challenges of finding new homes, establishing new and trustworthy relationships, and dealing with the results of trauma. Staying with the abuser, however, is hard and dangerous work. In fact, women's studies scholar Isabel Marcus (1994) described how domestic abuse can take the form of terrorism, through "unannounced and seemingly random but actually calculated attacks of violence," "psychological as well as physical warfare aimed at silencing protests," and "an atmosphere of intimidation in which there is no safe place of escape" (31). Such emotional abuse may destroy a victim's sense of agency.

Leaving the Abuser

Leaving the abuser, however, can be equally as challenging as staying and trying to "manage" that abuser. Based on her interviews with women who experienced housing instability after leaving their abusive partners, Australian researcher Silke Meyer (2016) concluded that these women entered "a state of homelessness when trading in their family home for temporary shelter with family, friends or in crisis accommodation," a state that occurred "very real, very quickly for many women and children" (199; see also Tutty, Ogden, Giurgui, and Weaver-Dunlop 2014; Williams 1998). Such women and their families might require, as proposed Charlene Baker, Kris Billhardt, Joseph Warren, Chiquita Rollins, and Nancy Glass (2010) from the Johns Hopkins

University School of Nursing, not only food and shelter for a few months but also long-term "assistance in overcoming the emotional and psychological impact of domestic violence on themselves and their children, and assistance related to economic security and housing stability" (431). Establishing economic security and housing stability is challenging but tangible. Managing and overcoming the trauma of abuse may be much more difficult to achieve.

Jessica, for example, related in her blog the way in which her therapist helped her understand the trauma she experienced from domestic abuse and why she had stayed with her abuser for so long: "She [the therapist] explained it's very similar to bi-polar disorder. My brain is still stuck in these crazy extremes, throw some PTSD on top of that and any trigger could send me spiraling in any direction" (2.29.2020). Moreover, Jessica's abuser had isolated her so that he seemed "the only one I thought I could go to for comfort, he was still my grounding point." When Jessica offered the blog entry "The Night [L] Tried to Kill Me," she shared with her readers that this entry "took a lot out of me to write. I cried a lot. It took several different sessions and breaks and many hours to write," and she warned those readers that before and after they read the entry to "take the time to do your own self care and make sure you are in a safe place mentally" (3.1.2020). Leaving the abuser may be just the start of healing from trauma.

Also, the children of abuse victims may experience long-term trauma. By the time blogger Susie left her abuser, for example, her youngest daughter had been diagnosed with PTSD: "My daughter grew up knowing fear. Real fear. Like fear that her dad was going to kill her mum one day or maybe herself kind of fear." As a result of that fear, the child had been "peeing in garbage cans at home, sucking on her hair, rocking and talking to herself" as well as experiencing "nightmares, panic attacks and at one point she did go catatonic. . . . Something inside of her broke" (11.20.2015). Therefore, upon leaving an abuser, the victim of domestic violence may face extraordinary challenges to establish a home that may contrast greatly not only to the ideal home she once may have envisioned but also to the actual one she fled.

Excluding the Abuser from the Home

Ultimately, as did bloggers Jessica and Susie, a victim of domestic violence might turn to the law to exclude the abuser from that home. Such a choice may start with filing a form but then requires depending on law enforcement to keep the victim safe. In a way, obtaining a restraining order is not only a way to enhance the agency of the victim and also a way to relinquish that agency to the courts and law enforcement. But leaving an abuser may also lead to homelessness.

One evening, for example, while volunteering at Tubman, I was helping clients prepare to meet with the volunteer attorney when one client explained how she did not want to leave her home because she owned the house—but her abuser would not agree to leave. She wanted to claim her property but felt she would not be safe if she stayed. Although I am never privy to consultations between a client and the attorney, I knew that she would probably have the option of filing a restraining order against her abuser, an order for protection (OFP) as it is called in Minnesota. An OFP is filed in civil court by the victim petitioner to help prevent the abuser from committing further acts of domestic violence by excluding that abuser from a shared residence or the residence of the petitioner, from a "reasonable area" surrounding that residence, and from the petitioner's place of employment, education, church, and such. The OFP also specifies that the abusing party must have no contact with the petitioner in person, by telephone, by mail, or by electronic messaging, and that even if the petitioner contacts the abuser, the abuser must not respond. Moreover, by federal law the abuser cannot have or buy a gun while subject to an OFP (see, for example, Minnesota Statutes 518B.01 2020; Texas Statutes Family Code Title 4. 2020; Washington Courts Domestic Violence Protective Order Process 2020). In turn, a Domestic Abuse No Contact Order (DANCO) may be issued by a court against a defendant in a criminal proceeding for domestic abuse, which also prohibits contact between the victim and abuser, despite a victim's wishes or her recantation.

Thus, violation of either an OFP or a DANCO is considered a crime, and the violator is subject to arrest—but, in essence, when issuing either an OFP or a DANCO, the victim relinquishes her agency or choice to the courts and law enforcement. Moreover, although these legal means may exclude abusers from the family home and thus help protect victims, they can present personal challenges for those victims. On the one hand, Susie described calling the police when her abuser started stalking and harassing her, only to be told, "Just keep calling when you hear him [outside her new home] and hopefully we'll get [t]here in time" (9.1.2013). Susie did not find this response reassuring. On the other hand, blogger Jessica obtained a restraining order not only to keep her abuser away from her but also to try to rediscover her own agency: "I bawled and retyped it a million times, but basically, I told [L] I would not accept any further contact from him" (4.3.2020). Jessica suffered emotional trauma but recovered her sense of agency. Ultimately, although Susie and Jessica were both dependent on others to protect them, neither remained in the family home.

Considering *Town of Castle Rock, Colorado v. Gonzales* (2005)

The challenge of depending on others to enforce the conditions and respond to any violations of a restraining order or an OFP is illustrated in the Supreme Court decision in *Town of Castle Rock, Colorado v. Gonzales* (2005), a decision that revealed problematic legal interpretations regarding the space we call home. In *Castle Rock*, the Court encountered a case in which, according to Suk (2008), the Court failed to acknowledge two essential issues. The first issue involved "the full implications of the contemporary reformist domestic violence regime now embraced in established legal circles," particularly that domestic violence abusers should be subject to mandatory arrest and other means to protect the victim and to eliminate violence from the home. The second issue concerned the principle that "the home should be subject to *public* control and the criminal law to *private* control"; in other words, it was of public and social interest to prevent domestic violence in the home, and victims of domestic violence relinquished their private sense of agency to be protected by criminal ordinances as endorsed by society (emphasis added, 292). With domestic violence now being discussed publicly, the state could intervene in what were once considered private affairs. As Suk warned regarding domestic violence, the nature of the home, as once supposedly "utterly familiar and comfortable" had become "unfamiliar and frightening"—indeed, "the figure [usually the male] meant to provide for the home's safety turns out to be the most terrifying threat to it" (291, 302). The *Castle Rock* decision unfortunately challenged a significant legal protection from domestic violence.

The facts of the *Castle Rock* case are quite disturbing. Jessica Gonzales, a resident of Castle Rock, Colorado, obtained a temporary restraining order (TRO) against her estranged husband Simon, who had been stalking her. The TRO was served upon Simon and commanded him not to "molest or disturb the peace" of Jessica or of any of her children and "to remain at least 100 yards from the family home at all times." The order also contained a warning to Simon that a violation of the order would "constitute contempt of court" and that he might be arrested without notice if a law enforcement officer "has probable cause to believe that you have knowingly violated this order." Finally, the order contained a notice to law enforcement officials: "You *shall* use every *reasonable means* to enforce this restraining order. You *shall* arrest, or, if an arrest would be impractical under the circumstances, seek a warrant for the arrest of the restrained person when you have information amounting to *probable cause* that the restrained person has violated or attempted to violate the order." (emphasis added). The Castle Rock Police Department received a copy of the TRO, and on June 4, 1999, the state trial court made the TRO permanent.

As summarized in the respondent's complaint and in the Supreme Court's decision, at about 5:30 pm on June 22, 1999, Simon indeed violated the restraining order by taking his three daughters away from where they were playing outside the family home. Jessica called the Castle Rock Police Department at 7:30 pm that evening, and when two officers arrived at the home, she showed them the restraining order and requested that it be enforced and the children returned to her. The responding officers said that "there was nothing they could do" at that moment about enforcing the restraining order and to call the police department again if the children were not returned by 10:00 pm. When Simon called Jessica at approximately 8:30 pm, he told her that he "had the three children [at an] amusement park in Denver," and Jessica called the police department again to request that someone "check for" her husband and his vehicle at the amusement park and "put out an [all-points bulletin] for her husband." The officer whom Jessica spoke with "refused to do so" and told her again to wait until 10:30 pm to see if Simon returned the girls. When Jessica called near that time, she was to wait until midnight. According to the complaint, the officer who took Jessica's report "made no reasonable effort" to enforce the restraining order or locate the three children—"Instead, he went to dinner." Then, at about 3:20 am, Simon arrived at the police department and opened fire with a semiautomatic handgun. The police shot back and killed him—and inside the cab of his pickup truck, they found the bodies of all three daughters whom Simon had murdered earlier.

Jessica filed suit in the US District Court for the District of Colorado against the town of Castle Rock, the Castle Rock Police Department, and the three officers involved. Her attorneys claimed that Jessica indeed had a federally protected property interest in the enforcement of the restraining order and alleged that this police department customarily failed to respond to violations of restraining orders. A protected property interest means that the person has a legitimate claim of entitlement under the Fourteenth Amendment—therefore, by not fulfilling the promised protection as indicated in the restraining order, the state was depriving Jessica of not only due process but also her "property." As Suk (2008) put it, "Taking away that promised protection was in effect taking away the home" (307). Then, when a motion to dismiss Jessica's complaint was granted, she appealed to the Tenth Circuit Court of Appeals, which found Jessica had a valid Due Process claim but affirmed that the individual police officers had qualified immunity, customary in most states, and therefore they could not be sued. The town of Castle Rock then appealed to the US Supreme Court. As led by Justice Scalia, the majority of the Court reversed the Tenth Circuit's decision and reinstated the District Court's order of dismissal of Jessica's complaint.

Ultimately, the Supreme Court's decision became a matter of discourse analysis—defining and interpreting the words commonly used in restraining orders and the statutes that created them, including the words that I italicized in the language of Jessica's restraining order. First, the Supreme Court found that restraining orders had no protected benefit or value because government officials "may grant or deny it" at their discretion. The directive addressed to police officials as printed on Jessica's restraining order—"You shall use every reasonable means to enforce this restraining order"—meant that, according to the Court, such officers indeed could decide whether to enforce the restraining order and whether such enforcement was reasonable. Second, the Court decided that the Colorado Legislature did not mean to make enforcement mandatory because the legislature had not used more forceful language, and therefore a police officer could decide whether there was probable cause that a restraining order had been violated—such as, had Simon Gonzales really taken the children with no intention of returning them? Finally, the Court debated the meaning of the word "shall" in the directions to police officers printed on the restraining order: "shall use every reasonable means" and "shall arrest." Was "shall" deliberately used instead of "may" or "will" or even "is authorized," the Court pondered. Ultimately, recalling the American Bar Association's cautions that similar state statutes could not "be interpreted literally," and therefore deciding that the word "shall" did not make enforcement of restraining orders mandatory, the Court dismissed the argument that a flexible interpretation "would render domestic abuse restraining orders utterly valueless" as "sheer hyperbole." Thus, the Supreme Court greatly weakened the protection that restraining orders or OFPs could provide a victim of domestic violence.

Justices Stevens and Ginsberg did write a dissent in the *Castle Rock* decision, and they noted that it was indeed plausible to construe use of "shall" to indicate mandatory directives to the police, that the majority of justices in this decision had placed "undue weight" on how other state statutes were interpreted, and that the state of Colorado had joined those states in creating mandatory arrest statutes, a show of support for enforcing restraining orders in domestic violence cases. Certainly, this minority of justices in *Castle Rock* as well as law scholars and practitioners were dismayed by the Court's decision not to make enforcement of restraining orders mandatory. Nicole Quester (2015), for example, concluded that given this decision, "American law has failed to provide women with a meaningful remedy against spousal abuse" (441). In turn, Kathleen Curtis (2006) reviewed the court decisions following *Castle Rock* and found conflicting results (see also Snead 2009). On the one hand, Curtis revealed that in *Starr v. Price* (2005), a federal district court relied on *Castle Rock* to conclude that nothing in Pennsylvania statutes "eliminated police discretion in enforcing protective orders." On the other hand, she found in *Hudson v. Hudson* (2007) that although the Sixth Circuit Court recognized the Supreme Court's reading of discretion in *Castle Rock,* the Sixth Circuit Court had held that, according to Tennessee statutes, arrest for violation of restraining orders or OFPs was "operational [and mandatory], not discretionary" (1185). In other words, in the *Starr* decision, the courts found that law enforcement could use their discretion in arresting violators of restraining orders for domestic violence such as Simon Gonzales, but in *Hudson*, the court found that officers like those in the Castle Rock Police Department must enforce restraining orders for domestic violence. Finally, law scholars Lynn Combs (2006) determined that the *Castle Rock* decision represented "a step backward for abuse victims who rely on restraining orders" (389), and Carrie Clingan (2007) concluded that the Court's decision "sends a message to victims of domestic violence that mandatory arrest statutes do not mean what they say" (326–27). Moreover, Amber Fink (2006) warned that the language in statutes such as those of Colorado indicated that the police "do not hold the discretion to do *nothing*" (emphasis in original, 391). Overall, the *Castle Rock* decision, the court decisions that followed, and the analysis of these legal scholars illustrate how complicated and risky is the third choice a victim of domestic violence might make—to stay at home but exclude the abuser.

Finally, along with bloggers Susie, Jessica, and Nancy, memoir writer Murray (2010) reflected on how that control can still be assumed by an abuser: "I was used to . . . sensing my feelings only in relation to others. If he was content, then so was I. Carlos had been calling the shots all along because I let him. I caught myself at this moment, ready to do the same, and it sickened me" (222). And, Lowe (2016) described in her memoir, how her abuser groomed her to obey him. He directed Lowe after she was raped on the streets, "I need to know where you are at all times. . . . I worry about your safety. I don't need you to be seen hanging out with the wrong people" (77). What he meant, determined Lowe, was that "he didn't want to look like he couldn't control me" (100). Staying with the abuser and living with violence, leaving the abuser but possibly encountering homelessness, or legally excluding the abuser from the home but risking violation and even revenge all illustrate the challenges of maintaining that space called home, once private but now of public interest. The seeds of domestic violence were seen in past principles such as coverture as well as the control and agency granted to the male head of the household rather than the female "helpmate." Victims of domestic violence are challenged to maintain their safety and that of their families and yet are limited in their choices, and they are particularly vulnerable to homelessness should they elect or be forced to leave their homes.

HOMELESSNESS AND YOUNG PEOPLE

Unaccompanied youth are also particularly vulnerable to homelessness. The Homeless Hub (2019b), sponsored by the Canadian Observation on Homelessness, noted that many youth experiencing homelessness not only have no stable or consistent residence but also have inadequate access to support networks necessary to transition into "the responsibilities of adulthood." Initially, such youth may live in hostels, stay with friends, live in "squats," share rooms in boarding houses or low-income hotels, or live in homeless shelters or on the streets, but what they have in common is housing instability. And typically, they have left behind homes that were "defined by relationships (both social and economic) in which they were typically dependent upon adult caregivers," or they may have been involved in child protective services, lived in foster homes, and aged out of a system without continuing support or the maturity to live independently. However, they face the adult challenges of being employed, paying rent, purchasing homes, and raising families, expectations of the so-called normal community. Therefore, helping these young people involves some major challenges: They have very different needs based on age, they likely have been affected by intergenerational poverty, and they are six times more likely to be victimized in contrast to the general population. Additionally, because of the stigma of homelessness as well as possible confusion about identity, lack of a sense of agency, and the trauma of street life or even of foster or group home care, many of these youth find regular school difficult. Programs for youth experiencing homelessness are greatly needed to help young people earn a Graduate Equivalency Degree (GED) (see, for example, covenanthouse.org), and successful programs link every young person with support staff to help with education and employment or career paths.

Additionally, as Katherine Meerse (2020), Executive Director of Avenues for Youth, stated in her interview with me, young people came into that organization "with trauma that is related to many things that happen to them, including stigma and bias." They might have experienced "the bias of racism and institutional racism" as well as that stigma assigned to them because of their homeless and economic situation. Thus, Ryan Berg (2021), ConneQT Program Manager, found that many of the young people who come to Avenues for Youth avoid identifying as homeless—resisting the stigma of homeless: "I think that our kind of cultural identifier of someone experiencing homelessness is the white man in his 40s or 50s looking ragged, suffering from chronic and pervasive mental health issues, someone who is chronically experiencing homelessness. I think that is a misnomer, and I think a lot of youth rightly don't categorize themselves in that way." Instead, as Berg went on, "A lot of youth, maybe in high school, don't see themselves as experiencing homelessness. They often see their unstable housing situation as something temporary until they get on their feet. They would say that they are staying on their friend's couch. They will say, 'I have got to find a place to stay tonight; I will find a place, but I am not homeless.'" And so, for these young people, concluded Berg, "It's dodging the stigma, so no one knows their experience. I am sure that it's rooted in shame, but I don't know if it's explicit." Youth experiencing homelessness are often traumatized not only by unstable housing but also by social stigmatization.

In his interview with me, Berg (2021) added that many of these young people have also encountered intergenerational poverty, often stemming from the historical effects of racial zoning, redlining, and restrictive deed covenants. According to Berg, "We live in a society where you are penalized and criminalized for being poor. Often times we see parents struggling to keep the family together, working three jobs in order to pay the rent, but then there is no adult supervision for the young people and so that is criminalized." In these cases, the young person might be removed from the home and placed in a group or foster home—or the family of those young people might elect to have them temporarily shelter with such organizations as Avenues for Youth. Certainly, memoir writer Gaulden (2017) made clear that poverty as well as addiction "plagued" him from an early age: "I had never had a chance to screw up in life. I started at the bottom" (33). According to former resident with ConneQT Mason Persons (2021) in his interview with me, such intergenerational poverty means that "if you grow up poor, you are very likely to stay poor. And when you experience unstable housing, you are likely to stay in it. All through my life we had unstable housing . . . shelters, friend's housing, and such . . . stuck in the cycle of poverty." Finally, as Brandon Robinson (2020) wrote in his memoir, poverty and instability are "two sides of the same coin" and have "devastating consequences for families" (35). Therefore, young people who experience homelessness may suffer not only from intergenerational trauma but also from intergenerational poverty—one affects the other. But these young people frequently avoid the label of homeless because of the stigma it carries, a stigma that derails their sense of agency and threatens their personal identity.

Longing for Home and Family

Each year, an estimated 4.2 million youth and young adults experience homelessness, 700,000 of whom are minors who are without a parent or guardian (National Law Center on Homelessness & Poverty 2019a; see also National Alliance to End Homelessness 2020e; National Conference of State Legislatures 2019; PEW Trusts 2017). Young people who experience homelessness are considered to be twelve to twenty-four years of age, some just entering their teenage years and some on the brink of adulthood. Writing for the National Center on Family Homelessness, Bassuk et al. (2014) considered children experiencing homelessness "among the most invisible and neglected individuals in our nation" (10). And as Justin Reed Early (2013) reminded his memoir readers, more than 80 percent "will be physically or sexually abused," and therefore their "tumbling spirits will become so injured that they will need to use mind-altering substances to sooth their slowly dying souls" (217). In response, youth experiencing housing instability may also create a variety of new homes and families, and their personal interpretations of those homes and families are complex and varied.

During my interview with Mason Persons (2021), for example, he recalled longing for home and family even though he had voluntarily left his family home: "I remember when like that first summer of being homeless, I was riding the bus up and down because I have nothing else to do, and I was wanting so badly to go home, but I had no clue where that meant, because I had literally nowhere, but I wanted to go home so badly." At various times, Persons had lived on the street, with friends, in a shelter, in two Host Homes through ConneQT, and finally in a shared and then his own apartment. Persons also distinguished between his two families—his "bio-mom" and his "chosen family," the latter consisting of nonrelatives whom he called his "mother" and "father," along with their minor child and a grandmother whom he called "Nonnie." His chosen family were acquaintances of his bio-mom and met Persons when he was a child. Later, he was dismayed when his chosen family had no room for him in their new house, but he could not live with the tension in his bio-mom's home, and so he was homeless for two years. After his disappointment of not being able to live with his chosen family, Persons reconciled with them but continued to avoid his "mentally abusive and manipulative" bio-mom. Eventually he found a space to call home through the ConneQT program, which is "youth driven," in that the young people review applications and select potential places to live where they can figure out their "next steps and receive education and career support." Persons had to leave his first Host Home family, however, when his basement room proved too cold to stay in during the winter—and although the move to another Host Home "felt a little traumatic in the moment," Persons trusted that his first host family "wanted the best for him." They had initially provided a "safe, calm environment" for him and wanted a new safe and warm place for him to live. Persons's experiences with homelessness, then, were grounded in a desire for that stability, safety, and loving support—for home and family.

Moreover, seeking a home seems never to be simply substituting one place for another but instead looking for emotional support and stability—all that the rhetorical trope represents. Memoir writer Kenisha Anthony (2020), for example, who was removed from her parents' house and lived in foster care at a young age, continued to long for her original but unstable family home: "I wanted my mother and father. I just wanted to be a child for once. I wanted to be loved and cared for." However, Anthony knew that she "needed to grow up fast to fend for myself—with no knowledge and guidance for how to do that" (109). On the one hand, when Anthony became a social worker herself, she remembered that a trainer had cautioned the group: "Keep in mind, no matter how unfit they are to you, a child will always love and want to be with their parents" (201). On the other hand, some young people experiencing homelessness may be certain that returning home would be traumatic and therefore express little longing for that family home. Persons was never homesick for his bio-mom, whom he saw as the reason he was homeless. He just wanted to go to a "home," wherever and whatever space that might mean—where he might discover his identity as well as exercise agency. Otherwise, as memoir writer Juarez (2018) concluded in looking back on his own experience with homelessness, "Growing up as a homeless teenager can really strip you of an identity. You get lost in the streets of survival by becoming whoever and whatever others want you to be. Even if you try to hold on to your identity, the need is real. It becomes easy to throw your values out the window when you're hungry" (186). According to blogger "Ralph" (B7), for the young person then, homelessness may mean "that you will be exploited, you will be stolen from, you will be victimized" (12.6.2004), but as blogger "Dan" (B5) simply concluded, home can be "a bad mess" (2.9.2007). To Juarez, Persons, Ralph, and Dan, home represented family and family represented home—but home and family could mean either life in or escape from an unsafe environment.

Another impulse of many young people experiencing homelessness may be not only to run from their original homes but also to create a new family among their peers—one that may be imagined as secure but may instead prove to be very temporary. Susan Ruddick (1995), a scholar of geography and social and political philosophy, traced youth subcultures in Hollywood who engage in "punk squatting" in a space that they claim as home. The families in these newly created homes often take on traditional roles. In his memoir, Early (2013) recalled Marcy who served as "Mother" to the community of young street people in Seattle as well as big "sister" Lou Lou who defended the younger children in that "street family," children who might otherwise be treated as "prey" (28, 53). Eventually, Early lost track of Marcy, and Lou Lou died, and so the members of these newly created families might never quite fit the image of the normal home, a disconnect that Early realized. Early also described a man who sexually abused him in exchange for shelter from "normal people," but while at his social worker's home for Thanksgiving, he also realized that he was "uncomfortable about sharing such a traditional family ritual with normal people" (60, 92). Moreover, in foster or group homes, such as memoir writer Anthony (2020) occupied, "normalcy was non-existent" (93). Home and family somehow represent normalcy regardless of the instability and abuse that unaccompanied youth might suffer, and it takes hard work on the part of not only advocates but also the youth themselves to turn a place into a new home.

Finally, sociologists Chris Chamberlain and Guy Johnson (2011), who supplemented a database of 3,941 homeless adults with sixty-five in-depth interviews, warned that the final typical pathway into adult homelessness was youth homelessness. Thirty-five percent of the adults they studied had first become homeless when they were eighteen or younger and suffered from "traumatic family experiences, including sexual and physical abuse, parental drug addiction and family violence" (67). And, as Persons pointed out, although youth experiencing homelessness are "strong and powerful and smart," they need help from adults who might guide them to resources and yet employ youth experience "to help create system change" (2021). When that help comes, it also might bring a personal sense of home and family— and of agency. Regarding the brick-and-mortar Avenues for Youth shelters and the physical presence of adults helping youth, Meerse (2020) described how Avenues for Youth was designed to contain "certain spaces as office and certain spaces as youth space to allow it to feel like their home." Meerse gave two examples of success in establishing that new sense of home. During the 2020–2021 COVID-19 pandemic, both youth and staff put together a one thousand piece jigsaw puzzle, taking turns to go down to the recreation room at Avenues for Youth and putting down one or two pieces at a time. Meerse saw that they were "getting very excited when it was their turn, to see how much had been added" to the puzzle, affirming a sense of community. Meerse also recalled how one day when she was leaving her office in the Minneapolis Avenues for Youth shelter, she overheard a young resident talking on the phone in the hallway. He said to his listener, "No, I haven't left yet. I am still at home." Meerse did not know if this young person did not want to share that he was in a homeless shelter and so masked his location, but then she realized, "What we are doing to make it [Avenues for Youth] feel like home is working." And so, young people may leave Avenues for Youth, said Meerse, but "they don't necessarily leave us." The staff say to young people, "We are never done with you until you are done with us," and they refer to residents and staff "as a family," with "all the good and bad that comes with that, the closeness and the tension, the laughter and the fighting with each other. We see all of that." Overall, youth experiencing homelessness and housing instability may be torn between returning to their original family homes and creating new ones, and some of those new ones may offer long-term stability and comfort while others last only a short time. These youth recognize what society considers normal and how at the moment they might lack normative competence. Without housing and family stability, youth find it difficult to maintain agency, to resist stigma, to avoid further victimization, to grow toward independent adulthood, and, for some, to accept gender identity.

Struggling with Gender Identity

The ages between twelve to twenty-four are often the period in which youth realize gender identity, a significant challenge that youth experiencing homelessness might face. According to social psychologist Naomi Ellemers (2018), gender is considered a "primary feature in person perception," the first thing that we may notice and remember about an individual and one of the earliest things we may realize about ourselves. Therefore, gender categories "are immediately detected, are chronically salient, seem relatively fixed, and are easily polarized" (275). Those people who do not conform to the stereotypical expectations of these binary gender categories—male/female and masculine/feminine—are devalued, or as Ellemers said, "We decide that they are not representative for their gender group rather than revising [our] stereotypical expectations" (286). Thus, they carry the normative stigma of difference and nonconformity.

In particular, LGBTQ+ youth experiencing homelessness may experience stigmatization not only because of their housing instability and intergenerational poverty but also because of their gender identity, an identity that might not be accepted in their home. This identity may include expansive expressions of gender, expanding upon typical perspectives of male/female and masculinity/femininity; gender fluidity, flexibility about gender identity rather than committing to a single definition; and/or gender dysphoria, discomfort and distress experienced and perhaps expressed when gender identity differs from sex assigned at birth. Because of the social bias toward masculine gender identity and its attributes of power, strength, and reasoning, transgender women in particular, or those who were assigned male at birth but who transition into women, may not only experience a loss of status but also be particularly at risk of assault at home and on the streets (see, for example, Bockting, Miner, Swinburne Romine, Hamilton, and Coleman 2013; Boskey 2021). Berg (2015), for example, shared how the father of one transgender youth "found God in prison" and decided that as long as his son "lived this way, he's dead to him" (58). And, memoir writer Robinson (2020) offered similar effects as a twenty-three-year-old Hispanic heterosexual transgender woman: "My dad was getting his suspicions about me being gay. And he did threaten to kill me. He said, 'I'm going to kill you, then I'm going to kill myself. Because I'd rather die, than people know that I have a faggot for a son.' So, I took the initiative. I ran away at seventeen" (31). Gender expansion, fluidity, and so-called dysphoria dangerous, for the young person who remains at home and for the young person who flees home despite the likely trauma of homelessness.

Researchers Virginia Pendleton et al. (2020) confirmed that in Minnesota 76 percent of LGBTQ+ youth said that "frequent fighting with parents or guardians was the main or partial cause of becoming homeless." According to scholars and practitioners in gender, sexuality, and health Walter Bockting et al. (2020), transgender individuals may also experience *enacted stigma*—actual experiences of discrimination—as well as *felt stigma*—perceived rejection and expectation of being stereotyped or discriminated against. The result of experiencing such stigma might be internalized transphobia, manifested as experiencing "intense shame and guilt"; attempts to conform to the sex assigned at birth or to "pass as a cisgender member of the other sex"; or avoidance of other transgender people "to avoid exposure of their own gender variance" (16). Moreover, law scholar Jessica DiBacco (2016) found that transgender youth faced discrimination at shelters, which may classify them according to their biological sex rather than gender identity, and in cities such as Philadelphia where there were three youth shelters, none were dedicated to LGBTQ+ youth. In terms of intersectionality, Robinson (2020) noted in his memoir that quality-of-life ordinances and urban policing "contribute to homelessness and the subjugation of LGBTQ+ people, especially Black and Brown LGBTQ youth" and classify poor LGBTQ+ people of color in the public sphere "as deviants and as criminals" (86). Among those LGBTQ+ youth experiencing homelessness, 58.7 percent reported victimization, and 41.3 percent reported depression, including suicidal ideation (4; see also Cochran et al. 2002). Finally, Persons (2021) confirmed this impression based on his personal observations while experiencing homelessness—Black and Brown "queers," he concluded, had the most difficult time getting housed because housing was often White and cisgender prioritized. And so, issues of gender identity, stigma, and trauma are pervasive in the LGBTQ+ youth community experiencing homelessness. According to LGBTQ+ youth themselves, they experience parental disapproval and rejection, bullying by peers, relegation to state child custody systems, criminal treatment of their everyday expressions of gender, lack of a safe place to shower and sleep, and overall systemic marginalization and social stigmatization. Resisting the stigma associated with both homelessness and so-called different gender identity presents a sometimes overwhelming challenge for such youth.

Using Social Media

Social media can play a role in helping LGBTQ+ youth establish a positive identity—at least one that relieves the stigma and stress that they might be feeling—or social media can endanger them further. In a stable family home, according to Berg (2015), social media may allow young people "still grappling with who they are to step outside the limits of their communities, to exercise their agency while still being reliant financially on their families" (xviii). While experiencing homelessness, LGBTQ+ youth may also use such self-reflection and personal exploration to explore their options. Persons (2021), for example, turned to journal writing as a cathartic release from the trauma of housing instability, "venting my frustration and seeking validation because I was pretty alone during that time." When he turned to social media, he found that he was "alone on the internet too." However, according to Berg (2021), most recently social media has helped LGBTQ+ youth experiencing homelessness "build within their activist communities," such as their uprising and subsequent civil rights response to the murder of George Floyd in spring 2020 in Minneapolis (see, for example, Taylor 2021). More and more, through social media LGBTQ+ youth may share their life stories, find accepting readers, and build *communitas*.

Lucie's Place in Center Arkansas, for example, provides not only a brick-and-mortar drop-in center for young adults experiencing homelessness but also offers a blog to discuss challenges as well as events and resources. In the blog entry on the death of George Floyd, for example, Lucie's Place affirmed #Black Lives Matter and #Black Trans Lives Matter as well as supported "those working towards justice and ending the serious, unresolved issues of police brutality, white supremacy and systemic racism in our country" (6.6.2020). Moreover, according to scholars in sexuality and gender and in social work Shelley Craig and Lauren McInroy (2014), LGBTQ+ youth are able to "cultivate a sexual minority identity online while their offline lives may require them to present as heterosexual or limit the presentation of their ideal sexuality in some way" (95–96; see also Miller 2017). This cultivation of identity is not without risk, however, as social media scholars Diane Felmlee, Paulina Inara Rodis, and Amy Zhang (2020) discovered. Sexist online harassment may try to reinforce gender inequity and is particularly directed toward those who do not display the classic gender stereotype of femininity, associated with displaying warmth and incompetence, being nice and emotional, and assuming morality and sexual inexperience. These scholars located 2.9 million tweets over a week's time that used at least one of four key feminine slurs (see also Felmlee and Faris 2016).

Also, online applications (apps) may advertise themselves, as does Grindr. com, as "a safe space where you can discover, navigate, and get zero feet away from the queer world around you"—or they may link young people with someone who offers a place to stay for sex. Based on her study of youth experiencing homelessness in Hollywood, Ruddick (1995) found that at least 30 percent of street youths engaged in so-called survival sex, trading sex for cash, shelter, food, or drugs. Moreover, Walls and Bell (2011) found that, in particular, Black LGBTQ+ youth "were significantly more likely than heterosexually identified youth to have engaged in survival sex" (432; see also Kattari and Begun 2017). And so, memoir writer Early (2013) proposed that among youth experiencing homelessness, "Selling your body for money to get drugs was also a normal way of life in my new community" and did not "really come with a moral stigma" (34). At Avenues for Youth, counselors offer no judgment about the need for such youth exchanging sex for housing in a street economy that is "kind of nuanced and varied," although these counselors do talk about alternatives, safety, choice, and autonomy (Berg 2021). Thus, social media may play a role in connecting for survival sex, seen by both advocates and youth as a matter of choice as long as such choices are made with safety in mind. Such are the many challenges that face unaccompanied youth, who may experience intergenerational homelessness and poverty, who may long for their original families and the ideal home and/or create new families from street peers, and who may turn to social media to find identity and a sense of agency—and such is the power of home as a trope, a space where safety and support are expected but are illusive for many such youth.

Overall, the space called home is contested by the actual voices and experiences of those who face or struggle with homelessness. Home is created not only by our expectations but also by restrictions. Those women with limited power in the home were historically restricted by such principles as coverture but now contest the echoes of that principle when they face such challenges as domestic violence, including assessing their right to stay safely in the home, to leave the home without repercussions, or to exclude the abuser from the home. *The Town of Castle Rock v. Gonzales* (2005) US Supreme Court decision and the resulting reactions to that decision demonstrate the fragility of the agency of the domestic violence victim. Unaccompanied young people also face the stigma of homelessness and may be expelled from their homes because of their substance abuse, gender identity, or lifestyle choices. As blogger Ralph warned, "If you are a teen runaway, you have people actively trying to exploit you. If you are a young woman without family resources, you really ought to prepare for this possibility before you have any idea that you might become homeless" (10.20.2004). In the next chapter, I extend my analysis of the ideal or imagined home, the home as trope, to other housing choices for people experiencing homelessness. I return to the "Wall of Forgotten Natives" encampment and the Minneapolis Navigation Center created to provide shelter and services to former "Wall" residents, and I illustrate how people experiencing homelessness often reject homeless shelters as well as how neighborhoods renounce the presence of such shelters. I add to this analysis the 2019 devastating fire in the Drake Hotel in Minneapolis, which housed people waiting for shelter beds and affordable housing, and the effects of the 2020–2021 COVID-19 on the homeless community—again focusing on the sometimes illusive search for a safe, secure, and supportive space called home.

Chapter Four

Displacement and Containment

The Encampment, the Shelter, the Fire, and the Virus

Homeless shelters are notoriously unpopular among people experiencing homelessness, a perspective expressed in social media and published memoirs. Blogger "Ralph" (B7), for example, used his own experience with homelessness to conclude, "Shelter life is a life of waiting. You wait on the charity, the good feeling, and on the whim of others. You wait, and you wait, and you wait, and all the while tension builds, as you wonder whether you will get what you need. . . . There are rules everywhere. . . . Everything, it seems, was punishable by thirty days expulsion. . . . You don't choose when the day is over. You don't choose when the day begins" (10.30.2004). In turn, "Clare" (B6) blogged some practical considerations for families experiencing homelessness and needing shelter as an alternative to living on the streets, in encampments, with relatives, or in cars or vans: "Ahh . . . the shelter system, first thing that comes to mind for people to go to who are about to become or already are homeless . . . right? Wrong!" This impulse to rely on the shelter system was "wrong," according to Clare, because "shelters may not be an option if there's a lack of shelters," and she warned that "families are split up because there are men only or women and children only shelters" (4.4.2011). In the context of these negative or cautionary reactions to the shelter system, it is important to note that the National Alliance to End Homelessness (2020d) reported 291,837 people experiencing homelessness found beds in emergency shelters in 2019, an increase of 38 percent since 2007. Of the estimated 567,715 people experiencing homelessness in 2019, however, more than 200,000 people (or 37 percent of that total population) remained unsheltered, sleeping outside or in other locations "not meant for human habitation." For many such as blogger Ralph, the homeless shelter has become a metaphor or rhetorical trope for loss of freedom, sense of agency, privacy, and dignity, a trope that is constructed by those experiencing homelessness rather than one imposed upon them and that reflects their resistance and, at times, rebellion against such shelters. This resistance and rebellion occur in part because shelters cannot fit the image of the ideal home—or as Rai (2016) reminded us, "Within the context of American democracy, housing is understood as both a commodity and a universal welfare right, as private property and a public good, as a literal place where we dwell and the conceptually rich place we call home" (31). Therefore, shelters represent deprivation for many who must stay in them.

Emergency shelters do provide people experiencing homelessness with a safe place to sleep, but many are open only overnight, often on a first-come, first-served basis. So-called transitional shelters offer temporary residence, typically anywhere from six to twenty-four months, and include supportive services to find permanent and affordable housing. But there are many more emergency than transitional shelters, and in their rejection of homeless shelters in general, bloggers, memoir writers, and video interviewees often do not distinguish between the two. To further Clare's points about the problems with shelters, for example, she provided her blog readers with links to two sources that explained how shelter rules might discourage or even endanger residents. First, Clare repeated an entry by blogger "Tick Tock Sheptock" in which he described how a shelter staffer insisted on putting women residents out for the day at 7:00 am when the temperature was 30 degrees: "Granted the hypothermia alert was called off . . . [but] it would have satisfied the residents to simply hear her express remorse for having to put them out" (quoted in 2.8.2011). Again, it is not unusual for shelter residents to have to leave for the day and to carry their belongings while wandering the streets or taking refuge in a library, park, or coffee shop until their shelter opens again that evening. Clare then provided a link to columnist Carey Roberts's (2008) description of the fate of a woman who fled an abusive relationship and tried to take refuge in a domestic violence shelter: "Pregnant with child, she was assigned to a room with another woman who seldom bathed. And the room itself smelled." When the woman complained, she was "exited [sic]" from the shelter. Roberts went on to relate how shelters may "turn away the persons who need help the most," citing another example, this one of a rape victim who was refused admission to a shelter "because she didn't fall within its poverty guidelines" (quoted in 2.8.2011). Resistance to homeless shelters, according to people experiencing homelessness, often comes from the desire for a space with the attributes that one might find in the ideal home—understanding, safety, support, and a sense of agency and identity.

Additionally, two foundational studies of people experiencing homelessness found the contrast between the home and the shelter to be extreme. In his study of single women residing in homeless shelters in a city outside of Washington, DC, urban anthropologist and ethnographer Elliot Liebow (1993) concluded, "Thus it is that shelters begin to make physical life possible. But these supports alone are not enough to stave off the devastation and despair of homelessness" (11). Liebow's research participants contributed to his assessment, including one woman who offered: "A shelter's not a home. A shelter is a dumping ground. Shelters are dumps created by the government so they don't have to provide low-cost housing" (211). Even more succinct is the following comment offered by another shelter resident: *"No one can live this way and be normal, no matter how they were when they first came"* (emphasis in original, 210). Several of Liebow's study participants asserted that they had changed for the worse since coming to the shelter. In turn, writer and activist Jonathan Kozol (1988) described the life of residents housed in the "welfare" Martinique Hotel in New York City in the mid-1980s: "Shelter, if it's warm and safe, may keep a family from dying. Only a home allows a family to flourish and to breathe. When breath becomes hard, when privacy is scarce, when chaos and crisis are on every side, it is difficult to live at peace, even with someone whom we love" (1). More recently, sociologists Amy Donley and James Wright (2012), who conducted focus groups with thirty-nine people living in tent encampments in Florida, offered a similar contrast of shelters to homes: "A couple who has spent every night of their last 10 years embraced in each other's arms is not going to forego that warmth, security, and love so she can go to one shelter and he to another." Both a home and a homeless shelter are distinct spaces, and, for many, a shelter cannot provide what a home is imagined to offer, or as Donley and Wright concluded, "the common and understandable desire . . . to be treated as actual human beings" (304). The shelter may offer tangible physical support, but only the home is imagined to provide emotional sustenance.

In this chapter, I extend my analysis of the ideal or imagined home offered in the previous chapter, this time in direct contrast to the homeless shelter. In doing so, I rely again on the tropes of "home" and "homeless," but I also describe further how the latter trope is both imposed upon and altered by those experiencing homelessness. I return to the "Wall of Forgotten Natives" tent encampment in Minneapolis at the time it was dismantled, and I analyze the challenges associated with the newly created Minneapolis Navigation Center that housed many former "Wall" residents. I reveal the almost immediate reemergence of tent encampments across the Twin Cities after the navigation center closed, and I look in depth at the spatial segregation that homeless shelters create; the rules and regulations that such shelters impose; and the boredom, substance abuse, lack of privacy, and unhealthy and unsafe conditions that plague shelter residents. These are the features that sociologists Sarah DeWard and Angela Moe (2010) proposed make the homeless shelter a "total institution," a system that negates what geneticist Louisa

Stark (1994) considered the "most basic human roles—those of friend, lover, husband, wife, parent, and so forth" (557).

Next in this chapter, I include a description of the Minnesota District Court decision of *Berry v. Hennepin* County (2020) regarding the due process and property rights of those people experiencing homelessness who select encampments as alternative shelter but whose tents and personal possessions are destroyed during "sweeps"—or evictions usually ordered by city officials and conducted by law enforcement. I also analyze the motivation of city planners in St. Paul, Minnesota, to create "Freedom House," a new homeless day shelter, as well as the mixed reactions of neighbors to such a project, based on my own observations and analysis of transcriptions of public informational meetings held in 2020 and 2021. I end this chapter with the history and conditions of the Martinique Hotel in New York City to contextualize the effects of the recent fire in the Drake Hotel in Minneapolis, a residence for many who could not find rooms at shelters or places in affordable housing, and I trace the effects of COVID-19, the 2020–2021 novel coronavirus, on the housing options and choices among people experiencing homelessness.

Ultimately, I extend what feminist geographer Ayona Datta (2005) concluded from her interviews with those living in a homeless shelter in Phoenix: "Home can be conceived as the social location formed by a family living together—the focus of one's domestic attention, which finds its spatial manifestation in a domestic dwelling." In contrast, homelessness "can be found in a variety of settings—streets, hostels, emergency shelters, and transitional shelters," but overall, both home and homelessness are "social and cultural constructions" (537). And, I argue that although some social media may enable *communitas* among the homeless, most bloggers, video interviewees, and memoir writers use these means of communication to express their desire for all that "home" represents and to challenge or alter the trope of homelessness assigned to them.

THE MINNEAPOLIS NAVIGATION CENTER

The City of Minneapolis was somewhat unique in working with Simpson Housing Services to create a navigation center where all former "Wall of Forgotten Natives" residents could be temporarily housed as of late December 2018 and until these residents could be placed in more permanent housing in early summer 2019. Thus, the Minneapolis Navigation Center was designed to keep its residents warm, well-fed, and safe—and it was considered not only transitional space but also a sort of buffer between marginalized and domiciled citizens. In essence, however, what had become home to some "Wall" residents was traded for a differently named homeless shelter, acceptable to the city but suspect to some residents, particularly those who had previously avoided the shelter system by moving to the "Wall" encampment in the first place. Moreover, despite the potentially positive features of this option, navigation centers across the United States have struggled to find a space in which to build such centers—and to meet the needs of all their residents as well as to appease the concerns of neighbors. Based on research involving the navigation centers in San Francisco, for example, where such centers were first established, Rebecca Cohen, Will Yetvin, and Jill Khadduri (2019) in writing for the US Department of Housing and Urban Development found that there was "no strong evidence" that such centers are ultimately effective (21). To be effective, these authors concluded, navigation centers would have to help their residents secure permanent housing through "intensive case management" and, quite often, expedite entry into drug treatment programs, both expensive and long-term efforts. Also, as journalist Emma Ockerman (2019) recalled, wealthy residents in San Francisco "fought tooth-and-nail" against placing such a navigation center near them (see also Har 2019).

The spaces proposed for the Minneapolis Navigation Center also were met with initial resistance. The first site proposed was in the Minnehaha neighborhood and seemed ideal as it was near Hiawatha Avenue where the "Wall" encampment had been located. However, this site was close to the popular Minnehaha Falls Regional Park, and, perhaps more unsettling for neighbors, it was near two schools. Locating the navigation center near the schools was "of very real concern," as Camille Gage blogged, given that some residents at the "Wall" site had been "wrestling with addiction," and neighbors feared the problems with crime and drug dealing that such addiction brings (9.20.2018). The second proposed site would have to be acquired through a Public Works expansion and so would be costly and not obtainable until after the cold Minnesota winter set in. Finally, the Red Lake Band of Chippewa offered use of a piece of their land, which lay across Hiawatha Avenue from the "Wall" encampment. Sam Strong, tribal secretary, considered this final selection indicative of "governments coming together, tribes, local units of the government, community leaders. And it's a powerful thing" (quoted in Nesterak 2018). To Strong and others, the Minneapolis Navigation Center seemed to provide a way to shelter former "Wall" residents in an acceptable and functional environment until more permanent housing could be found.

The Minneapolis Navigation Center was meant to be "low barrier." Although families with minor children would be guided to other housing options, adult partners could live together, and residents could even bring their pets. The center would be open 24/7 and would not have a curfew, a common restriction in most homeless shelters in the rest of the city. In fact, sobriety was not a requirement at the center. Drug users would be welcomed (or tolerated) although they could not use drugs in the center itself, and they would have access to support programs designed to help them gain sobriety. Overall, other than rules against violent and "highly disruptive" behavior, there would be few restrictions for those living in the center. Moreover, located in each of the three large heated tents that comprised the center, forty beds would each have a storage locker underneath, and residents were encouraged to personalize their spaces. Health care, meals, and showers would be provided, and Native healing practitioners would be available. And so, in mid-December 2018, about 162 residents from the "Wall" encampment began to move into the Minneapolis Navigation Center.

At that time, Camille Gage predicted in her blog that "better days lie ahead" (12.16.2018), and there would be "big changes at the ['Wall'] camp—that's a good thing" (12.17.2018). By the next day, however, Gage found herself answering allegations from the Communities United Against Police Brutality (CUAPB) as expressed via Facebook. Gage clarified that the City of Minneapolis would not force evictions from the encampment and would not destroy the possessions of people still living there. Then CUAPB alleged that the new navigation center was "practically a prison camp," surrounded by concrete barriers and high chain-link fencing with only one way in and out. Gage explained that those barriers were designed to keep drug dealers, predators, and sex traffickers out of the center; center residents could come and go freely. Ultimately, Gage used her blog to recommend, "We challenge ourselves to let go of fear and suspicion and the rumors that were constantly swirling around and simply trust each other." Such rumors could lead to "destabilization of the most vulnerable among us" (12.27.2018). In turn, the public media captured some positive voices of "Wall" encampment residents as they left for the Minneapolis Navigation Center. One of the last to leave, for example, was Teresa Martin who shared, "I feel sad and relieved at the same time. We lost a community but we no longer feel invisible. At least now we know that everyone here is getting help" (quoted in Serres 2018a). Then after a feast on January 11, 2019, at the Minneapolis American Indian Center, Gage blogged that the navigation center's success was made probable because of the collaborative effort of the Red Lake Band of Chippewa, the Minneapolis Urban Indian Directors (MUID) and its affiliates, the Minneapolis Police and Fire Departments, various governmental agencies, and the journalists who "took the time to educate themselves on the issues and truly engage everyone involved" (1.16.2019). The optimism about and commitment to the Minneapolis Navigation Center was overall quite strong despite some uncomfortable exchanges documented via social media. Moreover, community organizations such as Avivo (2021) were prepared to offer vocational rehabilitation services and seek more stable housing options for former "Wall" residents while they resided in the navigation center.

When the navigation center closed down on June 3, 2019, Steve Horsfield, the executive director of Simpson Housing Services, estimated that 60 percent of the residents there had "gone to what we would call positive outcomes" (quoted in Nesterak 2019b). However, despite the low-barrier standard set by Minneapolis Navigation Center, it proved impossible to control the violence surrounding drug use there. About forty residents were deemed a threat to others and were asked to leave, two people died of overdoses, and police were called to the center more than 480 times after its opening. By October 2019, MPR News estimated that after the center closed at least seven hundred of its former residents were still living on the streets with no place to go (Burks 2019). In response, the Red Lake Band of Chippewa explored building another tent emergency shelter and/or breaking ground on a new 110-unit affordable housing complex. In the meantime, some former residents of the "Wall" encampment as well as of the navigation center elected to live outside once again, and new tents appeared in various locations in the Twin Cities. Darrell Seki, Tribal Chairman of the Red Lake Band of Chippewa, said the following about these emerging tent encampments, "I never thought it would be like this. There's still people out there." Seki concluded that rent was so high in the Twin Cities that many former "Wall" residents could not afford to move from the navigation center into houses and apartments, and so "they end up homeless, they end up in a tent city" (quoted in Lee 2019). One married couple, for example, added that they wished they "could've stayed sleeping outside because it felt safer" than the center proved to be. Seki and others' disappointment became tangible as these former residents set up encampments in public spaces around the Twin Cities. Despite the efforts put into and the optimism about the Minneapolis Navigation Center, many people experiencing homelessness still elected to seek an alternative to shelters and find a home and community in tent encampments.

In response to the disappointment in Minneapolis Navigation Center and the difficulties in rehousing all of its residents, in December 2019 about fifty activists from the Native community walked through a gap in the metal fence surrounding the former "Wall" encampment and erected a symbolic teepee in the center of the space—a form of material rhetoric to not only reclaim the space but also to send a message about their disappointment in the efforts of the navigation center and their continuing homeless state. These activists read a statement in which they demanded a stronger response to the housing crisis and a "culturally specific" overnight shelter for Natives experiencing homelessness: "Our First Nations people continue to suffer and are sleeping outside tonight. The slow pace towards finding a solution is unacceptable and the community can no longer stand idle" (quoted in Serres 2019b). If this pace toward safer and secure housing did not improve, the Native activists told officials that they would establish a permanent tent encampment, most likely at the "Wall" site. On the one hand, others began to agree with these activists. According to Hennepin County District Four Commissioner Angela Conly, "People are in tents with their loved ones and their pets and if we don't have shelters that can accommodate for that, and if we don't have enough permanent, supportive, service-rich housing at the end of coming out of shelter then we [will] continue to see the numbers grow" (quoted in Perez 2019). On the other hand, Patina Park, who spoke on behalf of MUID, seemed cautiously optimistic: "We're not going to solve a problem that is literally hundreds of years in its design, but we are making excellent steps now to come up with true solutions with everyone at the table" (quoted in Evans 2019). The protests at the former "Wall" site lasted for two days until the Native community and Minneapolis officials reached a verbal agreement to establish an overnight shelter that respected Native culture—a partial triumph for those who wanted not only a homelike shelter but also one that acknowledged their heritage associated with ancestral space and land.

Keiji Narikawa, a Native community member, asserted that providing this overnight shelter was the "least the government can do . . . to help them reconnect with who they are as indigenous peoples and feel empowered again" (quoted Serres 2019a). By January 2020, however, these activists had to repeat their demand for a culturally attentive shelter and protested what the media identified as the "constant relocation and eviction of Natives experiencing homelessness from sleeping in public places" (Serres 2020b). Thus, the Native community, particularly those experiencing homelessness, resented their continued stigmatization as marginalized people without adequate and acceptable shelter, let alone what they would consider a home. Overall, the Native people had created the "Wall" encampment, which was then traded for a navigation center that promised a low-barrier, supportive, and resource-rich atmosphere but that for many residents proved too unsafe, ineffective, and chaotic. Former "Wall" and center residents were then joined by other people experiencing homelessness to build and occupy tent encampments throughout public spaces in the Twin Cities, to the dismay of the local neighborhoods and city officials. But these encampments appeared to many of their residents to have the potential to support a sense of agency as well as a space reflecting cultural identity and values.

Tent Encampments as Alternative Housing

Although it is difficult to count the number of such encampments in the country, which vary from a cluster of shanties to extensive groups of tents, the advocacy group Invisible People (2020) reported that they had observed nineteen highly visible encampments in 2007, but by 2017, that number had grown to 255 such encampments. Many more encampments, according to this source, were likely hidden beneath highway overpasses, in wooded areas, and alongside bridges and viaducts. According to the National Law Center on Homelessness & Poverty (2017), homeless tent encampments increased dramatically across the United States over the last few years, a 1,342 percent increase, for example, from 2007 to 2016. These encampments were often considered by many as unsafe, unwelcome, and unhealthy, and the vast majority (three-quarters) of them were illegal according to trespass and disorderly conduct city ordinances. Therefore, a great many encampment residents faced the threat of eviction. Those residents, however, had frequently rejected the option of a homeless shelter in favor of life in an encampment, a preference that shines light on the renewed action to dismantle such encampments across the United States and on the alternative definitions of "home."

Correspondent Eric Westervelt (2020), for example, offered a National Public Radio program that covered the "modern Hoovervilles" in Santa Rosa, California. This encampment epithet not only alluded to the shanty towns where hundreds of thousands of poor people lived during the Great Depression but also stressed how much poverty contributed to homelessness. In turn, Reuters writer Michelle Conlin (2020) described a tent encampment that had been functioning in downtown Phoenix, Arizona, "just down the road from Luxury high-rise apartments," an example of the growing number of such encampments across the county. And, Courtney Cole (2021) reported for WBTV in Charlotte, North Carolina, on a "Tent City" where the residents were given only seventy-two hours to leave what was described as a rat-infested encampment.

To counter the problems that such encampments might create and to appease the complaints of housed neighbors and nearby school officials, encampment residents are often vulnerable to what is called a sweep, conducted when a city or property owner such as MnDOT evicts those residents and clears away their shelters and belongings. Such sweeps were traumatic to encampment residents, related one homeless man when interviewed by Terrence McCoy from the *Washington Post* (2019). He said that he was emotionally "crushed" after a recent cleanup took away all his possessions: "They're taking what little we got." Such sweeps, according to McCoy, were basically "dehumanizing exercises that do little to redress homelessness and leave the people experiencing it worse off, materially and psychologically." To justify further such policies as sweeps, federal and local governmental agencies across the United States often point out health and safety problems within homeless encampments. The US Department of Justice (DOJ) (Chamard 2010), for example, offered an extensive list of harms caused by homeless encampments, including unhealthy conditions that were dangerous to the environment, to the larger community, and to the residents. The DOJ's study concluded, "The longer someone is unsheltered and chronically homeless, the more involved he or she becomes in criminal behavior, largely due to the increased use of 'non-institutionalized survivor strategies,' such as panhandling, street peddling, and theft" (8). Additionally, those living adjacent to the encampment might experience an increased level of crime, including drug dealing, vandalism, sexual misconduct, physical assault, and theft. Finally, the DOJ highlighted what it called "illegitimate use of public space," in that "regular citizens" could not use public parks or other spaces that were "controlled by transients" (10). Not only might the residents of an encampment illegally occupy public space but according to the DOJ, they might vandalize park facilities such as barbeque pits, sinks, and faucets to make the space untenable for those "regular citizens." Finally, the Vice Media Group reported that in Stockton, California, firefighters complained that they "constantly put out blazes at the homeless encampments" and that a father worried because two of his children went to a school next to a large encampment (Ockerman 2019).

Thus, the Twin Cities was not the only place where people experiencing homelessness created tent encampments in 2019, 2020, and 2021 and where cities and states were concerned with the growing number of tent encampments and attempted to limit this growth through ordinances, regulations, and evictions. Overall, these encampment residents faced an environment of limited shelter beds as well as increasingly restricted public spaces—and their preferences as to where to establish a new sort of space to reside were threatened. Some sought support for their choices in the court system.

The *Berry v. Hennepin County* (2020) Minnesota District Court Decision

In October 2020, seven people sued Hennepin County and Minneapolis officials because they were forced to leave their tent encampments in a sweep or eviction. These complainants in *Berry v. Hennepin County* (2020) requested a temporary restraining order to end not only the sweeps but also the seizure and destruction of the personal property of encampment residents, particularly those living in the encampments established in public parks. The basis for the suit was the violation of the Fourth and Fourteenth Amendments to the US Constitution as well as of sections of the Minnesota Constitution and applicable laws. The suit was not successful, and the sweeps continued. The District Court decision, however, illuminated how complicated, confusing, and ineffective state and city reactions to tent encampments could be—as well as the somewhat understandable reluctance of people experiencing homelessness to leave them.

On April 2, 2020, for example, Minnesota Governor Tim Walz issued Emergency Executive Order 20–33, which stated that tent encampments should not be subject to sweeps or disbandment because such actions increased the potential risk and spread of COVID-19. Then, on April 29, 2020, Walz issued Emergency Executive Order 20–47, which was designed to "clarify" the previous order by adding that if a local government entity was providing sufficient alternative shelters or if an encampment had reached a size that was a "threat to the health, safety, or security of the residents," then state or local governments could restrict or close the encampment. Finally, on May 13, 2020, Walz issued Emergency Executive Order 20–55, which reiterated his guidance regarding encampments set forth in Order 20–47. However, the imagined "threat" of such encampments was not fully defined, and the quick revision of the emergency executive orders was confusing to both encampment residents and those enforcing these evacuation orders.

Similar to the state reaction to tent encampments, on June 17, 2020, Resolution 2020–253 was adopted by the Minneapolis Park & Recreation Board (MPRB) and declared that Minneapolis parks could be a refuge space for people experiencing homelessness. Less than a month later, on July 15, 2020, the MPRB adopted Resolution 2020–267, which limited the number of Minneapolis parks that could be such refuge sites to twenty and the number of tents located at each site to twenty-five, all controlled through a permit process. Subsequently, in August and September 2020, the Minneapolis Park Police disbanded encampments in three parks along with one of several encampments in the 468-acre Powderhorn Park, and the MPRB stated that, because of "health and safety concerns," encampment permits would not be extended "into cold weather, anticipated to be sometime in October." The encampments in Powderhorn Park were also significant because they resulted from the Minneapolis Sanctuary Movement, which began after the murder of George Floyd on May 25, 2020, and the imposition of a curfew in reaction to the unrest that followed Floyd's death. First called the Powderhorn Sanctuary, neighbors and community members worked to provide tents, meals, first aid, and refuge during this time of unrest. As stated on the Minneapolis Sanctuary Movement website (2021), the movement was a "community care experiment fighting for housing justice, abolition, and land reclamation by supporting the most impacted people to take the lead." Thus, encampment residents tried to establish a safe and secure place to shelter and a newly created community as the COVID-19 pandemic grew, as civil unrest following the death of George Floyd continued, and as the national economy faltered, but they encountered a shifting environment of executive orders, resolutions, and, at times, community support—all reflective of the dilemma of satisfying both the homeless and the housed communities.

The original complaint in *Berry v. Hennepin County* (2020) as received by the Minnesota District Court did illuminate how each of the seven complainants became homeless and the effect of encampment eviction on them all.

For example, forty-one-year-old Patrick Berry was described as a member of the Ho Chunk Nation who became homeless after having to leave his apartment when his roommate became violent. Berry's parents were dead, and after he was robbed, he could not find affordable housing and so pitched a tent in Powderhorn Park. Within this encampment community, he found a home and community of sorts; he became a camp facilitator, helped other residents obtain medical care, and worked with volunteers in organizing supplies for the encampment. But in August 2020, when the police arrived to clear the park, Berry and others claimed that they had received no eviction notices. Berry had to grab his backpack from his tent but could carry nothing else as he ran to a friend's house. When he returned to the encampment, he saw a dumpster full of tents and other items, most likely containing his own abandoned tent, sleeping bag, and mattress. The complaint noted that Berry "did not try to go to a shelter because he was afraid of contracting COVID-19 in an enclosed and crowded space. He had also heard that staff at shelters exploited and even assaulted people who stay there." Berry's sense of agency was most likely undermined as his choices and support system became once again limited.

In turn, complainant Henrietta Brown, a member of the Oglala Sioux Nation, had become homeless when she struggled with depression and addiction after her daughter died from having been given the wrong medication in a hospital emergency room. Brown also had to leave her boyfriend's home, the original complaint noted, when it "became a hostile place." She moved into the Peavey Park tent encampment after she had tried unsuccessfully to enter two full homeless shelters. But in September 2020, she woke to find officers removing the stakes of her tent before she even was able to get out of it. Brown managed to grab her purse and blanket but was turned away when she attempted to collect other belongings, including her birth certificate, her application for medical assistance, a photocopy of her ID, and family photos. As a result, Brown could not get into a homeless shelter because she no longer had any form of required ID. Her tent had been thrown into a garbage truck during the sweep, and subsequently she lived under a bridge and on the streets. Certainly, both Berry and Brown fit the profile of many people experiencing homelessness and needing shelter—and through the lawsuit they joined others who protested the destruction of the community and homes they had created.

Indeed, all of the *Berry* complainants noted and the Court agreed that the tents encampment residents pitched in Minneapolis parks became their homes, containing "life's necessities," and that losing these possessions would "imperil" their health and safety—moreover, without adequate shelter space or affordable housing, the "cycle of homelessness between sleeping in public spaces, in cars, on friend's couches, or in inexpensive hotels, repeats indefinitely," noted the Court. However, the Court did not accept the complainants' argument that seizing the tent encampment residents' personal possessions violated their Fourth Amendment property and privacy rights or that such action was a violation of the residents' procedural due process rights under the Fourteenth Amendment. Moreover, the Court declined to issue a temporary restraining order against such sweeps because the complaint did not meet the requirements of a civil action—for example, not all of the complaining residents could have suffered the same "irreparable harm," any possible harm might have been "mitigated" by the county finding shelters for them, and that harm was not "certain or concrete." Thus, city and state actions in clearing tent encampments in public parks were confusing and inconsistent but were permitted by the courts, and complainants lost not only their possessions but also the community they may have established in this alternative home.

Encampment Growth and Displacement

In contrast, the tent encampment in Logan Park in northeast Minneapolis had obtained the necessary permit to be established, and the residents and supporters worked to find alternative housing in shelters, hotel rooms, newly built tiny homes, apartments, and even other stable and safe tent encampments. Also, Strong Tower Parish, the church overlooking Logan Park, planned to open a new twenty-four-hour shelter. Indeed, the Logan Park encampment fulfilled the requirements of the governor's Emergency Executive Orders as well as the MPRB's resolutions. As encampment resident Brandon Harris noted, after first living in the park and then following the rest of the campers to a hotel and eventually to the parish shelter, he and his girlfriend wanted next to join a sober-living house. There they hoped to "finally [be] able to achieve the sense of balance and reward for the basic simple things that a normal person does in life" (quoted in Otárola 2020). Harris felt less marginalized and stigmatized as he and his girlfriend moved toward that socially constructed normalcy that the housed citizen enjoys. In turn, Logan Park resident Sadie Laynn noted that she had been harassed and robbed in homeless shelters in the past but that this encampment was the one place where she could leave her belongings unattended: "I call this *luxury homelessness*. I've never had it like this before" (emphasis added, quoted in Otárola 2020). Despite the state and city efforts to sweep away homeless encampments within public spaces, these encampments continued to exist, and the number of residents grew—moreover, some of these encampment residents continued to decline shelter beds even when they became available, and they sought the support and structure of such places as Logan Park and the Strong Tower Parish.

The dangers to health and life in such encampments, however, continued to catch the attention of city officials all over the Twin Cities. By December 2020, for example, the St. Paul Fire Department had responded to thirty fires in tent encampments where propane cylinders and other heat sources caught fire and easily ignited nylon tents. In addition, emergency crews responded to seventy-five medical calls at the camps, including one person who died of exposure. In response, Ramsey County, in which St. Paul is located, explored opening a temporary homeless shelter, leased a vacant dormitory at Luther Seminary, and reopened the older Bethesda Hospital to house people experiencing homelessness (see, for example, Harlow 2020; Prather and Chanen 2020). By the beginning of 2021, more fires and deaths among encampment residents were reported and yet resistance to shelters persisted. Some St. Paul city council members expressed reservations about encampment sweeps, calling them "removals" and "evictions," while neighbors complained about the overcrowding in the camps, the growing violence in the area, and the presence of trash and discarded needles near their homes, all attributed to mismanagement by the MPRB. At the same time, activists demanded more resources for people experiencing homelessness (see, for example, Du 2021; Prather 2021).

During this time, the negative responses to homeless shelters by many encampment residents were remarkably consistent. Kelly Gwin, for example, a resident of the Minnehaha Park encampment site, said that she would rather sleep "under a bush" than go to a shelter: "You have to be out by a certain time. You have to be in by a certain time. You can't bring your personal items. What are we supposed to do with this stuff? This [encampment] is our home" (quoted in Roper 2021). And, bloggers such as "Patrick" (B3) offered their own views of life in an encampment:

> Seeing homeless people living in these large camps is misleading because the homeless don't create such communities because they want to live that way, but only because it is necessary for survival. There is safety in numbers. There is also the benefit of networking with other homeless people to keep apprised of services, for knowing when the next feeding will be, for learning that some shelter has closed down for the weekend. . . . There is nothing quaint or endearing about a homeless camp. (4.13.2015)

Displacement from the public space of tent encampments remains an issue among people experiencing homelessness, but spatial segregation in shelters is resented and often resisted. The homeless shelter represents containment that diminishes its residents' sense of agency and identity, and those who avoid becoming shelter residents may establish a new community, a different type of family, and an alternative home in encampments as long as they are allowed to remain there.

CONTAINMENT IN HOMELESS SHELTERS

Goffman (1961) not only wrote about stigma, but he also defined the total institution: "A place of residence . . . where a large number of like-situated individuals, cut off from the wider society for an appreciable period of time, together lead an enclosed formally administered round of life" (xiii). When DeWard and Moe (2010) applied Goffman's definition to their study of one Midwestern homeless shelter, they found a "clear demarcation" between those in power "in terms of decision making and the administration of the institution," and those who were dependent on that institution and were therefore powerless (117). In order for the total institution to function, DeWard and Moe found that a rigid set of rules and regulations must "systemically exert control over residents and reinforce hierarchy," a hierarchy that must be understood by all residents, a form of normative competence, and that punishment must be administered for anyone who questioned that hierarchy. In turn, responses from shelter residents might take one of three possible forms: (1) submission or "complete deference" to those in power; (2) adaptation or "acknowledgement of their subjugated role within the shelter hierarchy" as well as possible changes in their identities "in ways that allowed them to define for themselves where they fit within the hierarchy"; or (3) resistance or opposition to this subordination (119). Indeed, the staff of homeless shelters might so stigmatize and repress their residents that only the first response, submission, seems safe. Urban geographers Sarah Johnsen, Paul Cloke, and Jon May (2005), for example, found that shelters could become "spaces of care" where "an individual's homeless status—conferred 'other' in most contexts—becomes the 'norm'" (796), or shelters could be "spaces of fear" where users "commonly alter their behaviour [sic] in an attempt to 'fit in' and avoid transgressing the boundaries of acceptability" (798). Thus, a process of othering can occur within the shelters, which reflects mainstream understandings and stigmatization of people experiencing homelessness. And so, the staff at one shelter identified some residents as "lackers," considered not responsible for their predicament because of some form of incompetence, and other residents as "slackers," considered competent and therefore responsible for their homelessness and undeserving of help (804). The homeless shelter, then, could either create a safe and supportive place for residents or re-enact the stigmatization that the residents found in general society.

To do its job, the homeless shelter hierarchy might feel it has to contain and confine those people experiencing homelessness through enforced spatial segregation, but bloggers and memoir writers often critiqued their own and others' required submission and adaptation while in homeless shelters, their resistance and opposition to these shelters, and/or at times, their recommendations for improving the shelters. Their reactions and insights centered on unreasonable rules and regulations; lack of personal space, privacy, and safety; and inadequate services for achieving sobriety and transition into more secure housing. However, they also celebrated the unexpected companionship that they might achieve in the shelter setting, perhaps as a result of resistance and opposition. In these reflections, we must listen to the voices of people experiencing homelessness as they most specifically describe life in such shelters and as they take on the role of advocates and even activists in pointing out what the "legitimate" citizen might wrongly assume was an acceptable place to live.

Unreasonable Rules and Regulations

The most common complaints about homeless shelters address what are perceived as unreasonable rules and regulations. Shelter residents resent loss of agency and identity as well as lack of trust that they will make wise choices without such restrictions—so much so it is difficult for residents to see the homeless shelter as a "home." Blogger "Elaine" (B12), for example, resented the rules in a shelter that housed both men and women in Eugene, Oregon:

> Women are not allowed to wear shorts above the knee. At all. Knees are considered an erotic part of the female anatomy and therefore must be hidden at all cost. Women are not allowed to sit, eat or socialize with the male residents. Women are not allowed to keep their belongings with them. Baggage is practically confiscated and access to the bag is controlled by schedule. Women are only allowed to take a fifteen-minute shower. Women must put on certain shelter pajamas before going to bed. (6.16.2005)

These rules seem designed to eliminate any possibility of attraction or intimacy between the residents, to restrict free access to personal possessions, to create uniformity, and to limit the time for personal hygiene, all in favor of moving residents through a set schedule and of maintaining anonymity among them. In turn, shelter residents complain that such rules dehumanize them and mask their identities. Blogger Elaine, for example, who had traveled constantly while experiencing homelessness, criticized the dehumanizing and marginalizing regulations at a shelter in Sarasota, Florida. One evening when she attempted to reenter the shelter, she was told that she "'had used up all my nights' for that particular month," and she had to spend the night sleeping outside on a pier (1.24.2005). Memoir writer Gaulden (2017) complained about the shock of having to leave a shelter because of what seemed arbitrary limits on how long a resident could stay: "Timing out of shelters was like speeding down a raceway and running out of room" (93). Not only did residents have to obey the rules while in a shelter, but also they might not have another housing option if they had to leave. As Gaulden concluded, "The staff directly controlled our lives" (95).

Similarly, Ralph warned his blog readers by way of an analogy: "You move through the shelter like a cog on an assembly line, from soup kitchen to bed, with no freedom to vary from the program. . . . And more important than any of that, homeless shelters deprive you of dignity. They scream out that you have failed to take care of yourself, that you *need*" (emphasis added, 10.25.2004). According to Ralph, shelter residents were blamed for their own state, the features reinforced by the trope of homelessness. Lamatt (2011) shared in her memoir that the residents of a women's homeless shelter where she stayed for a great many months displayed a "dead look" on their faces because the women were not asked to do something—instead they did what they were told to do or they were given "violations" (55). In a more extreme analogy, memoir writer Murphy (2018) considered the shelters he entered "like a concentration camp"—"The rules were absolute, and the enforcement merciless" (41). And so, these shelter residents felt contained and confined, and they were spatially segregated from the so-considered legitimate citizen not only by the physical structure of the shelter but also by the hierarchy that did not permit them to make choices or secure separate identities from that constructed by the trope of homelessness.

Finally, Rich Hebron (2018) devoted much of his personal memoir to a description of the rules and regulations at the "Gym" and the "Rawls," separate spaces in one homeless shelter system that he called "Inspired Horizons." At the Gym, the men had to sign in to reserve one of the sixty beds for the night: "As long as you don't miss a day, you'll get the same bed, sheet, blanket, and pillow. Otherwise, you go on the overflow list" (19). Men on that overflow list went to the Rawls where they were required to take showers but were sometimes provided very small towels and no soap, and they were given a thin mat and one sheet for sleeping. At the Rawls, Hebron learned first-hand that persistent bed bugs would come out of the wooden walls at night so it was best to claim a space to sleep toward the center of the room. Moreover, in the journal entries that Hebron integrated into his memoir, he chronicled his growing mental deterioration while staying at the Rawls: "The repetition of everything is taking the biggest toll. I feel like I've gradually been stripped of my freedom. . . . The order and structure tire me. Having to be at particular places at specific times is a drag. Each day moves slower and slower" (9.18.2011). The Rawls residents had a rigidly set time to get up, to have breakfast, and to catch the bus into town and return to the shelter to get a place for the night. Finally, these residents were spatially segregated from many public spaces as well as the private homes of so-called normal citizens—they might view these spaces from the bus windows, but they were not encouraged to get off the bus in these neighborhoods.

Lack of Personal Space, Privacy, and Safety

In addition to complaints about overly strict rules and regulations, those living in homeless shelters resented their lack of personal space, diminished privacy, and unsafe conditions. There was always a need for additional homeless shelters, according to bloggers and memoir writers, but also such shelters provided very little personal space. "George" (B9), for example, wrote an extensive blog entry about shelter space in his Canadian city:

> There are not enough emergency beds for the homeless here, and the street population is growing steadily. While 40 new shelter beds will be added soon, and 50 permanent housing arrangements are in the works, these simply will not address the sheer number of homeless that huddle in doorways, or set up tents in park bushes. (10.15.2006)

Within existing shelters, George reflected that he had heard "the line that we can't 'warehouse' people by setting up massive dormitories where people sleep on the floor, but the reality of an increasing street population is making this band-aid solution more and more popular" (10.15.2006). Because not enough homeless shelters existed, and the space within those that did exist was limited, life in a shelter could be very unpleasant. In fact, blogger Elaine offered her readers a detailed description of one homeless shelter in downtown Denver where the residents had to sleep in chairs once all the beds were taken:

> The lights snap on over the crowd of sleepy men and women in the St. Francis Center. I look around and watch row-upon-row of people begin to rise from their chairs to face another day. Yes, I said chairs. . . . Everyone who checks in [late] at night sits at a chair at a long table all night. Some people sleep on their arms, or jackets or backpacks. When they sleep. (1.25.2005)

As a result of this arrangement, many residents suffered from severely swollen ankles as they "wander into the bathroom" in the morning, a bathroom where only two toilets were available. Such are the specific complaints of those occupying homeless shelters—a lack of available shelters as well as personal space if one indeed is admitted to a shelter.

Shelter residents also complain that they have little personal privacy. Hebron, for example, commented, "In the last month and a half, I haven't had a private moment" (9.22.2011). Moreover, Liebow (1993) attributed lack of privacy to not only the spatial closeness of other residents but also to what he perceived as the intrusive nature of the staff. According to Liebow, shelter residents complained that they were "never left alone with your thoughts, never time to collect your thoughts or plan anything because the staff is always there probing," but having to answer such questions "was part of the price" that residents "paid for being powerless" in such settings (137). In such face-to-face encounters with shelter staff, the residents were unable to keep their personal information private. Finally, that lack of privacy and personal space contributed to lack of safety in homeless shelters according to the residents. Blogger Ralph, for example, warned his readers that in such shelters "personal security is low, and you are likely to have things stolen as you sleep" (10.25.2004). And, blogger "Dan" (B5) simply stated why he did not go to homeless shelters even in cold weather: "Don't use them. They're too dangerous" (12.4.2006). Women in particular feared the lack of security in shelters, not only from other residents and outside intruders but also from their abusers who might find them within a shelter. In fact, Jasinski et al. (2010) discovered that 14 percent of women they interviewed reported victimization, including theft and assault, while they were staying in homeless shelters. Although other women might believe that they were safer in a shelter than on the streets, these scholars found that shelters "do not always provide high levels of physical safety" and they "are full of potential offenders" (59). In fact, one young homeless girl interviewed by Invisible People shared the result of this lack of shelter security when she said simply: "I don't like shelters. They are pretty brutal. I was in a shelter once, and I got beat up there" ("Hit By a Train" September 12, 2011). Overall, residents of homeless shelters often report that they are unpleasant and unsafe places—not at all imagined as "home."

Inadequate Services for Achieving Sobriety and Transition

Finally, residents of homeless shelters who do not or cannot overcome addiction are often critical of the services offered in rehabilitation (rehab) programs affiliated with the shelters. Although many homeless bloggers and memoir writers attribute their addictions to family background and abuse, personal challenges with sobriety, and the trauma that homelessness causes, they may also complain that shelters do not help them transition to a better way of life.

Patrick, for example, offered a number of detailed blog entries in which he complained about the lack of success and limited number of case managers in shelter rehab programs. His complaints were partially inspired when one shelter made "a big deal" over 250 people completing their rehab program, but as Patrick noted, "what they don't say is how many people they were unable to help" (3.7.2015). Such programs, according to Patrick, should pay attention to what people struggling with addiction in addition to homelessness need, rather than "thinking in terms of what they want to give to the homeless" (9.5.2015). In other words, according to Patrick, a sobriety program should honor the sense of agency and identity of each participant, without the threat of "No Not Return" punishments if a program participant breaks a rule. Additionally, blogger "Lawrence" (B4) commented that "the only thing that *really* ends homelessness for a person is whatever facilitates their becoming financially self-sufficient—having an I.D., a real job, a bank account, paying their own rent and being entirely free of government assistance" (emphasis in original, 11.27.2016). Lawrence praised Housing First, a program that did not consider drug addiction and mental illness as barriers to shelter residents receiving housing and instead seemed to understand that a sense of agency and dignity can provide a foundation for sobriety and eventual employment. Bloggers such as Patrick and Lawrence were indeed outspoken in their recommendations for how shelter programs could be improved.

Finally, although people experiencing homelessness might complain about the restrictions within and ineffectiveness of shelter rehab programs, some do celebrate when they are able to transition into more stable housing. "John" (B2), for example, blogged about first moving into a subsidized low-rent home and encountering unreliable roommates but then about his success in finding more suitable housing. In fact, leaving a homeless shelter should be a cause for celebration among other residents, as Hebron proposed: "Living in the shelter is the only place where friends look each other in the eye and say, usually with a laugh, 'Well, I hope I never see you again!'" (10.25.2011). Hebron's comments exemplify the possible beneficial side of homeless shelters. Despite lack of personal space, privacy, and safety; despite exclusion from public spaces and the spatial segregation from so-called normal citizens; despite what are perceived as unreasonable rules and regulations; and despite potentially inadequate services for sobriety and transition into more stable housing, at times companionship can flourish in homeless shelters—friendships, personal support systems, and a new sense of family and even of home. Therefore, some of the social media entries and the published memoirs of those experiencing homelessness offer not only a critical but also a balanced view of life in homeless shelters.

Unexpected Companionship

Living homeless outside a shelter can certainly provide friendships, support systems, and different kinds of families, although they might be short term and difficult to achieve and they might distort reentry into so-called normal society. Blogger "Norman" (B10), for example, confessed to his readers, "One of the problems I will have to overcome before I see myself making friends [upon finding stable housing] is I still don't feel very comfortable hanging out with non-street people" (8.7.2004). Norman believed that only people experiencing homelessness would accept rather than stigmatize him. In contrast, Lamatt (2011) wrote in her memoir about "an extended family" that she developed in her homeless shelter, a family "that keeps me going" (333). She told her readers that the women in her family shelter gave "what little they have to others cutting something in half to share, or giving it all to another. This is the most beautiful love, caring for another human being" (335). Lamatt lived for quite a while among these other residents and wrote about how she tried to give as much to them as they gave to her. In fact, two decades before Lamatt published her memoir, Liebow (1993) found similar responses among some of the women whom he had studied as they looked back on their prior shelter life: "Thus it was that shelter life sometimes made it possible for the women to be part of a human community in which one could give and take aid and comfort—from each according to her ability; with luck, to each according to her need" (220). In the midst of constraints on freedom, possible damage to dignity, and a sense of loss of agency, at times shelter life might provide companionship and *communitas*.

Hebron (2018) wrote extensively about the companionship he enjoyed in the two months he lived in the Rawls homeless shelter. His story, however, was unique. When he was 21 and had just graduated from college, Hebron dropped off "the grid," leaving behind his family as well as his phone and other means of communication to better understand homelessness by becoming homeless: "Gaining an enlightened perspective on a marginalized community, seemingly so misunderstood by society, energized me. The redundant images and stereotypes of homelessness bored me" (6). Living homeless, Hebron felt, "could enrich my perspective more than any entry-level job" (7). And so, Hebron spent the first month of this experiment on the streets, trying to find shelter from the weather and having to sleep in parks. During this time, he found, "My loneliness surprised me the most. . . . I longed for companionship." As a result, he joined an overnight shelter, hoping to "curb" that loneliness (16–17). At the Rawls, Hebron found that the men there "reminded me of the guys I grew up with in Wisconsin. They razzed and teased each other. It was part of the culture" (97). His shelter friends constantly joked about the degree to which his hair and beard grew, asking him why he did not want to achieve the appearance of a "gentleman" and how he would ever survive an employment interview without improving his appearance. In the midst of such teasing, these other residents taught Hebron how to network and follow job leads, even though at the end of his experiment he probably would not need them given his education and family support system. When his shelter friends were not around, Hebron concluded that he didn't "do so hot" and that he would "get down, in these depressive negative moods" (10.1.2011). Companionship helped negate Hebron's trauma of living homeless, even though he knew that he could eventually go home. Thus, bloggers and memoir writers often critiqued the oppressive rules and regulations of homeless shelters, the lack of privacy as well as of personal space and safety, and the sometimes inadequate services that addressed sobriety and transition into more stable housing—even though they might celebrate friendships, develop support systems, and create a new sense of family while they lived in a shelter. After all, that is what people experiencing homelessness are looking for—a "real" home with emotional support.

RESPONSES TO THE "FREEDOM HOUSE" HOMELESS DAY SHELTER

Again, the primary complaints by homeless shelter residents address the rule that they must leave the shelter early in the day, often taking their possessions with them, and then must return to sign up for a bed in the evening. In response to when libraries, coffee shops, and other places of comfort for people experiencing homelessness closed during the 2020–2021 COVID-19 pandemic, a low-barrier homeless day shelter, called Freedom House, was created in a vacant fire station in the West 7th Street neighborhood of St. Paul, Minnesota. Freedom House was designed to give unsheltered people a place to avoid the virus, escape harsh weather, use bathrooms and showers, catch up on sleep, and connect with social services during the day, particularly after the night shelters closed in the morning and before they reopened in the evening (Nelson 2020). In this neighborhood stood Irvine Park, complete with an ornamental fountain and gazebo, a popular place for outdoor weddings and surrounded by craft breweries, trendy cafes, galleries, antique stores, and Victorian mansions. On a regular basis, people experiencing homelessness were already spending their days in the park—to the dismay of the neighbors. And so, arguments against Freedom House addressed what was perceived as necessary spatial segregation of people experiencing homelessness from the public spaces in the neighborhood as well as the protection of housed residents in their private homes. In the minds of many such residents, these homes were meant to be not only safe, quiet, and solid investments in the future, but also located in space solely for their comfort and within their control.

Establishing Freedom House had necessitated a reinterpretation in the city zoning regulations that protected such residential neighborhoods from being overwhelmed by businesses and industries. For that reason, discussions regarding Freedom House were conducted in a series of public information meetings during which testimony was given and questions answered, as well as dozens of letters and phone calls from neighbors, local businesses, and nonprofits organizations either in support or opposition to the day shelter were given consideration. The initial letter from the Comprehensive & Neighborhood Planning Committees to the City of St. Paul Planning Commission had already expressed the benefits and challenges of such a homeless day shelter. On the one hand, the committees wrote, "It is evident that such daytime services [are needed] as a part of a functioning city." On the other hand, the committees remarked that the numbers of people who need such services "suggest that a homeless services facility may not be appropriate in residential zoning districts . . . which are embedded among residences" (Comprehensive & Neighborhood Planning Committees Letter 2021). Therefore, the St. Paul Planning Commission was alerted to expect both understanding and support as well as opposition from those owning and renting houses in that area.

To address these concerns and remind neighborhood residents of the challenges faced during the pandemic and the homeless crisis, Dana DeMaster, Supervisor of the Research and Evaluation Unit at Ramsey County Health and Wellness Department, opened the first informational meeting held on November 10, 2020, by inviting neighbors to ask the City of St. Paul any "challenging questions" about the proposed homeless day shelter (Freedom House First Meeting 2020). Then St. Paul Council member Rebecca Noecker stressed the "humanitarian crisis" that the city faced with "far too many residents without a home." Deputy Mayor Jaime Tincher of St. Paul showed slides to depict the number of tent encampment sites and the rising number of people living "outdoors" in the Twin Cities. Tincher argued that, with social distancing directives in response to the COVID-19 virus limiting the number of night shelter beds, this new day center seemed to be the "best place" for the city to address this homeless crisis. Finally, Ricardo Cervantes, St. Paul Director of Safety and Inspections, seconded this notion by calling the alternative of tent encampments "a serious health and safety risk" and "not a dignified form of shelter." Overall, Freedom House would provide day services for users, and the space was appropriately near Dorothy Day Center–Catholic Charities Higher Ground, which provided a pay-for-stay overnight shelter ($7 per night), as well as Listening House, which was a day and an evening shelter as well as a community resource center. Listening House, however, could take only twenty-five to sixty-five people daily during the COVID-19 pandemic and was not open seven days a week. In contrast, Freedom House would be open from 8:00 am to 8:00 pm, seven days a week and accommodate double the number of users that Listening House could. According to Cervantes, Freedom House had the capacity for "individual privacy" and offered access to people experiencing homelessness, including night workers, to come during the day for showers, bathrooms, and "respite and food." In turn, Cervantes and others were working with St. Paul police, who were prepared to respond to any "safety issues" among the "vulnerable people," such as those who had mental health issues, who might use Freedom House.

Despite these reassurances, several neighbors expressed concerns. One resident said that they were already experiencing "a tremendous increase in issues" instigated by people experiencing homelessness, such as sleeping in residents' cars if they were left unlocked and urinating in the Irvine Park gazebo. Moreover, neighborhood residents could not "leave their garages open for even five minutes to take their groceries inside" because their bikes and other items would be stolen. These problems were made clear during testimony. But perhaps more significant but less obvious, in this meeting the voices of people experiencing homelessness were not directly present. As a result, they could not establish credibility or *ethos* in speaking during a meeting. Instead, their needs had to be represented by the city officials who presented statistics and zoning regulations, and their identities were at times stigmatized by residents in the neighborhood who considered people experiencing homelessness problematic and unreliable in respecting the public park and the private homes in the neighborhood.

In preparation for the second information meeting held on May 28, 2021, the St. Paul Planning Commission solicited letters and phone calls in support for or in opposition of Freedom House, but their reactions were similar to those offered in the first meeting. For example, one counselor at nearby Minnesota Community Care, the largest community health center in the city, wrote supportively:

> This is a space where people experiencing homelessness can spend their days. Because I mean they [other spaces] are almost non-existent because of the pandemic. Freedom House is a safe, welcoming, supportive space for unsheltered adults to spend daytime hours and access services like mental health and medical care as well as rest, store their belongings, get food and supplies. (Freedom House Letters 2021)

In contrast, a neighborhood resident seemed to rely on the broken-windows theory in his letter to discredit Freedom House users:

> The broken and boarded up windows at [Freedom House and throughout the community] . . . do not project a safe, thriving neighborhood, either. One of my neighbors shared that she's had to call the police more times this year than in the past thirty years. Just this weekend a violent, mentally ill person had an outburst at a building site in the neighborhood and burned a piece of property of the builder. (Freedom House Letters 2021)

Also, business owners from the West 7th Street Neighborhood & Re-Zoning group sent photos of fires, trash, syringes, and crack pipes to illustrate the negative actions of Freedom House residents. These visual images served as metaphors for the destruction of private property by people experiencing homelessness. As could be expected during the second informational meeting, a representative from Listening House reminded those attending that "people who live in extreme poverty live very, very public lives," and therefore, "to hold people who have less to a higher standard is unreasonable." In contrast, a resident of the neighborhood expressed dismay about having more people experiencing homelessness in the neighborhood: "Swearing, yelling, and fighting in the night, as early as 5 am. Gunshots. Rocks thrown at cars and windows. . . . This is my neighborhood. I work from home. My family is not going to be able to continue living here if Freedom House remains" (Freedom House Second Meeting 2021). This neighbor seemed positioned to flee to the suburbs should Freedom House remain and should spatial segregation of the homeless continue to be violated.

However, in this second meeting, neighbors did raise one concern that was so far unaddressed and perhaps unsurmountable. What would happen to those who left Freedom House by the 8:00 pm deadline but before night homeless shelters opened at 10:00 pm? And how would those needing to get to night shelters such as Safe Space in downtown St. Paul get there from Freedom House? Would they try to walk there in the winter? Would city buses be available? Could St. Paul officials partner with the Lite Rail system to accommodate them? Also, would the sometimes overwhelming intake system at night shelters, a system that forced those seeking a bed for that night to wait for up to two hours before the shelter opened, mean that Freedom House users would hurry out of the neighborhood when the day shelter closed? After all, Safe Space could only serve up to sixty-four residents each night, and "folks stand in line" to get into this shelter. Or would Irvine Park neighborhood be a place for Freedom House residents to wait out that two-hour gap? These all seemed reasonable concerns because the hours of night shelters were in conflict with those of day shelters. After all, the users of both types of shelters might intrude on both private spaces of neighbors and public spaces of parks, and the solutions proposed in this meeting needed to either reassure the neighbors or contain the shelter users—or both. The crisis of homelessness was recognized, the concern about the increasing number of tent encampments raised, and the need for day shelters affirmed, but simply coordinating the opening and closing times of day and night shelters were unresolved at the end of the meeting.

The opening of Freedom House was celebrated later that winter, and its existence noted on the shelter's website as "due to a successful collaboration between stakeholders who care deeply about all residents of the community we share." Those stakeholders consisted of Ramsey County, the City of St. Paul, the St. Paul Fire Department, the St. Paul City Council, partner agencies, community members, local businesses, the Listening House Board of Directors, and the donors and funders ("Welcome to Listening House & Freedom House" 2018/2020). But spatial segregation remained a challenge not only for people experiencing homelessness whose voices still were not directly heard and for the neighbors around Freedom House who did not want their investments in and control over their homes disrupted.

SPATIAL DISPLACEMENT BY FIRE AND A VIRUS

In the final section of this chapter, I turn to two events involving abrupt and emergency spatial displacement of people experiencing homelessness and the reactions to them not only by those people facing homelessness but also by public officials, advocates, and activists. While these events again challenged the trope of the ideal home, they also illuminated the adaptability of the homeless. A 1986 fire at the Brooklyn Arms Hotel in the Fort Greene area of east Brooklyn, New York, provides the context for the first event—a 2019 devastating fire in a similar hotel in downtown Minneapolis. The second event involves the public health response to the 2020–2021 novel coronavirus or COVID-19 as well as predictions about the number of infections that people experiencing homelessness would contract.

Life and Death in the Brooklyn Arms and the Martinique Hotels

The Brooklyn Arms Hotel fire killed four children who were left alone in their family's one-room apartment and set the context for life and death in such "welfare" hotels. About 1,500 people lived in the Brooklyn Arms at the time of the fire, most of whom received public assistance until more permanent shelter was available for them. Significantly, after the fire the children's parents, Edwin Alvarez, Sr., and Susana Alvarez, were arrested for "knowingly" jeopardizing their children's welfare. Later it was revealed that during the time of the fire the parents were out collecting returnable bottles and cans in order to earn much needed spending money. In response to the charges filed against the parents, Robert M. Hayes, counsel for the Coalition for the Homeless at the time, said that although he did not know the details of this particular case, "the city was partly to blame for the harm that children suffer" at these so-called welfare hotels because the city "refused to provide day care, recreational facilities or other services for homeless families." Hayes concluded, "Virtually every child in this homeless shelter system is routinely neglected by necessity" ("Parents Arrested" 1986; see also "Brooklyn

Welfare Hotel" 1986). Moreover, the owners of the Brooklyn Arms had been cited for a number of violations of the city fire, building, and safety codes, endangering residents who were dependent on the cheap hotel rooms they rented there.

Such hotels in New York City and other major metropolitan areas, often once elegant and later in decline, seemed prevalent in the 1980s. During that decade, the Prince George Hotel, the Latham Hotel, and the Granada Hotel were among the fifty-five-some hotels in New York City that provided shelter for more than two thousand families facing homelessness. In his book based on the months he spent among such hotel residents, Kozol (1988) made the Martinique Hotel infamous. Noting that he found the Martinique "the saddest place that I have been in my entire life," Kozol reported that the city paid the hotel $20,000 a year for a room and was "powerless to strike a better bargain with the hotel owners" (44). In turn, to rent one room, a family of four paid $1,800 a month, a higher rent than regular rooms in most tourist hotels at the time. Families who lived in the Martinique did receive a combination of twice-monthly Aid to Families with Dependent Children, a monthly food stamp allocation, a restaurant allowance of about 71 cents per meal per person (there were no cooking facilities in the rooms), a very small sum to pay transportation costs to help in the search for housing, and finally an allocation for nutritional supplements to pregnant women and children under five—but these amounts seldom could sustain a family. The average family staying at the Martinique consisted of a mother with three children, and 19 percent of the residents had become homeless after living in substandard housing, 34 percent after being evicted by a landlord, and 47 percent after first doubling up for a short time with other families. Moreover, 70 percent of these hotel residents had seen at minimum five vacant units that they could not afford or that would not accept children or welfare recipients. Kozol also found that the Martinique residents were often terrorized upon arrival at the hotel, given the chaos and disorder that reigned there, and they experienced "nearly absolute bewilderment" about the number of rules and regulations imposed upon them by the hotel manager (63). The hotel was a well-known site for drug use and sales. One resident, for example, who had been made homeless when a new landlord raised the rent on her Queens apartment, noted the large number of drug pushers outside the hotel who would "sell drugs in broad daylight. People in the hotels buy them. The guards, all of them, smoke crack" (Kurtz 1987; see also Maranes 2021). The hotel residents also noted the number of drug users residing in the hotel itself and were concerned about the children who played unsupervised in the hallways and witnessed violent outbursts that disrupted the nights.

Shortly after the Brooklyn Arms Hotel fire and given the deteriorating shape of such welfare hotels and the expense to maintain them, New York

City Mayor Ed Koch pledged to empty the forty-six most problematic welfare hotels in the city by July 1990, and the Martinique was chosen to be the first to go. This hotel had become, according to the *New York Times*, "a symbol of the horrors of a system that paid exorbitant sums to warehouse families" in "shabby, crowded hotels" ("As a Hotel is Emptied" 1988; see also "City Closed Door" 1988). And so, some of the former Martinique residents were moved into apartments in city-owned buildings or housing projects, at times not much safer or quieter than the hotel. Additionally, Koch committed to building 10 homeless shelters in the boroughs outside of Manhattan, but local leaders in Brooklyn, Queens, and the Bronx argued that the shelters would "ruin middle-class neighborhoods without making a dent in the homeless population," a population that at the time numbered 57,000 in New York City alone (Kurtz 1987). Finally, Manhattan Borough President David Dinkins commissioned a study called "A Shelter Is Not a Home" and urged Koch to drop one of the two new shelters slated for Manhattan as well as empty five downtown welfare hotels in lieu of providing more affordable housing. When Dinkins became mayor of New York City, he ordered homeless tent encampments bulldozed, barred "unauthorized persons" from public spaces, and supported the transit authority's eviction of people sheltering in the subways (Roberts 1991; see also Bardanel 1987). City officials not only disagreed but seemed stymied by how to address the homelessness crisis. Equally disturbing was the continued existence of and dangers in such hotels, including the Drake Hotel in downtown Minneapolis.

Fire at the Drake Hotel

During Thanksgiving week in 2019, a fire in a twenty-five-story Minneapolis Public Housing Authority complex left five people dead and dozens more without shelter. Then on Christmas Day that year, a fire in the Drake Hotel displaced about 250 people, and the hotel was completely destroyed. Much like the Martinique and the Brooklyn Arms, the Drake Hotel had been built in 1926 as a luxury traditional and residential hotel and was now being used as a temporary shelter until shelter beds or more stable housing could be found for its residents—thus, the terminology used to label such a place changed from a "welfare" hotel to a "spillover" hotel. Initially called the Francis Drake Hotel, the building had 180 apartments and 50 "transient" chambers, now known as hotel rooms, and was maintained as such over five and a half decades. Then in 1983, People Serving People, a large and comprehensive homeless shelter system for families in Minnesota, started operating the hotel for emergency and transitional housing. By 1997, the hotel offered low-cost rooms, and a few residents worked in the hotel or in the community to pay their own rent. At the time of the four-alarm fire on Christmas Day 2019, Hennepin County and other social service agencies such as Mary's Place were using the hotel for overflow from homeless shelters and gave people money to stay in the hotel temporarily.

There was not a sprinkler system in the Drake Hotel, as there was not in the Public Housing Authority complex, but the fire alarms were working in the hotel. Even though firefighters were able to evacuate all of the Drake residents, three people were injured and taken to the hospital. One hotel resident reported, "I told my wife we've got to get out now. I mean I didn't even grab my wallet. Because there was smoke in the hallway already starting to come through the building. And there were a lot of people, it was pretty chaotic. But it was fairly organized chaos, people were pretty calm walking out" (Combs 2019; see also Moen 2019). Loss of clothing and other personal effects, including forms of identification such as driver's licenses, would create major problems for these Drake residents even though donations immediately started pouring in from the community. A hotel resident stated, "I already lost everything once. Now I just lost absolutely everything" (quoted in Spewak 2019).

Thirty families with children who had been living at the Drake were relocated by Hennepin County to a hotel in the suburb of Bloomington, ten miles south of downtown Minneapolis. Sixty to seventy adults who were living at the Drake took shelter at the First Covenant Church, not ideal in that although the Red Cross served three meals a day there and the church gymnasium could accommodate beds for all, there were few showers and not enough washers and dryers. Moreover, according to a letter sent by the church leadership to the congregation, the church was only meant to shelter displaced Drake residents for two weeks. Thus, Minneapolis Mayor Frey and other city and county officials admitted that it would be difficult to find shelter for all those evacuated from the Drake. In May 2019, a number of such officials had reported to the Minnesota legislature that emergency shelter was needed for three hundred to six hundred additional people in the Twin Cities metropolitan area, and by November 2019, the Minnesota Department of Human Services had planned to issue grants to twenty-five organizations serving people experiencing homelessness, but that money would not be available until July 2020. And so, the former residents of the Drake Hotel found themselves in a state of emergency and dependent on the city and nonprofit organizations to find them homes and replace their possessions. Despite the conditions at such hotels, they had been home for many people experiencing homelessness.

These former residents of the Drake Hotel were not submissive or silent about their needs and options. They actively disagreed, for example, about the method of distribution of monetary donations coming from individuals, organizations, and state and city agencies. The Minnesota Vikings donated $50,000 to help the victims of the fire, and the Minneapolis Foundation raised nearly $400,000, $10,000 of which went to Target gift cards distributed among the victims and $40,000 to help the First Covenant Church temporarily house fire victims. However, those former residents who had lived independently in the Drake Hotel complained that they could not benefit from these donations because they were not considered homeless—they had been employed in the hotel or elsewhere and had paid their own rent. One such resident, Ron Tolbert, commented that he was grateful for help from the Red Cross, but noted that other donations were "only going to help the families on government assistance" (Raddatz 2019). Similarly, former Drake resident Jeffrey Jones explained how his sense of agency was negated given the system of donations: "I would like to see the money coming directly to us. Not to state agencies, because people are making it impossible for us. They think we're not able to control our own money. And we are" (quoted in Williams 2020). Jones was responding to how people living with homelessness are frequently stigmatized as incompetent and irresponsible—again, the "lackers" as Johnsen, Cloke, and May (2005) found they might be called. Both Jones and Tolbert were penalized even though they had already found stability and independence at the Drake Hotel. Overall, such spillover hotels offer temporary housing to people experiencing homelessness, for whom there is no room in homeless shelters or no means of finding affordable housing. This type of containment indeed seemed more acceptable to the city and to neighbors than tent encampments, but the majority of hotel residents were stigmatized and marginalized as responsible for their own situation and perceived incompetent in resolving that situation even though they had established a temporary and tenuous home.

The Novel Coronavirus or COVID-19

The arrival of the novel coronavirus, COVID-19, also created a demand for alternative shelters and led to uneasiness among not only people experiencing homelessness but also among housed citizens. At the point when news of COVID-19 was just reaching people experiencing homelessness and in a series of video interviews, interviewees summed up the effects of the virus on their already marginalized and stigmatized positions: "We are not a priority, are we? They don't tell you anything, no solution. They see a homeless man and directly think that we are more likely to be infected with the virus, and that's bad. The homeless ain't [sic] got nowhere to isolate. We all care for each other. We always do" (Redfish 2020). However, with the arrival of the virus, immediately questions arose about people living on the streets, in encampments, and in shelters: Should the homeless be isolated or contained even further because they might endanger whole communities given that they often entered public spaces? Could they become ill quickly because they often lived in close quarters in shelters? And, what measures could possibly protect them from the virus given the characteristics attributed to them—unhealthy, unclean, and unstable? People experiencing homelessness represented potential contagion in the eyes of many.

And so, the print and electronic media initially agreed on the dangers of the virus that prevailed because of or among people experiencing homelessness. Just after the first 234 people had been diagnosed with COVID-19 in the United States, for example, Andrew Selsky (2020) reported for ABC News in Salem, Oregon, that because people experiencing homelessness did not have places to wash their hands, struggled with existing health problems, and were often "crowd[ed] together in grimy camps," they were particularly vulnerable to the virus. In turn, Chunhuei Chi, Director of the Center for Global Health at Oregon State University in Corvallis, Oregon, stated, "They are [at] double risk. One is risk for themselves, the other is a risk to society" (quoted in Selsky 2020). A week and a half later, Jennifer Loving, CEO of "Designation: Home," an organization addressing homelessness in Santa Clara County, California, commented in an article for Vox news: "The idea [of helping people in other crises such as a flood or fire] is to have as many people together as possible [to 'co-locate' them]. But in this situation, we have to do everything opposite" (quoted in Kim 2020). Finally, Emma Grey Ellis (2020), a staff writer at WIRED, reported that for people experiencing homelessness, either in the long term or newly affected given the faltering economy, COVID-19 was "horror on top of horror." Just a few weeks after Loving had offered her assessment, Ellis reported,

> The shelters are full, or closed, or too fraught with coronavirus to consider sleeping in. They have no access to toilets, much less toilet paper. They've been laid off, and there's nobody on the street so they can't even panhandle. Common places to find shelter and a bathroom—libraries, gyms, fast food restaurants—are closed. Soup kitchens are closing, out of food, out of workers.

Also, Ellis noted that it was "nearly impossible for homeless people to maintain social distance. Their needs are met en masse" (see also Jorge 2020; Serres, Chanen, and Galioto 2020). Overall, the usual conditions of homelessness were perceived as leaving unhoused people particularly vulnerable to the virus, and those experiencing homelessness were stigmatized as an even greater problem than usual—a threat to the so-called normal citizen, a dilemma for advocates and activists, but somehow responsible for their own situation.

However, eight months after Ellis published her account, Thomas Fuller (2020), writing for the *New York Times*, reported that health officials were finding that people living in tent encampments and even in homeless shelters did not suffer the same devastation wrought by the virus in similarly confined places, such as nursing homes and prisons. Health experts, such as Dr. Helen Chu, an infectious-disease doctor in Seattle, Washington, who helped conduct 2,500 COVID-19 tests in homeless shelters there, found that less than 1 percent (fifteen tests) came back positive for the virus. Dr. Chu admitted "it pretty much had turned out to be not as bad as I would have thought" (quoted in Fuller 2020). And, later during the pandemic, the medical community's reports on the virus's effect on the homeless changed over time in such professional publications as the *Journal of the American Medical Association* (*JAMA*) and the weekly report *Morbidity and Mortality*. Early on in *JAMA: News from the Centers for Disease Control and Prevention* (CDC), for example, investigators had warned, "Homeless shelters are often crowded, making social distancing difficult. Many persons experiencing homelessness are older and have underlying medical conditions" (Kuehn 2020; see also Lima et al. 2020; Mosites, Parker, and Stoltey 2020). And, around the same time, public health experts Jack Tsai and Michal Wilson (2020) warned in *The Lancet*, "People experiencing homelessness live in environments that are conducive to a disease epidemic . . . in congregate living settings—be it formal (i.e., shelters or halfway houses) or informal (i.e., encampments or abandoned buildings)." By January 2021, however, Julia Rogers (2021) with the Purdue University Northwest College of Nursing, reported in the *Annals of Internal Medicine* that only one person tested positive for COVID-19 while living in a homeless shelter in King County, Washington.

Then a health care practitioner, educator, and researcher wondered on the PBS News Hour (2020), "Where Do Homeless Patients Go After Being Treated for COVID-19?" and concluded that there was a "dire need" for them to have medical respite in homeless shelters, nursing homes, transitional housing, or freestanding facilities. And, by February 2021, the CDC offered recommendations for health departments on how to vaccinate people experiencing homelessness. That guidance included administering the vaccine in locations such as homeless shelters, meal service sites, and public libraries, as well as advertising vaccination availability in encampments, on public transportation, and via social media ("Interim Guidance for Health Departments" 2021; see also Noguchi 2021). Overall, however, when medical experts continued to monitor people experiencing homelessness for what was predicted to be a health disaster for them, they found that those experiencing homelessness often escaped the virus. This escape from contracting the virus might be explained by three reasons: (1) Large cities such as those in California, Minnesota, and New York rented hotel rooms for the most vulnerable people experiencing homelessness; (2) tent encampment residents spent a lot of their time outdoors and avoided crowds; and (3) people experiencing homelessness avoided crowded shelters on a regular basis and now for fear of the virus. Thus, we might speculate that their choice of alternative shelters, their establishment of homes and communities in tent encampments, and the actions of certain public health advocates could explain how many people experiencing homelessness avoided contracting the virus than as initially predicted. Contrary to this evidence, however, they continued to be stigmatized as victims and carriers of COVID-19 by the media and the general public.

Certainly, in the midst of concerns about the virus, homeless tent encampments began to grow again. Minnesota Governor Walz decided that those people experiencing homelessness were necessarily exempt from his COVID-19 "stay-at-home" order, and homeless shelters were encouraged to stay open for twenty-four hours a day. In addition, Minneapolis installed four hygiene facilities to provide bathrooms and handwashing stations throughout the city, and some park bathrooms were made accessible for people experiencing unsheltered homelessness. Across the United States, more and more city and state agencies as well as homeless organizations began to rent hotel rooms to house people experiencing homelessness at a time when these rooms were not generally needed because of restrictions on vacations and travel. In New Orleans, Louisiana, for example, where most shelters stopped accepting new residents and when nearly two hundred people were living in tents under a nearby freeway, the Hilton Garden Inn, one block off Canal Street, opened its doors to people experiencing homelessness. As Martha Kegel, Executive Director of Unity of Greater New Orleans, the city's largest provider of homeless services, offered, "Folks who sleep on the street, a large percentage of them won't go into a congregate shelter. But if you offer them an individual hotel room, virtually no one refuses" (quoted in Webster 2020). California Governor Gavin Newson secured almost seven thousand such hotel rooms to house people who were homeless and had been exposed to COVID-19, were at risk of contracting the virus, or had tested positive. During the civil unrest following the death of George Floyd in Minneapolis, people experiencing homelessness had also sheltered in the empty nearby hotels. Douglas Pyle, who had been homeless for eighteen months, slept in a bed in a private hotel room with a locked door and "without fear that someone would roust him at night or steal his few belongings." The next day, Pyle shared, "It felt like I was sleeping on a cloud. The best part is, I can face the world with a clear mind" (quoted in Serres 2020a). In some hotels, such residents could cook in their rooms, bring food in, and even shelter along with their pets. But most significant was that their sense of identity and agency was restored in this supportive new home, a lesson for all those who addressed the homelessness crisis.

In the meantime, the number of people experiencing homelessness and using social media dropped radically during the pandemic. Public spaces closed, such as the libraries and coffee houses where they could use computers and have access to the internet. Thus, their voices were often silent except as captured by the news media. The responses to Fuller's (2020) article for the *New York Times* in which he speculated that the normal tendency to isolate might protect people experiencing homelessness from contracting COVID-19 reflected the extremes of societal reaction to homelessness during this time. One respondent to Fuller's article concluded, "Good news, kind of. These days any good news is welcome. I'm glad that those who are down on their luck are at least not being slaughtered wholesale by this damned virus." Another respondent offered a similar insight: "It removes a bit of the stigma when we encounter the bearded guys on the bus hauling their garbage bags of [returnable] cans." However, a third respondent suggested, "The solution to the homeless problem is to declare them social parasites and sentence them to thirty year contracts aboard Chinese fishing trawlers." Reactions to how people experiencing homelessness were weathering the virus varied from concern and insight to stigmatization as usual. However, people experiencing homelessness might seem particularly vulnerable during crisis, such as fires and disease, but they might prove to be less helpless, less silent, and more competent than they are often perceived. The environments in which they create and recreate their homes might bring chaos and impermanency but also might bring peace, safety, and *communitas*.

Overall, the voices of people experiencing homelessness reflect on how the tropes of home and homelessness are imposed upon them as they are spatially segregated and stigmatized—or altered by them as they exercise agency in selecting where and how to shelter. They may also resist those who negatively characterize homeless encampments, such as blogger Lawrence who criticized the Vancouver Police Department's approach to a homeless encampment in Canada as "a less-than-honest campaign of harassment and vilification, intended to build that public perception that the homeless camp is a hotbed of crime and violence that must be stamped out" (12.16.2019). Or, they may share their impressions of homeless shelters, as did blogger Ralph: "The most dismal thing about a lack of privacy is that it forbids expression of dissent or resentment. . . . On a purely aesthetic level, fourteen old men sleeping on the floor of a church snore more than I would have ever believed" (10.30.2004). Contrary to public perception, those experiencing homelessness have made such shelters a trope for loss of freedom, dignity, and privacy, as well as a challenge to a sense of agency and identity—all the negative characteristics of a "total institution." The street may be experienced as a center of brutality and the home as a provider of psychological and emotional support, but for many experiencing homelessness, the encampment can become a sort of in-between space—a temporary place of instability and vulnerability but also space for freedom and community. Finally, during eviction, fire, or pandemic, people experiencing homelessness have proved to be resilient and unique, resourceful and outspoken. In the next and final chapter in this book, I return to the theoretical perspectives and the case studies that comprised my research, all to offer some concluding impressions and recommendations regarding homelessness.

Chapter Five

Final Reflections

Activists and advocates, policy makers and scholars, and many people experiencing homelessness seek to understand this situation in order to create some lasting solutions—only to see rising numbers among those who live unsheltered, those who face intergenerational poverty and trauma, and those who are spatially segregated and stigmatized. The causes of homelessness are varied, often seem unavoidable, and sometimes appear illusive. As seventeen-year-old Michelle, the eldest of five children staying with their mother at a Union Rescue Mission in Los Angeles, shared in her video interview: "I can't help but wonder how this happened to us. My mom isn't abusive, she is not an alcoholic, she has never done drugs. And sometimes that's the most difficult thing to deal with—realizing that there are times when your life isn't in your hands" ("Homeless Teenagers" May 26, 2011). No universal or singular reason for homelessness exists, just as no comprehensive solution emerges despite our efforts to address the issue. The perspectives of stigma, space, and social media do offer ways to increase our understanding of homelessness, and, in this book, I have worked to illuminate and add to those perspectives through a series of case studies. Overall, I discovered the significance and power of spatial segregation, which is often imposed upon people experiencing homelessness and used as a tool to marginalize them, and I have illuminated the universality of the tropes of home and homelessness, which originated over a century ago and now are maintained most often by those who enjoy secure housing. Again, I hope to have achieved what Koerber (2018a) stated was the goal of such research: "After a good rhetorical analysis, the world should never look the same as it did before" (199)—homelessness should never appear the same as it does to those who experience it and to those who have thus far avoided it.

Certainly, an important part of my work was "listening" to people experiencing homelessness because they often offered a multitude of concrete solutions, such as did blogger "George" (B7):

I've thought a long time about what would be useful to the homeless. We need public toilets. Not filthy porta potties, but proper restrooms that are private and clean. We need safe places to sleep. Capsule hotels, which are found in Tokyo and some other places in the world, would be excellent. The rooms should be very cheap, and I mean five bucks is too much. They should be subsidized, and there would be twice as many as there is demand for them. They should be extremely secure, and you should be allowed to stay for as long as you want. We need showers. Safe, secure, single occupancy showers. Those are answers that would help people. (4.23.2011)

Also, they wanted enduring approaches to homelessness, as Karp (2011) described in her memoir:

Sustainability is the key to any lifestyle. Sure, I would sell my phone and my laptop for the price of a few hamburgers. But, then, the hamburgers would soon be gone, and so would my phone and laptop. I would have absolutely no phone so an employer could contact me. And without a laptop, I would only be able to search and apply for work online during the hours the public library was open . . . a phone and internet access are no longer "luxury" items. (109–10)

And, almost every one of them want a mentor to help them discover a path out of homelessness—or they offer to be a mentor themselves. Memoir writer Fabian (2013), for example, revealed the importance of Miss Jackson, a teacher in her high school English class:

More than anything I needed someone to listen and understand what I was going through. I told her about the apartment and how dark it was. I told her about my auntie and her husband and how cruel they were. I told her everything I had kept inside for so long. Miss Jackson listened without judgement. She made me feel like I wasn't a failure. She made me feel strong. (81)

Finally, the blogs and memoirs created by those experiencing or who had experienced homelessness often provided a better sense of self and optimism for change, as blogger "James" (B1) shared: "[W]riting on this blog has brought out a part of me that is genuine and honest and actually I am impressed with the difference I am seeing in my life because of it. . . . I feel as though this blog has in a way saved my life! I now have a purpose and a passion" (4.12.2010). James's purpose was to have a home and reunite with his children: "The hope that I will eventually see my kids. The hope that I will eventually be in my own place. The hope that my life will be filled with good things surrounding me" (7.15.2010). Thus, my goal in this book was to discover what Robinson (2020) identified as "lived experience" or the "first-hand, everyday accounts of how marginalized people experience the world and the personal knowledge they gain from these experiences" (4). Within the previous chapters and to use Britt's (2018) terms again, I have attempted to capture and analyze the lived experience of people enduring homelessness to not only establish my own productive nonidentification stance, or a new identification and understanding of those experiencing homelessness, but also to enhance the following three theoretical perspectives.

STIGMA, OR MARGINALIZATION AND OTHERING

Stigmatization, marginalization, and othering disadvantage those of a race, ethnic group, gender, or religious affiliation as well as those living in poverty and experiencing homelessness. In doing so, these strategies provide those who consider themselves "normal," or those who are indeed dominant within social, economic, and political hierarchies, with an excuse to exclude those who are perceived as different from them. As Donald Burnes (2016), founder and executive director of the Burnes Institute for Poverty and Homelessness, noted about people panhandling on street corners, "We tend to create stereotypes based on these contacts made when the traffic light turns red, and most of us do our best to avoid interactions. . . . Many of us argue that they choose to live that way, that they have made bad choices, and that they are lazy people who just need to get a job" (287). Such stigmatization might be based on misunderstanding, fear, or maintenance of socioeconomic power—and those stigmatized struggle to achieve any *ethos* or credibility in living and talking about their lives.

Such stigmatization can be used to justify segregation, ethnocide, and even genocide. Generations of Native people, for example, have been stigmatized to the extent that their beliefs and culture are often not valued or considered useful in so-called civilized society. Moreover, the acts and laws that addressed Native people historically found them expendable because they did not conform to the goals established in the early colonization of the United States—goals such as individual land ownership and adjustment to urban life and work. As a result, Native people often suffer intergenerational trauma as well as spiritual and physical homelessness. Stigmatization of Native people also diminishes their *ethos* in protesting their treatment by dominant groups and in establishing their own spaces and homes. Within the "Wall of Forgotten Natives" encampment in Minneapolis, residents inherited this stigma and were identified by the trope for drunkenness and drug use, violence, irresponsibility, lack of hygiene, and inability to "evolve" because of their homelessness.

That same kind of stigma carries over to other minority groups, such as the Black individuals and families who settled in and were confined to the Five

Points neighborhood of Denver. Throughout the United States, racial zoning, redlining, deed covenants, and gentrification all supported that same goal of individual land ownership that affected Native people but added new means to control who could buy and rent homes. Certain groups were stigmatized as disruptive to the value of land and the stability of neighborhoods, and therefore they were encouraged or permitted to live in less valuable, more unstable, and usually rundown and overcrowded areas of a city. In these undesirable neighborhoods, crowded apartments and major industry might coexist while single-family homes and suburban subdivisions were established elsewhere. Moreover, marginalized groups, such as those convicted of felony sexual offenses, regardless of the circumstances of their crimes and their progress in treatment, were so stigmatized by community ordinances that they were, in essence, made homeless and so were more likely to engage in recidivism and subsequent recommitment.

In general, people experiencing homelessness are assigned the trope of moral, economic, and personal failure as well as propensity to spread disease, engage in substance abuse, and break any number of quality-of-life laws that perpetuate the broken-windows theory of evolving misbehavior. In contrast, the home serves as a metaphor or trope for private, contained, concrete, and stable life, even though the history of the home reflects how women were considered less capable than men and their identities and sense of agency were consequently diminished. And eventually, those who conform to normative behavior might still encounter stigmatization and even violence within the home for not performing up to the standards imposed by a dominate and usually male occupant. Moreover, unsheltered youth, particularly LBGTQ+ youth, may suffer from intergenerational poverty, systemic racism and classism, and trauma, stigma, and abuse in the home and on the streets.

Finally, people experiencing homelessness often avoid the homeless shelter, which for them has become a trope for loss of freedom, agency, privacy, and dignity, a trope constructed by those experiencing homelessness rather than imposed upon them. They may reject homeless shelters because of the results of marginalization and, very likely, spatial segregation. The rules and regulations of the shelter, the lack of privacy and safety, the unhealthy conditions, the overcrowding, and even the boredom and depression may be the result of hierarchical oversight as well as stigmatization of many who are homeless—again the "slackers" as staff at one shelter called them. Although tent encampments are often considered by their residents to provide more freedom, agency, and choice, these residents face disruption in the form of sweeps or evictions. Finally, the speculation that people facing homelessness would succumb more easily to the COVID-19 pandemic was most likely the result of the stigmatization of their supposed overcrowding and poor hygiene, even though both their voluntary and publicly subsidized isolation may have kept them safe in encampments and in hotels.

Overall, stigmatization narrows our abilities to know and consider others and to understand their different life challenges—and cripples our ability to listen to the voices of people experiencing homelessness and to accept their stories. Stigmatization offers a false sense of security for the so-called normal or legitimate housed citizen who sets boundaries and spatially segregates those who are misunderstood and disadvantaged.

SPACE, OR BOUNDARIES AND SEGREGATION

Space is both discursively and materially constructed, therefore subject to dispute regarding possession and ownership. Certainly, Thistle's grandfather experienced this concept when the government seized the homes and lands occupied by the Métis people. At times, Native people simply got in the way of the profits that colonists and settlers hoped to gain from the land they seized. Centuries later when Native people occupied the "Wall of Forgotten Natives" encampment in a space near the land still owned by the Red Lake Band of Chippewa, their encampment became a potential material text or texture to celebrate their voices, to shelter their bodies, to overcome their *kakoethos*, and to visibly and materially challenge their marginalization. After the "Wall" encampment was dismantled and after the Minneapolis Navigation Center closed and in part because all residents could not be rehoused, tent encampments continued to grow in Minnesota and across the United States. In turn, the Black residents of the Five Points neighborhood in Denver might have been spatially segregated for decades, but they had created an appealing and alluring cultural space, the "Harlem of the West," before it became subject to gentrification. Five Points residents also faced spatial segregation created by racial zoning, redlining, and restrictive deed covenants that excluded them from renting and buying housing throughout the rest of the city, and the courts were very hesitant and very late in overturning any of those spatial boundaries.

The scholarly impulse often involves classifying or categorizing space, whether spaces are called pleasure, refuse, or functional spaces, according to Wright (1992), or whether they are called prime, marginal, or transitional spaces, according to Snow and Mulcathy (2001). This impulse helps us recognize such phenomena as when prime or pleasure spaces increase, marginal or functional spaces decrease. And so, people experiencing homelessness have been confined to shrinking and constantly monitored public space, sometimes claimed by businesses such as entertainment and shopping centers, and excluded from private space occupied by housed citizens. Also, young people as well as victims of domestic violence who flee their abusers might occupy that public space by living on the streets or in shelters, and so they encounter city ordinances and shelter rules that restrict them. These are the people for whom home, socially conceived as a firm division between private and public space and between safety and danger, may become untenable because of poverty, violence, or rejection. Even legal restraining orders may not protect those occupants who experience violence in that space called home.

And so, when a new homeless day shelter was proposed, residents of the Irvine Park neighborhood in St. Paul, Minnesota, were so concerned that some focused on how both private and public spaces might be negatively affected by the continued and increased presence of people experiencing homelessness. To ease that concern, they wanted a solution for where users of Freedom House, seen as potential neighborhood disruptors, would go in the two hours between the time the day shelter closed and night shelters opened. Would those users invade the neighbors' private spaces as well as the public space of Irvine Park? In turn, people experiencing homelessness often resent the features of homeless shelters that matched those of a "total institution," including casting them out for twelve hours a day into public spaces where they were unwelcome and in private spaces where they were expected to find their own solutions to being so unwelcome. It would seem that these two groups, the housed and the homeless, wanted the same thing—a safe and warm place to reside—where privacy and agency were honored. But a common solution seemed almost impossible for each group in the Irvine Park area.

Overall, the propensity to protect private space, and to use public space to attract businesses to bring revenue into the city, leads to the inclination to exclude people experiencing homelessness—to set such spatial as well as social boundaries around them so that they are contained and unseen. And yet, those people experiencing homelessness seek freedom and dignity, agency and choice, privacy, and companionship that alternative places and at times conventional homeless shelters may bring. The hotel rooms that people experiencing homelessness were offered during the COVID-19 pandemic fulfilled those desires, and in those spaces some people found clarity and motivation, just as public libraries and coffee shops had previously provided a way for them to express their voices in social media or perhaps to write their memoirs.

SOCIAL MEDIA AND MEMOIRS, OR
PERSONAL NARRATIVE AND TESTIMONY

In her blog, Camille Gage offered an inside look at life in the "Wall of Forgotten Natives" encampment as well as guidance to her readers when such things as trash threatened to be diminish livability in the space. She took the stance as a reporter when the Natives Against Heroin wished to expel drug sellers and users from the encampment, and she dispelled rumors about and alerted MUID and other Native organizations to just what was happening in the encampment. Also, the personal memoirs of Thistle (2019) and others often presented to their readers detailed descriptions of and stories about the lives of people experiencing homelessness. Such stories enlighten readers about what people experiencing homelessness face and how they succeed or fail in finding stable, safe, and affordable housing. Such writers often employ a narrative approach driven by plot, description, and dialogue, which engage readers and often end with analytical and even philosophical statements.

Karp (2011), for example, began her memoir by telling her readers the story of how she was thrown out of her home by her mother, a Jehovah's Witness who was physically, mentally, and emotionally abused herself. Karp found refuge in a travel trailer inherited from her father, a temporary shelter but a means of transportation too expensive to drive in the long term. She described how she discovered that she could park in the corner of a Walmart parking lot as long as she did not bother customers or draw attention to herself. Karp also explained that when her friend Brandon heard about her plight, he suggested that she should "totally start a blog or something about this" (92). And so, Karp did start her blog, a blog that turned into her memoir, and her first entry began as follows: "In three days, I will be homeless. This is not by choice. . . . Personally, I enjoy having a permanent residence and the sense of stability and security that it gives me. . . . [Soon] I will be making my way on the streets of Orange County as best I can, and I will be considered the most stigmatized of people—a homeless woman" (94). Such a "once upon a time" opening may have been somewhat startling but was certainly intriguing to her readers, and thus began Karp's personal narrative of homelessness.

Moreover, Karp recognized the bias of people "who had the stereotypical idea of a homeless man or woman, who believed that it would not, could not happen to them" (95). When Karp herself was a child, her mother instructed her not to "make eye contact" with the homeless because they were "just lazy bums. Too lazy to get a job. . . . They're just faking it to make money without actually having to do anything" (2). Again, being stigmatized as a socially unacceptable person is obviously painful, even traumatic to people experiencing homelessness, as Karp's memoir revealed. In turn, Early (2013) remarked in his self-published memoir of living on the streets, taking shelter in a YMCA, and being sent to a logging camp for boys facing homelessness: "Words are very powerful and when negativity is relayed repeatedly, it's easier for one to accept and believe it as true. It took a long time to reprogram all the negative garbage that was dumped on me over the years. But I would be lying if I said it didn't bother me at all. It still does" (6). Early went on to tell the story of how his father called him a "faggot," even though Early was too young to understand what the word meant: "I didn't really know the meaning of fag, but I was taught definitely that fags were *bad*, very, very bad" (emphasis in original, 8). Although not all people living with homelessness may have the desire and tools to express themselves through memoirs and blogs, those who do often critique the stigma assigned to them and the pain caused by that stigma by narrating about when they first encountered it.

Moreover, the traditional narrative approach may take a slightly different form for some blog writers. Often blog writers tell stories and create dialogue with their personal, direct, and authentic voices, voices that analyze family background and history, the causes and effects of their situation or trauma, attempts to find family or build community, and successes and failures in accomplishing goals such as sobriety and employment. Also, this approach as used by blog writers experiencing homelessness or who have experienced homelessness seems particularly confessional, highly personal, and particularly self-reflective, at times much like thoughts shared with a therapist or in a support group for substance abusers—and, at other times much like words used by an advocate for others experiencing homelessness. "Patrick" (B3), for example, first defined his blog as simply a "homeless blog," but then added, "No wait, it's a blog about homelessness, sort of. These things we call blogs can be all sorts of things, depending on the writer. If you've been following this blog for a while, you know that this blog is equal parts homeless advocacy, personal diary, political soapbox, and web-log" (1.16.2015). Also, after blogger "Clare" (B6) described how the teacher of her younger daughter "sounded stunned" to learn that there were children experiencing homelessness in the school, Clare concluded, "I hope that she does read my story and every story I post on here. There is a new brand of poverty out here. One marked by individuals finding their way to the internet via social websites to stay connected, to make that human contact with others in the same situation so that they know they aren't alone in hell" (10.12.2010). Finally, "Elaine" (B12), who maintained her blog for ten years, acknowledged that her own readers might fall into two groups: Individuals in a similar situation, "especially a single, vulnerable woman," or readers for whom "homelessness is a topic close to your heart, or maybe you just feel that you should cultivate some knowledge on survival skills, because with the economy the way it is now, who knows what will happen in the future?" Overall, Elaine just hoped that her blog entries would give her readers "something to think about and/or something to laugh about, for humor can be mined from even the most dire of circumstances" (2.23.2009). These blog writers made clear their investment in their entries and their hopes for enlightening their readers through storytelling and personal testimony.

Scholars and advocates have explored how people experiencing homelessness offer such narrative accounts of the causes and effects of their lack of stable housing—however, these accounts are often based on face-to-face interviews, some spontaneous but others quite controlled. Sociologist David Farrugia (2011), for example, looked for storytelling techniques in his twenty interviews with youth experiencing homelessness in Melbourne, Australia, and found two common responses. On the one hand, when telling of how they became homeless, the young people whom he interviewed expressed failure and shame, "consequences of their individualized understanding of their biography," finding fault for their choices and current situation. On the other hand, once the young people had moved out of homelessness, they expressed pride and strength, "while also describing those who remain homeless in ways that reflected the status of homelessness as a sigmatised [sic] difference . . . associated with personal failing" (761, 773). In turn, Toolis and Hammack (2015a) employed "life story interviews" in their research and also found a number of "resilience narratives" celebrating self-reliance, social networks, and street smarts (52). These studies are quite useful in understanding homelessness. However, by way of social media and memoir, people experiencing homelessness tell their own stories, in their own voices and in their own way, and often in great depth. Young people and female victims of domestic violence, in particular, may use this form of expression. Of the sixteen blogs I followed, five were written by women who had experienced violence in the home, on the streets, or both, and four were written by those who had experienced homelessness while young. Of the fifteen memoirs I analyzed, two were written by women who had experienced violence in the home, on the streets, or both, and five were written by youth who had experienced homelessness. This sampling may seem small but given limited access of people experiencing homelessness to social media and to self- or commercial publishing, given the qualitative nature of my study, and, finally, given the affirmation of many of my impressions by interdisciplinary scholarly work, I have confidence in my findings.

Finally, and somewhat unusual for the genre or affordance of social media, few readers responded to the blog entries I analyzed, perhaps again a result of less internet access for those experiencing homelessness or perhaps because of the rather exclusive use of the blog to self-affirm or self-comfort. In some cases, this lack of response frustrated the bloggers. Blogger Patrick, for example, was so disappointed that new personal connections did not materialize via his use of social media that he asked his readers whether he had been "talking to a brick wall these past 13 years" (7.22.2015). And, in other cases, the responses varied greatly. In his first blog entry "Lawrence" (B4), for example, admitted that he had been homeless for thirteen years but recently had quit smoking and could now say that he was neither "an alcoholic nor a drug addict" and so "being homeless is, for me, hardly the torment that it could be if I was a slave to street drugs." Lawrence confessed that he still earned money by "binning" (checking dumpsters for discarded food to eat and articles to sell), but he ultimately hoped that his blog would "entertain and inform" (12.2.2012). He received two comments in which the writers congratulated him for giving up smoking, and one that suggested Lawrence might suffer from ADHD given his tales about his periodic confusion. In a fourth very long comment, however, the respondent concluded that Lawrence was "the embodiment of the neoliberal citizen-entrepreneur ideal who turned his social status as a 'homeless person' into a commodity, much like a lifestyle celebrity." Lawrence's blog entries, concluded this respondent, enabled general society to feel secure in their conviction that homelessness was a choice and there was no "shame for dehumanizing people who are pushed out of society by circumstances that anyone could find themselves in." (12.2.2012). This respondent was definitely provoked by Lawrence's very personal blog entry and suggested that Lawrence had a wide readership, but no dialogue between the two followed the response, again perhaps because of the lack of resources among his readers.

Blogger Clare, however, encouraged her blog readers that social media could provide a new kind of personal and even family connection, regardless of where the person might be sheltering: "Your kids or grandkids are more 'connected' than you realize and who knows what the next generation in technology and media will bring to the human experience" (10.1.2010). For Clare, social media had the potential to build new or confirm past connections between homed and homeless family members. Those who did respond to a blog entry were often people who understood homelessness or were homeless themselves, or sometimes were those seeking to understand homelessness, perhaps a small community but a supportive or engaged one via this form of social media. In response to blogger Patrick when he wrote an entry about losing track of a friend, "Agent X" commented, "I have lost friends on the streets before. Sometimes they just go missing. . . . Sometimes they return. Sometimes we eventually learn that they have passed. All of those are sad departures." (10.22.2015). And, after Clare told of her own difficulty in getting into the shelter system with her children, one respondent shared that she too was "shocked to discover" that she would be separated from her teenage boy and he would be accommodated in an adult male shelter without her (4.24.2011). Another respondent, this one with stable housing, confessed to

Clare, "I have stereotypes. I don't like to admit it. You're [sic] honesty is helping me be honest with myself" (4.20.2011). Although the *communitas* formed by these bloggers might have been small in contrast to lifestyle or political blogs written for a greater audience, the blogging seems an effective activity for those experiencing homelessness.

PROPOSED APPROACHES OR SOLUTIONS TO HOMELESSNESS

Overall, these memoir and blog writers testified about the challenges to their sense of agency and dignity, offered advice to their readers, and confessed the trauma of and perhaps resisted the stigma of homelessness. Moreover, through social media and memoirs, people experiencing homelessness have suggested how to approach the homeless crisis and have recommended solutions to it—from rethinking the rules and regulations that govern homeless shelters to eliminating the cultural stigma attached to homelessness. Blogger George, for example, revealed that he worked in an emergency shelter on the night shift and handed out blankets and sandwiches to people who arrived after the shelter had filled. He noticed a difference when he handed out a blanket "with a smile instead of indifference":

> If I am tired and I plop the blanket in their arms, they don't seem to make much eye contact. I wouldn't either, were I receiving a blanket from someone who didn't seem to care. If, on the other hand, I express my genuine concern and say "that is the best I can do tonight" the response is one of appreciation and connection, even with those who have been judged as typically unresponsive. (3.8.2020)

This personal and sympathetic connection that George offered seemed to make a difference to those arriving too late at the shelter to get a bed—and may have countered the stigma they might frequently feel. Thus, those experiencing homelessness often propose solutions to their current state. When told about an experiment to pass out money to those living on the streets, blogger Dan commented, "Well that won't work. You've got too many of us who will just go off to find something like alcohol or whatever they want. . . . When you're homeless, it means you need a place to live. So if they can help homeless people get somewhere to live, then that could work" (5.16.2011). And, of course, housing is the ultimate practical and concrete solution to homelessness. As Sheila Crowley (2016), president and chief executive officer of the National Low Income Housing Coalition, put it, "Homelessness is not an inevitable or permanent condition of life in the United States. . . .

The primary cause of homelessness is an acute shortage of affordable and available housing for our poorest citizens. Among other challenges, ending homelessness will require a housing solution" (159). There are, however, numerous ways to identify, create, and offer that housing. In the final section of this book, I address the challenges and means of establishing such housing and then end with assessing the necessary cultural changes in our attitudes toward homelessness and the people who experience it.

Affordable and Available Housing

Economist Conor Dougherty (2020) proposed that homelessness "has nothing to do with lack of space. It's the concentration of opportunity and the rising cost of being near it . . . a dire shortage of available housing in places where people and companies want to live, along with tectonic changes in how today's technology-centric economy operates" (xii). According to Dougherty, rising housing costs, such as in spaces where people want to live and be near to their work, contribute to spatial segregation because of income inequity and generational wealth gaps. Anti-growth land-use policies and zoning laws, which dictate where industrial complexes, apartment units, and single-family houses may be built and how much space they can take up, limit such migration to be nearer to that work. In San Francisco, the city that Dougherty analyzed, the private market often dictates that the most expensive and most limited housing must be in the heart of the city where major companies reside, and there is "no way to rectify a housing shortage other than to build housing, and there's no way to take care of people whom the private market won't take care of other than subsidies or rent control, or both." Working out details about how to achieve such results "is democracy," Dougherty concluded (233).

One of those "democratic" details is the creation of affordable housing, or as Dougherty defined it: "[S]ubsidized buildings that are built with the help of the federal government and have apartments that are restricted to people who make below their area's median income," primarily homes that are "part of a government program and not the naturally cheap apartments that most people imagine them to be" (32). As blogger Patrick speculated, if "there were plenty of jobs to be had, and apartments were affordable" about half of the people experiencing homelessness "could get themselves off the streets" (9.26.2015). Often, however, we imagine such affordable housing to be those "naturally cheap" and most likely rundown apartments, as Dougherty cautioned, even places such as the Martinique Hotel in the mid-1980s in New York City.

In contrast, Douglas Massey et al. (2013) offered a study of how an affordable housing complex flourished in a suburb of New Jersey and became the genesis of the "Mount Lauren Doctrine," an "affirmative obligation" that each municipality in New Jersey would accommodate to meet its fair share of the regional need for affordable housing (1; see also *South Burlington County NAACP et al. v. Mount Laurel Township et al.* 1975). Again, one cause of homelessness is simply lack of housing, or as Massey et al. (2013) put it, when "markets do not provide housing to families at prices they can afford," a structural imposition is "foisted on individuals by a fundamental mismatch between the distribution of income and the distribution of rents" (9–10). A liberal "density zoning" policy, however, particularly in major cities and their suburbs, can decrease spatial segregation, curtail the "spatial concentration of poverty," and lower "the concentration of affluence" (19). In other words, avoiding zoning policies that limit the number of families that can reside in a community opens the door to building affordable housing in that community. Massey et al. (2013) focused their study on Ethel Lawrence Homes (ELH), a public housing project that offered affordable housing to families in the economically stable suburban township of Mount Laurel, New Jersey. In particular, this group of mainly sociologists considered the effect of the public housing project on (1) the current use value, or the more emotional connection to one's home, including fear of a rise in crime rates, as well as on (2) the exchange value of houses already in the neighborhood, including fear of a decline in property values. Put simply, Massey et al. (2013) discovered that the answer to whether either concern would be realized if ELH were to be built in the suburb of Mount Laurel was "No." One hundred percent of the units in the ELH complex were affordable, and Massey et al.'s analysis showed that not only could poor tenants be integrated into the neighborhood, "more effectively than many residents of those communities expect," but also these tenants benefited from a safe and quiet place to live with access to better schools. In fact, those benefits constituted "an important social mobility program capable of breaking the cycles of disadvantage they left being in poor neighborhoods" (99). Such affordable housing complexes could work for all involved.

Finally, Martha Burt, Laudan Aron, and Edgar Lee, with Jesse Valente (2001), writing for the Urban Institute Press, found such affordable and available housing, as provided through subsidies, tax incentives, and other mechanisms, could not only move toward ending homelessness but also far exceed the benefits of creating additional emergency shelters. Support for affordable housing might come from Section 8 subsidies, created in 1974 by the Housing and Community Development Act, a federal housing choice voucher program that required voucher holders to negotiate and compete in the private housing market. Also, support might come from public housing, which flourished mainly in the 1950s and 1960s and offered homes to mainly poor families in high-rise complexes, such as the one that unfortunately burned during the

2019 Thanksgiving week in Minneapolis. However, affordable housing complexes, such as ELH in Mount Laurel township, could thrive without spatial segregation. Any such housing choices, according to David Ellwood (1989), former dean of Harvard University's Kennedy School of Government, would be most welcomed and successful if they followed four "value tenets": "(1) the autonomy of the individual; (2) the virtue of work; (3) the primacy of family; and (4) the desire for and sense of community" (quoted in Burt et al. 2001, 324). Seldom would any of these value tenets be available in homeless shelters, a few might be available in public housing, and such subsidies as Section 8 are notoriously unavailable due to the demand. Blogger Clare, for example, told the story of her laughing "in a social worker's face when she suggested applying for Section 8 for housing help." Clare replied to the social worker, "You mean apply for a program that's closed in this state and awarded like the lottery? No thanks, I needed help yesterday, not the faint possibility at some unknown future date" (9.7.2010). If housing is the solution to homelessness, then the question remains of just how quickly people experiencing homelessness can move into stable housing in safe and desirable neighborhoods by way of efficient and effective government agency and nonprofit support—or if they need transitional services before they can do so.

Rapid Re-Housing and Housing First Programs

Victims of domestic violence and their children, according to Hilary Botein and Andrea Hetling (2016), experts in planning and public policy, need a "continuum of support," perhaps beginning with emergency shelters, continuing with trauma-informed services, and then ending with long-term housing (2; see also Boardman 2019). As Juarez noted in his memoir about homelessness, his sister "had seen our mother beaten many times and was so traumatized that the sound of a truck passing by would bring her to tears. She associated the sound with our father's truck and the violence that would occur each time he found us" (204). Thus, youth who are experiencing homelessness need ongoing support, such as psychological and trauma counseling, family counseling and reconciliation services, apprenticeship and education opportunities, and stress relief, according to Jeff Karabanow, Sean Kidd, Tyler Frederick, and Jean Hughes (2018), experts in social work, clinical psychology, and nursing. Again, the Host Homes program ConneQT provides such services in a stable and safe home. Without such help, youth are ill-prepared for what they might encounter living on the streets, in shelters, or in foster homes. As blogger Ralph described his experience with homelessness as a young person,

When I ran away from home, I knew nothing about how to make my way, home-less or sheltered. I had a few skills, but very few could easily be converted to money. I didn't know what challenges I would face, and I had no idea how much danger I was in. I was bullied in grade school, and I quit high school when I was sixteen, a year before I ran away. The alienation I'd learned from this fueled my decision to leave home, but did not teach me how to do it. (4.18.2011)

According to Ralph, teen homeless shelters resembled youth authority jails, and group homes were "miserable and dangerous."

The timing of when people experiencing homelessness can move to affordable housing is often critical. On the one hand, traditional transitional housing programs assumed that families experiencing homelessness must "demonstrate their readiness for permanent housing by meeting certain conditions," such as completing therapy, determining a path to employment and perhaps additional education, and even achieving sobriety. On the other hand, rapid-rehousing or Housing First programs are based on the supposition that families should receive permanent housing as soon as possible and then "address other needs when their housing situations are stable" (Botein and Hetling 2016, 56). According to the Housing First website (2021), the pro-gram is a "rights-based intervention rooted in the philosophy that all people deserve housing, and that adequate housing is a *precondition* for recovery" (emphasis in original). This approach assumes that once individuals and families are in safe and affordable housing, they can better "address their health and social service needs" and "decrease their reliance on government services," according to Botein and Hetling (85). Such programs, for example, move victims of domestic violence directly into alternative housing situations where they and their families can stay as long as they need in order to become stable and feel safe.

Therefore, for victims of domestic violence and youth experiencing home-lessness, the two groups I explored in depth in chapter three, as well as for a wide range of people living without stable and safe shelter, the Housing First program serves as a model for how we can better address homeless-ness. In fact, several nonprofit organizations and governmental agencies promote Housing First by name or rapid re-housing in principle. The US Interagency Council on Homelessness (2021), for example, recommended Housing First programs because they recognized that people experiencing homelessness, like all people, "need the safety and stability of a home in order to best address challenges and pursue opportunities." Moreover, the National Alliance to End Homelessness (2020c) stated, "Rapid re-housing is a primary solution for ending homelessness." The rapid re-housing pro-gram, concluded the National Alliance, has also been "effective for people traditionally perceived to be more difficult to serve, including people with limited or no income and survivors of domestic violence." Finally, such Housing First and rapid-re-housing programs across the United States and around the world have been increasingly identified as an effective solution to ending homelessness. The coalition for the Homeless in New York City (2021) identified Housing First as "another proven solution" particularly to street homelessness, moving people directly into subsidized housing and then linking them to support services. The Coalition also found the "majority of long-term street homeless people [who were] moved into 'housing first' apartments remain stably housed and experience significant improvement in their health problems." Additionally, the Housing First approach costs less to house people experiencing homelessness than do shelters, hospitals, and correctional facilities.

And so, Scott Carrier (2015), writing for *Mother Jones*, identified rapid re-housing programs as a "shockingly simple, surprisingly cost-effective way to end homelessness" (see also Semuels 2016). By focusing on such a program in Utah, which was supported by the LDS Church Welfare Department, Carrier proposed that any place could address homelessness more successfully by offering rapid re-housing. Carrier also quoted for his readers the conclusions of Sam Tsemberis and his associates, who developed and modeled such a program in New York City:

> Ironically, ending homelessness is actually cheaper than continuing to treat the problem. This would not only benefit the people who are homeless; it would be healing for the rest of us to live in a more compassionate and just nation. It's not a matter of whether we know how to fix the problem. Homelessness is not a disease like cancer or Alzheimer's where we don't yet have a cure. We have the cure for homelessness—it's housing. What we lack is political will.

These rapid re-housing and Housing First programs have proven successful outside of the United States. Alex Gray (2018), for example, analyzed for the *World Economic Forum* how Finland "solved its homeless problem." Using the Housing First program, Finland increased the supply of affordable rental housing by buying flats from the private market and by building new housing blocks. As a result of these efforts, "There are no more homeless shelters in Finland. They have all been turned into supported housing." In the words of one person who benefited from this Housing First program, "Homelessness also means daily alcohol use. It was not so much about getting drunk, but a way to pass the time. When I've had an apartment, I've spent several months without drinking. You can't get sober when you're homeless, no one can" (quoted in Gray 2018). The program, much as with ELH in New Jersey, builds connections with the local community through open house events and interaction with neighbors, such as mutual efforts to maintain green spaces and pick up litter in the neighborhood. Gray found that after about two years, both the neighborhood and the supported housing residents were accustomed and adjusted to each other.

Creative Measures to Address Homelessness

Finally, if affordable and permanent housing is not immediately available, creative measures have been initiated in the meantime. One such measure to address homelessness in the short term involves building tiny house villages, in cities such as Dallas, Texas; Detroit, Michigan; and Portland, Oregon, and as described by correspondent Jenny Xie for *New Frontier Design* (2017; see also Lee 2021). Xie explored ten such villages across the United States, and she found that Othello Village, in Seattle, Washington, provided twenty-eight tiny houses, each measuring ninety-six square feet, along with twelve tents on platforms, for up to one hundred people experiencing homelessness. The village residents shared a kitchen, shower trailer, donation hut, and security booth, and they benefit from water and garbage services, heat and electricity, and on-site counseling. The City of Seattle, in coordination with the Low Income Housing Institute, intended to build two more tiny house villages that would each serve up to seventy people.

Similarly, a group of tiny houses was set up as a "model community" at Woodland Hills Church in Maplewood, an eastern suburb of St. Paul, Minnesota, in January 2021. In expectation of living in one of the tiny houses, Paul Bloedorn stated, "One of the most important things we can give our family and our children is perspective, a different perspective, a different view of the world. This gives us a chance to see life from a different side" (quoted in Warren 2021). About the same time, the Minneapolis nonprofit Avivo, in partnership with the White Earth Nation, announced its intention to open a twenty-four-hour indoor village of tiny houses in an empty book-publishing warehouse. The seventy-square-foot rooms would offer adults living on the streets the alternative of a bed, closet, and some small furnishings, and were intended to provide a COVID-safe and secure place for up to one hundred residents. The residents would share showers and bathrooms, and meals would be provided along with common space for meditation, movies, and meetings. The facility would also provide security and be pet friendly. Fourteen of the first sixteen clients who moved into the Avivo Village were Natives, and the walls of the warehouse were painted in the four colors that represented the Native medicine wheel. As David Hewitt, director of Hennepin County's Office to End Homelessness, concluded, "Shelters need to play that critical role of being a place that people can stay safely and feel supported, but supported to get out into housing. Housing is what ends homelessness, not shelters" (quoted in Smith 2021b). Tiny houses, in essence, meet some of the requirements of a "home," a safe and secure space that has the potential to provide companionship and community.

Another creative measure to address homelessness emerged both in Portland, Oregon, and in Ulm, Germany, in reaction to the coronavirus pandemic and harsh winter weather. In December 2020, Portland offered people experiencing homelessness small white "pods" with enough electricity, heat, and room for two people. The pods, resembling garden sheds, appeared in three ad-hoc "villages," according to Associated Press correspondents Gillian Flaccus and Michael Hill (2020), and one pod resident proclaimed, "We just get to stay in our little place. We don't have to leave here unless we want to." Also, in January 2021, the City of Ulm set up "nests" on the streets for the second year to prevent people experiencing homelessness from dying from hypothermia. The nests were meant to address emergency housing situations, such as when homeless shelters were full or other forms of permanent housing were not available. Sophisticated technology regulated the temperatures inside the nests, and often upon seeing someone had used a nest for the night, neighbors would "offer a cup of hot tea in the morning" (Gatollari 2021). These creative solutions to address homelessness, along with rapid re-housing and Housing First programs, provide alternatives to homeless shelters, often avoided and resented by people experiencing homelessness. These alternatives offer a sense of agency, freedom, and dignity to their residents. For more permanent change, however, we need to address the cultural norms—the stigmatization and resulting spatial segregation—that often negatively influence our approach to homelessness.

CULTURAL CHANGE

Burnes (2016) suggested that to effectively address homelessness, policy makers and service providers must "ask persons experiencing homelessness to sit on boards and advisory groups, and some of us even pay attention to the comments and suggestions from those directly affected" (286). In other words, we must listen to the voices of those experiencing homelessness and value their "lived experience." Moreover, we must ask why we tolerate homelessness and admit that, as historian David DiLeo (2016) suggested, at "some cellular level, too many of us still believe that people experiencing homelessness are living in a way that corresponds to their value as human beings" (142). Our first instincts are to believe that they are lesser, that they are responsible for their situation, and that we would never find ourselves in that position. As DiLeo concluded, we must deconstruct and examine "[p]owerful dogmas like free will, free enterprise, and rugged individualism" as well as our mistaken "belief in the self-made man" (143). Otherwise, if we are lucky enough to be housed in a safe and secure home, we may tend to accept the spatial segregation of those experiencing homelessness and thus spatially segregate them as the other—dangerous and self-destructive. Therefore, the first step to such a reckoning is to, according to DiLeo, "acknowledge that homelessness is not a failure of character, but the failure of an otherwise dynamic system to provide enough gainful employment for people who can work and sufficient services for those who cannot" (154). And again, the first step is to house all who want to and need to be housed in spaces that they can call "home."

Moreover, remedial measures are necessary to remind us of how our history and culture have contributed to homelessness. A program in Minneapolis, for example, gives homeowners the opportunity to disavow the racial covenants they might find in their deeds, "to reclaim their homes as equitable spaces" and to raise awareness of these past discriminatory housing practices (Navratil 2021). A recent effort returned 114 acres to the Lower Sioux Native community, land along the Minnesota River bluffs. In response, Lower Sioux President Robert Larsen said, "Our ancestors paid for this land over and over with their blood, with their lives. It's not a sale; it's been paid for by the ones that aren't there anymore. . . . This isn't the end. We hope this is just a kick-start to showing people that it can be done" (quoted in Smith 2021a). Finally, personal encounters with individuals experiencing homelessness have the potential to raise our consciousness and to advocate for change. Judith Koll Healey (2020), in a letter to the editor of the Minneapolis *Star Tribune*, for example, described her walk about the north end of Lake of the Isles in south Minneapolis when she encountered a new homeless tent encampment. She asked herself: "How would it grow?" "What would it mean for the neighborhood?" "Who was living in these tents?" Later, a conversation with one woman seated in an open tent revealed to Healey, "Nothing I had assumed was actually the case." Those living in the encampment went to work, and all were waiting for affordable housing. Drugs and alcohol were not allowed in the encampment because of the problems realized in the Powderhorn Park encampment. And so, Healey concluded that "both those who used the tents and those who were helping them formed a community of need. And far from a blight on the neighborhood, those loose-knit, unofficial social organizations could teach us all something about life." Healey listened to the voices of people experiencing homelessness and learned from them.

Such are the small but necessary steps toward cultural change in terms of how we approach homelessness. And so, it seems appropriate to end this book with blogger Ralph's words, which should inspire us all to change our perception and understanding of homelessness: "There is nothing so bad that it will not pass. If there is one thing the world teaches, it is that all things change. If you cannot think of what to do, if you believe that all hope is gone, if you are tired of trying, then pause. Breathe deeply. . . . Abandon anger, desperation, depression, melancholy. Embrace confidence, strength, abilities, resources. Be positive, by all means" (10.26.2004).

Appendix A

Online Blogs and Video Interview Citations

With the exception of Camille Gage, from whom I have permission to use her name, I have listed the online blogs fully and alphabetically by blogger name to acknowledge copyright, but to preserve any privacy concerns, I have assigned randomly each blog a number (e.g., B2, B3, B4) and a pseudonym. When appropriate, I have given a brief description or history of the blogger. Also, I have avoided editing blog entries unless to correct for possible mis-understandings, and so in some cases I confirm a word or sentence by adding [sic]. These sources appear below, rather than in the References section, with the exception of the published blog by Dick Murphy-Scott. All published memoirs are listed in References section.

Anonymous 45. A contributor to "Living Homeless: Our Write to Speak." https://www.homelesshub.ca.

Barber, Tim. "Living Homeless: Our Write to Speak." https://www.homelesshub.ca.

Barbieux, Kevin. "The Homeless Guy." https://thehomelessguy.wordpress.com/author/thehomelessguy/.

Book, Derek M. "Formerly Homeless: A Journal of Lived Experience." http://housecanada.blogspot.com/2017/09/.

Clemens, Tony, with Phillip Stern. "Homeless Man Speaks." https://homelessmanspeaks.com.

Gage, Camille. "The Wall of Forgotten Natives: Blog." https://www.franklinhiawathacamp.org/#camp-blog.

Gage, Camille. "WiiDooKoDaaDiiWag: They Help Each Other." https://www.theyhelpeachother.org.

Gish. "Gish's Journal." http://www.homeless.org.au/gish/.

Invisibull. "Invisibull's Blog." https://invisibull.wordpress.com.

MeParallel. "Me Parallel: A True Story." https://www.meparallel.com.

Mobile Homemaker. "Survival Guide to Homelessness." http://guide2homelessness. blogspot.com/.

"['Name Redacted']: A Story on Surviving Domestic Violence." http:// nameredactedblog.wordpress.com.

Radar, Ruthie. "Ruthie in the Sky." http://ruthiessky.blogspot.com/.

Rhodes, Janet. "Freedom Within: My Journey Through Domestic Violence & PTSD." https://freedomwithinsite.wordpress.com.

Woodvine, Stanley Q. "Sqwabb." https://sqwabb.wordpress.com/about/.

Also, throughout this book, I have cited the video interviews by the short titles indicated in square brackets following each entry. These citations are below, rather than in the References section.

"Alayna's Story," YouTube video 5:30, posted by Union Rescue Mission, November 8, 2016. https://www.youtube.com/watch?v=CqwjaExT4wA. ["Alayna"]

"Escaping Homelessness," YouTube video 3:28, posted by AJ+, March 3, 2016 https://www.youtube.com/watch?v=d5vmzW_m-6w. ["Escaping"]

"Getting Deep with a Young Homeless Man," YouTube video 1:20, by The Periphery, March 27, 2019. https://www.youtube.com/watch?v=NpEJvhW_Yao. ["Getting Deep"]

"Homeless," YouTube video 5:20, posted by hkzproductions, September 12, 2010. https://www.youtube.com/watch?v=zWd1QN4cnNo. ["Homeless"]

"Homeless Alcoholic—Wolf," YouTube video 2:05, posted by Briandofilm, April 14, 2012. https://www.youtube.com/watch?v=BAFp5wdsMnI. ["Homeless Alcoholic—Wolf"]

"Homeless Interview: Homeless Man Explains to Us Why/How He Became Homeless," YouTube video 4:08, posted by Maketreks, Toronto, July 22, 2011. https://www.youtube.com/watch?v=O5LZPuREnyg. ["Homeless Interview"]

"Homeless Man Tells His Story While Getting Haircut," YouTube video 3:07, posted by Street Cuts, February 24, 2015. https://www.youtube.com/watch?v=jM-h10UmP7w. ["Homeless Man Tells His Story"]

"Homeless Teenagers Living on LA's Skid Row," YouTube video 5:07, posted by Union Rescue Mission, May 26, 2011. https://www.youtube.com/watch?v=2rUpe-bjtl4. ["Homeless Teenagers"]

"Homeless Woman Sleeping Rough In London After Domestic Violence," YouTube video 10:14, posted by Invisible People, October 26, 2019. https://www.youtube.com/watch?v=luK55xEiCrQ. ["Homeless Woman Sleeping Rough"]

"#Homeless Interview #Denver," YouTube video 2:18, posted by Inquisitive303, June 29, 2013. https://www.youtube.com/watch?v=wGinwaF5lxE. ["#Denver"]

"Indigenous Homeless Woman Cries for Her People to Have a Home," YouTube video 4:48, posted by Invisible People, August 6, 2011. https://www.youtube.com/watch?v=0cTJeIuPeu0. ["Indigenous Homeless Woman"]

"Interviewing the Homeless of Detroit: Episode 2 William," YouTube video 10:15, posted by Invisible People, November 1, 2016. https://www.youtube.com/watch?v=SRs02YefT4M. ["Homeless of Detroit"]

"Interviews: Homelessness During COVID-19," YouTube video 3:47, posted by Redfish, March 20, 2020. https://www.youtube.com/watch?v=VB164EYhoYI. ["COVID-19"]

"Invisible: A Portrait of Bristol's Homeless," YouTube video 7:54, documentary by Arthur Cauty, June 7, 2018. https://www.youtube.com/watch?v=WoAzzghXtEw. ["Invisible"]

"Los Angeles Homeless Man Works Full Time and Sleeps in Venice Beach," YouTube video 20:52, posted by Invisible People, January 14, 2019. https://www.youtube.com/watch?v=k7s7k6gxGD0. ["Los Angeles Homeless Man"]

"Lovely Is Homeless for Reasons You Won't Expect," YouTube video 1:20, posted by Downtown Streets Team, February 2, 2015. Downtown Streets Team, San Rafael, CA. https://www.youtube.com/watch?v=s5gKPPHDUAI. ["Lovely"]

"Native Americans—Homeless in Their Homeland." YouTube video 45:35, posted by IndianCountryTV.com, April 2, 2012. https://www.youtube.com/watch?v=4dvbQVLv5KY. ["Native Americans"]

"Natives Against Heroin." Video 6:08, posted by Brandon Ferdig on The Periphery, November 10, 2019. https://www.facebook.com/theperipherydotcom/videos/472270720361774. ["Natives Against Heroin"]

"Native Americans Tent City's Minneapolis." YouTube video 5:56, posted on by Dahir Shali, September 26, 2018. https://www.youtube.com/watch?v=wM4c1F2FQT8. ["Native Americans Tent City's Minneapolis"]

"The Group Leading the Way at the Native American Homeless Camp in Minnesota," YouTube video 6:08, posted by Natives Against Heroin vs. Homeless and Addiction, November 10, 2019. https://www.youtube.com/watch?v=kKTA4S7aVlM. ["The Group Leading the Way"]

"Stories from the Wall," YouTube video 20:58, posted by Minnesota Indian Women's Resource Center, September 20, 2018. https://www.youtube.com/watch?v=jP3i1dQsq30. ["Stories from the Wall"]

"Young Homeless Girl Lived in 57 Different Foster Home Placements," YouTube video 4:34, posted by Invisible People, September 8, 2013. https://www.youtube.com/watch?v=SWcxaoEDG1E. ["Young Homeless Girl"]

"Young Homeless Girl Was Hit by a Train and Died Shortly After This Interview," YouTube video 6:16, posted by Invisible People, September 12, 2011. https://www.youtube.com/watch?v=v1sT44x4BXw. ["Hit by Train"]

"Winter Warriors: Native American Homeless Camp in Minneapolis," YouTube video 24:10, posted by Freedom Radio and TV, December 11, 2018. https://www.youtube.com/watch?v=_jFhwpBUPlI. ["Winter Warriors"]

Appendix B

Fair Use and Privacy Concerns Regarding Social Media—Personal Positioning

Blogs as well as video interviews on YouTube and other platforms exist in the public arena even though their creators may tell their own personal stories and convey the stories of others. Authors of those blogs that have been published as books obviously retain copyright, just as do any published memoir writers. However, I have followed the statutory guidelines of fair use in quoting from all sources throughout this book, and I have respected the privacy of bloggers while giving them credit for their work.

Fair use guidelines have been spelled out in such court opinions as *Campbell v. Acuff-Rose* (1994) and involve consideration, as a whole, of the following aspects: (1) purpose or character of the use; (2) nature of the original work; (3) amount and substantiality of the portion used; and (4) effect on the potential market for or value of the source work. These factors favor my fair use of blogs and video interviews as well as memoirs—in particular, because of the scholarly and research purpose of this book; my use of factual sources; my quoting of proportionally small excerpts; and the lack of negative impact on the market for original work (see also 17 US Code §107). In fact, I hope that my use of blogs will increase their readership and that my reference to memoirs will increase the profits authors make on these publications, many of which are self-published. Finally, these sources are certainly valuable to our understanding of homelessness.

At the same time, the bloggers as well as video interviewees might be concerned with privacy, given that they often share with their readers and viewers personal information, such as addiction problems and the trauma of sexual assault. However, as early as 1940, the Circuit Court of Appeals in the Second District noted in *Sidis v. F-R Publishing Corporation* that, according to the often quoted Warren and Brandeis (1890) article on the right to privacy, "the interest of the individual in privacy must inevitably conflict with the interest of the public in news." The *Sidis* court concluded that if individuals were newsworthy, their private stories were not barred from publication. Certainly, there is great public interest in the homeless crisis and in the stories of individuals and groups who are struggling with homelessness—indeed such interest and stories may add to public concern and action. Moreover, the courts created a standard by which to weigh whether privacy rights are violated: "the reasonable expectation of privacy" (see, for example, *Katz v. United States* 1967; *Kyllo v. US* 2001; Smith *v. Maryland* 1979; *US v. Jones* 2012). The participants in video interviews and the bloggers upon which I rely do not technically have a legal and reasonable expectation of privacy as defined by these court opinions. They might, however, have a personal and reasonable expectation of privacy—therefore, as a researcher, I protect as much as possible those expectations. (See again Appendix A for my citation style.) Indeed, various scholars have weighed in on this compromise and have recommended privacy accommodations when using social media sources, such as anonymizing and reidentifying, seeking informed consent, protecting vulnerable populations, and developing precautionary design stances.

According to researcher Linda Eastham (2011), blogs are "simultaneously private and yet quite public"; however, the "ability of anyone to retrieve the blog monologue/dialogue contributes to its public nature" (353, 355). And so, researchers can discern to what extent bloggers mean their blogs to be private by "knowing why bloggers blog,"—for example, the choices bloggers might make in setting up their blogs and their "perceptions of the privacy of their work" (355). Any blogger requiring the use of a password, restricting reader responses and comments, and hiding the blog from access by public search engines, for example, usually indicates that he or she wants to reserve privacy. In my research for this book, the blogs were all identified by a simple Google search, mentioned in the scholarship I read, recommended by the organizations that address homelessness and maintain blogs or websites, and/ or did not require a password—all indications that the blogger was not concerned with privacy. But again, I chose to anonymize the blogs even though some reidentification is possible through an internet search of the blog quotes I include. I did begin my research by asking bloggers for informed consent, knowing that several had stopped blogging, were unavailable for correspondence, or had passed away, but only one replied. Camille Gage, the author of the blog for the "Wall of Forgotten Natives" encampment, responded (positively) to me, and therefore I credited her with all her writings as well as my personal interview and correspondence with her.

In fact, rather than restricting reader responses and personal identification, the bloggers whom I studied often solicited them. Blogger "James" (B1), for example, shared the following with his readers:

> What I would like to know is, what do you want me to write about. Would you like to hear about a certain shelter, more about my life, where to go for resources and basically anything you think I might be able to tell you about. If it is something I cannot answer, I will be honest and tell you I cant [sic] answer. However, I would still like to get your comments and ideas on how I can make this a better blog. (6.22.2011)

Also, my own Institutional Review Board (IRB) simply looked at the project and determined that additional oversight was not needed (Study 00008526). I acknowledged to the IRB that this study might involve vulnerable populations, but I followed the guidance of Emma Rose (2016) and others in designing research projects that include advocacy for vulnerable populations, including people experiencing homelessness (see also Caruso and Frankel 2010; Grabill 2009; Margolin and Margolin 2002; Rose and Walton 2015). I hope that, by sharing the voices of those experiencing homelessness, I might benefit them in some way. Certainly, as Jill Woelfer and David Hendry (2011) caution, I wish to cause no harm.

I also want to share my personal positioning in conducting this analysis. As a white, middle-class, older academic, I recognize my privilege of being educated and employed for most of my life, even though my parents struggled economically at times. I was on the verge of poverty myself in the late 1960s, as I worked in a low-paying editorial job in New York City, and in the early 1970s as I took on both teaching and free-lance editorial work to supplement a fellowship in order to sustain myself through graduate school. My previous personal encounters with people experiencing homelessness, however, reveal how limited my own thinking was prior to beginning this research, as I make clear in the three experiences described below.

First, a few years ago, while waiting in line for the man in front of me to order his coffee at a bookstore café, I overheard him argue with the barista that surely his cup of coins should cover the cost. While he was falling short on nickels, dimes, and quarters, I offered to buy his coffee. In turn, he fist-bumped me, then shook my hand, and finally wanted and received a hug. I suspect that he often felt the stigma of not only being short of money but also being potentially rejected because of his appearance. In this case, I was pleased with what I did, but later realized my actions were just stop-gap measures for the moment. Second, my resolve was later tested and compromised when I noticed a man, most likely experiencing homelessness, sleeping in a study area on campus with what seemed all his possessions. My first thought was that I should report his presence, given the campus rules against this activity, but then I just left him alone as the students were doing. Then, I wished that I should have left a $20 bill on top of his pack, but I was already in the elevator going up to my office when I realized that my impulse was again to use money to address the issue of homelessness.

Finally, in my ongoing volunteer work for two nonprofit organizations, I have become more aware, as both an advocate and activist, of how domestic abuse and sexual violence may lead to homelessness for individuals and their families. Beginning in early 2000, I began serving as a volunteer courtroom observer for WATCH (We Are at the Courthouse), a court monitoring and judicial policy nonprofit now affiliated with The Advocates for Human Rights (https://www.theadvocatesforhumanrights.org). I was a principal investigator and research participant for WATCH's 2004 Order for Protection Report, their 2004–2006 Victim Impact Statement Study, and their 2009–2010 Guardian ad Litem Study. The three studies entailed my attending hearings and trials as well as interviewing judges, attorneys, and advocates. Most important was my personal education on how women experiencing domestic violence sought help from the legal system to find a safe and secure place to live.

Beginning in 2017, I served as a volunteer for Tubman Family Crisis and Support Services (https://www.tubman.org), an organization that helps people of all ages, sexes, gender identities, and racial and ethnic backgrounds who have experienced relationship violence, elder abuse, addiction, sexual exploitation, and other forms of trauma. As a Legal Counseling Advocate (LCA), I assist clients and attorneys at legal advice clinics that focus on safety, divorce, child custody, housing, services, and other family law issues. I help clients prioritize their legal issues before they meet with an attorney, and I provide appropriate information, referrals, emotional support, and supportive counseling before they leave the clinic. I often speak with victims of domestic violence who fear homelessness if they leave their abusers. My first instinct is to help them reach safety, but often they remind me of their psychological, emotional, financial, and legal costs if they and their children leave their home or claim their right to live in that home. They might have to start over in an uncertain future, despite all the resources that organizations such as Tubman provide. Finally, I cannot force any decision upon them but instead support their personal agency.

My LCA experience is enhanced by ongoing Tubman training and professional development, including the 2019 lecture "Read Your Deed: Housing Inequality in the Twin Cities" and the documentary *Jim Crow of the North*, cosponsored by HAVEN (Housing and Volunteer Engagement Network), People Services, Simpson Housing Services, and Union Gospel Mission Twin Cities. Attending that lecture was the first time I had ever been in a large emergency houseless shelter, let alone one that exclusively serviced men experiencing homelessness. The walls of the room where the lecture was held were lined with cots stacked one on top of each other to accommodate the up to fifty-two residents who took shelter there each night. My visit to Union Gospel Mission contrasted to and yet contextualized my tour of the Minneapolis location of Avenues for Youth, where twenty-one youth can find emergency or transitional housing in double or single rooms, are provided with crisis and basic needs, and are given support that ranges "from cooking meals together, playing games and watching movies in the evening, and having tough conversations in the middle of the night," according to the Avenues for Youth website (https://avenuesforyouth.org).

I realize that my own personal experiences with homelessness are limited although they have certainly been enhanced by my volunteer experience and my observations of where adults and youth experiencing homelessness may take shelter. Therefore, in doing this project, I was careful to listen to the voices of those experiencing homelessness and to learn from those voices, whether those voices came in the form of blogs, video interviews and narratives, or memoirs.

References

17 US Code §107. 2020. "Limitations on Exclusive Rights: Fair Use." Legal Information Institute. https://www.law.cornell.edu/uscode/text/17/107.

Ackerman, Alissa, and Meghan Sacks. 2018. "Disproportionate Minority Presence on U.S. Sex Offender Registries." *Justice Policy Journal* 16: 1–20.

Addiction Center. 2020. "The Connection Between Homelessness and Addiction." https://www.addictioncenter.com/addiction/homelessness/.

Adler, Erin. 2018. "West St. Paul Votes To Loosen Rules on Where Sex Offenders Can Live." *Star Tribune*, March 12, 2018. https://www.startribune.com/west-st-paul-votes-to-loosen-rules-on-where-sex-offenders-can-live/476619363/.

Adler, Erin, and Chris Serres. 2018. "Homeless Camp Residents, American Indian Leaders Discuss Tensions, Plans to Move This Week." *Star Tribune*, December 10, 2018. http://www.startribune.com/homeless-camp-residents-american-indian-leaders-discuss-tensions-plans-to-move-this-week/502308991/.

Administration for Children & Families. US Department of Health and Human Services. 2016. "Domestic Violence and Homelessness: Statistics (2016)." https://www.acf.hhs.gov/fysb/resource/dv-homelessness-stats-2016.

Ahmed, Sara. 2000. *Strange Encounters: Embodied Others in the Post-Coloniality*. London: Routledge.

American Bar Association Commission on Domestic Violence. 2018. "Domestic Violence Arrest Policies by State." https://leg.mt.gov/content/Committees/Interim/2017-2018/Law-and-Justice/Meetings/July-2018/Exhibits/LJIC-July16-2018-Ex30.pdf.

Amster, Randall. 2008. *Lost in Space: The Criminalization, Globalization, and Urban Ecology of Homelessness*. New York: LFB Scholarly Publishing.

Anthony, Kenisha A. 2020. *Labeled: A Ward of the State, a Memoir*. Self-published.

Anton, Corey, and Valerie V. Peterson. 2003. "Who Said What: Subject Positions, Rhetorical Strategies, and Good Faith." *Communication Studies* 54: 403–19.

Arduser, Lora. 2013. "The Care and Feeding of the D-Beast: Metaphors of Lived Experience of Diabetes." In *Rhetorical Accessability* [sic]: *At the Intersection* of *Technical Communication and Disability Studies*, edited by Lisa Melonçon, 95-114. New York: Routledge.

Aristotle. 1999. *Nicomachean Ethics*. Trans. Terence Irwin. Indianapolis, IN: Hackett Publishing.

Aristotle. 1991. *On Rhetoric: A Theory of Civil Discourse*. Trans. George A. Kennedy. New York: Oxford University Press.

"As a Hotel Is Emptied, the Poor Move Out." 1988. *New York Times*, December 27, 1988. https://www.nytimes.com/1988/12/27/nyregion/as-a-hotel-is-emptied-the-poor-move-on.html.

Associated Press. 2018. "In Minneapolis, Leaders Grapple with Sudden Homeless Camp." NBC News, September 27. https://www.nbcnews.com/news/us-news/minneapolis-leaders-grapple-sudden-homeless-camp-n913641.

Auerswald, Colette L., and Stephen L. Eyre. 2002. "Youth Homelessness in San Francisco: A Life Cycle Approach." *Journal of Social Science & Medicine* 54: 1497–512.

Aune, James Arnt. 1983. "Burke's Late Blooming: Trope, Defense, and Rhetoric." *Quarterly Journal of Speech* 69: 328–53.

Avivo. 2021. https://www.avivomn.org/about/.

Ayesh, Rashaan. 2020. "Domestic Violence Pushes Many Women to Homelessness." *AXIOS*, February 5. https://www.axios.com/homeless-women-domestic-violence-02646cf1-fa84-4ad9-8fcf-104e260bfa73.html?utm_source=twitter&utm_medium=social&utm_campaign=organic&utm_content=1100&fbclid=IwAR32TOYbsvMQ3Jjd2PGeh1DUBSmdVuK74VGAow4dfulJcqU6kIB7-cQBBtU.

Baake, Ken. 2003. *Metaphor and Knowledge: The Challenges of Writing Science*. Albany: State University of New York Press.

Bachelard, Gaston. 1992. *The Poetics of Space*. Trans. Maria Jolas. Boston: Beacon Press.

Baker, Charlene K., Kris A. Billhardt, Joseph Warren, Chiquita Rollins, and Nancy E. Glass. 2010. "Domestic Violence, Housing Instability, and Homelessness: A Review of Housing Policies and Program Practices for Meeting the Needs of Survivors." *Aggression and Violent Behavior* 15: 430–39.

Baldwin, James. 1956. *Giovanni's Room.* New York: Dell Publishing.

Bardanel, Josh. 1987. "Dinkins Proposes Repairing 40,000 Units for the Homeless." *New York Times*, March 25, 1987. https://www.nytimes.com/1987/03/25/nyregion/dinkins-proposes-repairing-40000-units-for-the-homeless.html.

Basnet, Minu. 2012. "Move, Get Out the Way." In *Women of Color and Social Media Multitasking*, edited by Keisha Edwards Tassie and Sonja M. Brown Givens, 113–30. Lanham, MD: Lexington Books.

Bassuk, Ellen L., Camela J. DeCandia, Corey Anne Beach, and Fred Berman. 2014. *America's Youngest Outcasts: A Report Card on Child Homelessness.* American Institutes for Research, The National Center on Family Homelessness, November 2014. https://www.air.org/sites/default/files/downloads/report/Americas-Youngest-Outcasts-Child-Homelessness-Nov2014.pdf.

Bell, Susan Groag, and Karen M. Offen. 1983. *Women, the Family, and Freedom: The Debate in Documents*. Stanford: Stanford University Press.

Benson, Paul. 1990. "Feminist Second Thoughts about Free Agency." *Hypatia* 5: 47–64.

Benson, T. B. 1915. "Segregation Ordinances." *The Virginia Law Review* 1: 330–56.

Berg, Ryan. 2015. *No House to Call My Home: Love, Family, and Other Transgressions*. New York: Bold Type Books.

Berg, Ryan. 2021. Personal Interview, January 5, 2021.

Berry v. Hennepin County, Case No. 20-cv-2189, US District Court, MN, October 29, 2020.

Blackstone, Sir William. 1765-1770. *Commentaries on the Laws of England*. Oxford: Clarendon Press.

Blair, Carole. 1999. "Contemporary U. S. Memorial Sites as Exemplars of Rhetoric's Materiality." In *Rhetorical Bodies*, edited by Jack Selzer and Sharon Crowley, 16–57. Madison: University of Wisconsin Press.

Bless, Jennifer. 2017. "Homelessness in Indian County Is a Hidden, but Critical, Problem." Urban Institute. https://www.urban.org/urban-wire/homelessness-indian-country-hidden-critical-problem.

Blood, Rebecca. 2000. "Weblogs: A History and Perspective." *Rebecca's Pocket. Perseus Publishing*, September 7, 2000. http://www.rebeccablood.net/essays/weblog_history.html.

Blood, Rebecca. 2002. *The Weblog Handbook*. New York: De Capo.

Boardman, Justin. 2019. "Trauma-Informed Training & Consulting." https://justin-boardman.com.

Bockting, Walter O., Michael H. Miner, Rebecca E. Swinburne Romine, Curtis Dolezal, Beatrice E. Robinson, Simon Rosser, and Eli Coleman. 2020. "The Transgender Identity Survey: A Measure of Internalized Transphobia." *LGBT Health* 7: 15–27.

Bockting, Walter O., Michael H. Miner, Rebecca E. Swinburne Romine, Autumn Hamilton, and Eli Coleman. 2013. "Stigma, Mental Health, and Resilience in an Online Sample of the US Transgender Population." *American Journal of Public Health* 103: 943–51.

Boskey, Elizabeth. 2021. "Understanding the Stigma Faced by Transgender Women." *Very Well Mind*. https://www.verywellmind.com/understanding-stigma-transgender-people-face-4120056.

Botein, Hilary, and Andrea Hetling. 2016. *Home Safe Home: Housing Solutions for Survivors of Intimate Partner Violence*. New Brunswick, NJ: Rutgers University Press.

Braylock, Breland, and Matthews v. the City of Dayton. 2018. District Court, Fourth Judicial District, Court File No. 27-Cv-18–199.

Brice-Sandler, Michael. 2019. "New York Is Shipping Its Homeless to Squalid Housing Out of State." *Washington Post*, December 3, 2019. https://www.washingtonpost.com/dc-md-va/2019/12/03/new-york-is-shipping-its-homeless-squalid-housing-out-state-newark-lawsuit-claims/.

Bridgett, Alayna. 2020. "Mandatory-Arrest Laws Hurt Survivors of Domestic Violence Rather Than Help Them." *Health Matrix: The Journal of Law-Medicine* 30: 438–73.

Britt, Elizabeth C. 2018. *Reimagining Advocacy: Rhetorical Education in the Legal Clinic*. University Park: The Pennsylvania State University Press.

Bronstein, Jenny. 2013. "Personal Blogs as Online Presences on the Internet: Exploring Self-Presentation and Self-Disclosure in Blogging." *Aslib Proceedings: New Information Perspectives* 65: 161–81.

"Brooklyn Welfare Hotel Fire Kills Family's Four Children." 1986. *New York Times*, July 12, 1986. https://www.nytimes.com/1986/07/12/nyregion/brooklyn-welfare-hotel-fire-kills-family-s-four-children.html.

Brown, Phil, Stephen Zavestoski, Sabrina McCormick, Brian Mayer, Rachel Morello-Forsch, and Rebecca Gasior Altman. 2004. "Embodied Health Movements: New Approaches to Social Movements in Health." *Sociology of Health & Illness* 26: 50–80.

Bryan v. Itasca County, Minnesota, 426 U.S. 373 (1976).

Byers, Kyle. 2019. "How Many Blogs Are There? (And 141 Other Blogging Stats)." *GrowthBadge*, January 2, 2019. https://growthbadger.com/blog-stats/.

Buchanan v. Warley, 245 U.S. 60 (1917).

Buck v. Bell, 272 U.S. 200 (1927).

Buel, Sarah M. 1999. "Fifty Obstacles to Leaving, a.k.a, Why Abuse Victims Stay." *The Colorado Lawyer* 28: 10–19.

Buchta, Jim, and Mary Jo Webster. 2021. "Racial Homeownership Gap in the Twin Cities Highest in the Nation." *Star Tribune*, June 27, 2021. https://www.startribune.com/racial-homeownership-gap-in-the-twin-cities-highest-in-the-nation/600072649/?utm_source=newsletter&utm_medium=email&utm_campaign=amnews.

Bureau of Indian Affairs. 2016. "American Indian Urban Relocation." Record Group 75. Chicago Field office Employment Assistance Case Files, 1952-1960. https://www.archives.gov/education/lessons/indian-relocation.html#page-header.

Burks, Megan. 2019. "Homeless Advocates Count 723 on Minneapolis Streets Since Encampment Disbanded." MPR News, October 22, 2019. https://www.mprnews.org/story/2019/10/22/homeless-advocates-count-723-on-minneapolis-streets-since-encampment-disbanded.

Burnes, Donald W. 2016. "Where Do We Go from Here." In *Ending Homelessness: Why We Haven't, How We Can*, edited by Donald W. Burnes and David L. DiLeo, 277–90. London: Lynne Rienner Publishers.

Burt, Martha, Laudan Y. Aron, Edgar Lee, and with Jesse Valente. 2001. *Helping America's Homeless: Emergency Shelter or Affordable Housing?* Washington, DC: The Urban Institute Press.

Butzer, Stephanie. 2019. "Point in Time Report: Homelessness up 8.2% in Denver Metro Area Compared to 2018." Denver Channel 7 News, August 8, 2019. https://www.thedenverchannel.com/news/local-news/point-in-time-report-homelessness-up-8-2-in-denver-metro-area-compared-to-2018.

Cambria, Allison J. 2006. "Defying a Dead End: The Ramifications of *Town of Castle Rock v. Gonzales* on Domestic Violence Law and How the States Can Ensure Police Enforcement of Mandatory Arrest Statutes." *Rutgers Law Review* 59: 155–90.

Campbell, aka Skyywalker, et al. v. Acuff Rose Music, Inc. No. 92-1296, US Court of Appeals for the Sixth Circuit (1994).

Campbell, Alexia Fernández. 2016. "How America's Past Shapes Native Americans' Present." *The Atlantic*, October 12, 2016. https://www.theatlantic.com/business/archive/2016/10/native-americans-minneapolis/503441/.

Caruso, Christine, and Lois Frankel. 2010. "Everyday People: Enabling User Expertise in Socially Responsible Design." *Digital Library.* http://www.drs2010.umontreal.ca/data/PDF/024.pdf.

Centers for Disease Control and Prevention. 2021."Interim Guidance for Health Departments: COVID-19 Vaccination Implementation for People Experiencing Homelessness." CDC, February 2, 2012. https://www.cdc.gov/coronavirus/2019-ncov/community/homeless-shelters/vaccination-guidance.html.

Certeau, Michel de. 1984. *The Practice of Everyday Life.* Trans. Steven Rendall. Berkeley: University of California Press.

Chamard, Sharon. 2010. "Homeless Encampments." U.S. Department of Justice, Office of Community Oriented Policing Services, No. 56. https://www.hsdl.org/?view&did=682342.

Chamberlain, Chris, and Guy Johnson. 2011. "Pathways into Adult Homelessness." *Journal of Sociology* 49: 60–77.

Chandler v. Zeigler, Supreme Court of Colorado, 291 P.882 (Colo. June 16, 1930).

Chávez, Karma R. 2015. "Beyond Inclusion: Rethinking Rhetoric's Historical Narrative." *Quarterly Journal of Speech* 101: 162–72.

Chávez, Karma R. 2011. "Counter-Public Enclaves and Understanding the Function of Rhetoric in Social Movement Coalition-Building." *Communication Quarterly* 59: 1–18.

Chávez, Karma R. 2013. *Queer Migration Politics: Activist Rhetoric and Coalitional Possibilities.* Urbana: University of Illinois Press, 2013.

Chavira, Danielle. 2020. "Denver Eyeing Area in Five Points Neighborhood for Sanctioned Homeless Camp." CBS Denver, September 13, 2020. https://denver.cbslocal.com/2020/09/13/denver-libary-homeless-camp/.

Christensen, Julia. 2013. "'Our Home, Our Way of Life': Spiritual Homelessness and the Sociocultural Dimensions of Indigenous Homelessness in the Northwest Territories (NWT), Canada." *Social & Cultural Geography* 14: 804–28.

City of Apple Valley Ordinance Amending Chapter 1030 of the City Code Entitled "General Offenses." 2017. Section 130.08. "Sexual Offender Residence Location Restriction." https://www.ci.apple-valley.mn.us/DocumentCenter/View/7663/Approved-Predatory-Offender-Ordinance?bidId=.

"City Closed Door on Notorious Welfare Hotel." 1988. *United Press International*, December 31, 1988. https://www.upi.com/Archives/1988/12/31/City-closes-door-on-notorious-welfare-hotel/3594599547600/.

City of Dayton Ordinance No. 2019-05. 2019. "An Ordinance Amending Chapter 130 of the Dayton Code of Ordinance, Revised." https://cityofdaytonmn.com/wp-content/uploads/2019/08/03-26-19_Council_Packet.pdf.

City of Sherrill v. Oneida Nation of Indians of NY et al, 544 US 197 (2005), 337 F3d 139.

City of West St. Paul Ordinance 97. 2020. "Predatory Offenders." Chapter 97. https://codelibrary.amlegal.com/codes/weststpaul/latest/weststpaul_mn/0-0-0-7712.

Clingan, Carrie. 2007. *"Town of Castle Rock, Colorado v. Gonzales*: The Value of a Restraining Order." *Journal of Gender, Race & Justice* 10: 315–48.

Coalition for the Homeless. 2020. "State of the Homeless 2020." https://www.coalitionforthehomeless.org/state-of-the-homeless-2.

Coalition for the Homeless. 2021. "Housing Based Solutions." 020/.https://www.coalitionforthehomeless.org/proven-solutions/.

Coates, John, and Sue McKenzie-Mohr. 2010. "Out of the Frying Pan into the First: Trauma in the Lives of Homeless Youth Prior to and During Homelessness." *Journal of Sociology & Social Welfare* 37: 65–96.

Cochran, Bryan N., Angela J. Steward, Joshua A. Ginzler, and Ana Mari Cause. 2002. "Challenges Faced by Homeless Sexual Minorities: Comparison of Gay, Lesbian, Bisexual, and Transgender Homeless Adolescents with Their Heterosexual Counterparts." *American Journal of Public Health* 92: 773–77.

Code, Lorraine. 1995. *Rhetorical Spaces: Essays on Gendered Locations*. New York: Routledge.

Cohen, Rebecca, Will Yetvin, and Jill Khadduri. 2019. "Understanding Encampments of People Experiencing Homelessness and Community Responses: Emerging Evidence as of Late 2018." U.S. Department of Housing and Urban Development. https://www.huduser.gov/portal/sites/default/files/pdf/Understanding-Encampments.pdf.

Cohn, Jenae. 2016. "'Devilish Smartphones' and the 'Stone-Cold' Internet: Implications of the Technology Addiction Trope in College Student Digital Literacy Narratives." *Computers and Composition* 42: 80–94.

Cole, Courtney. 2021. "Charlotte Homeless Encampment 'Tent City' Cleared Out Following Abatement Order." WBTV, February 21, 2021. https://www.wbtv.com/2021/02/21/charlotte-homeless-encampment-tent-city-cleared-out-following-abatement-order/.

Collins, Jon. 2016. "He Sold Drugs to His Own Community; Now He Fights for Redemption." MPR News, April 18, 2016. https://www.mprnews.org/story/2016/04/18/opioid-profiles-james-cross.

Colorado Encyclopedia. 2019. "Five Points." https://coloradoencyclopedia.org/article/five-points.

Combs, Lynn A. 2006. "Between a Rock and a Hard Place: The Legacy of *Castle Rock v. Gonzales.*" *Hastings Law Journal* 58: 387–412.

Combs, Marianne. 2019. "Outpouring of Donations, Scramble to Find Shelter after Minneapolis First Displaced 250." MPR News, December 25, 2019. https://www.mprnews.org/story/2019/12/25/firefighters-battling-blaze-at-francis-drake-hotel-apartments.

Comprehensive & Neighborhood Planning Committees Letter. 2021, March https://www.stpaul.gov/sites/default/files/2021-05/Homeless%20Services%20Zoning%20Study%20PC%2004.30.21.pdf.

Conlin, Michelle. 2020. "In Pandemic America's Tent Cities, a Grim Future Grows Darker." *Reuters*, December 23, 2020. https://www.

reuters.com/article/us-health-coronavirus-usa-homelessness-i/
in-pandemic-americas-tent-cities-a-grim-future-grows-darker-idUSKBN28X19Y.

Corrigan v. Buckley, 271 U.S. 323 (1926).

Corrigan, Patrick W., Amy Kerr, and Lisa Knudsen. 2005. "The Stigma of Mental
Illness: Explanatory Model and Methods for Change." *Applied and Preventive
Psychology* 11: 179–90.

Craig, Shelley L., and Lauren McInroy. 2014. "You Can Form a Part of Yourself
Online: The Influence of New Media on Identity Development and Coming Out of
LGBTQ Youth." *Journal of Gay & Lesbian Mental Health* 18: 95–109.

Crowley, Sheila. 2016. "Homelessness Is About Housing." In *Ending Homelessness:
Why We Haven't, How We Can,* edited by Donald W. Burns and David L. DiLeo,
159-75. London: Lynne Rienner Publishers.

Culler, Jonathan. 1978. "On Trope and Persuasion." *New Literary History* 9: 607–18.

Curtis, Kathleen K. 2006. "Comment: The Supreme Court's Attack on Domestic
Violence Legislation—Discretion, Entitlement, and Due Process in *Town of Castle
Rock v. Gonzales*." *William Mitchell Law Review* 32: 1181–216.

Datta, Ayona. 2005. "'Homed' in Arizona: The Architecture of Emergency Shelters."
Urban Geography 26: 536–57.

De Choudbury, Munmun, Scott Counts, and Michael Gamon. 2012. "Not All
Moods Are Created Equal! Exploring Human Emotional States in Social Media."
Proceedings of the Sixth AAAI Conference on Weblogs and Social Media: 66–73.

Denver Public Library. 2020. "Five Points-Whittier Neighborhood History." https://
history.denverlibrary.org/five-points-whittier-neighborhood-history.

Desmond, Matthew. 2016. *Evicted: Poverty and Profit in the American City*. New
York: Crown Publishers.

DeWard, Sarah, and Angela M. Moe. 2010. "'Like a Prison!' Homeless Women's
Narratives of Surviving Shelter." *Journal of Sociology and Social Welfare* 37:
115–36.

DiBacco, Jessica. 2016. "The Sexual Exploitation of Homeless LGBTQ Youth."
Villanova University Charles Widger School of Law, Student Blog Series. https://
cseinstitute.org/sexual-exploitation-homeless-lgbtq-youth/.

Dickinson, Greg. 2020. "Space, Place, and the Textures of Rhetorical Criticism."
Western Journal of Communication 84: 297–313.

Dickinson, Greg, and Casey Malone Maugh. 2004. "Placing Visual Rhetoric: Finding
Material Comfort in Wild Oats Market." In *Defining Visual Rhetorics*, edited by
Charles A. Hill and Marguerite Helmers, 259–76. Mahwah, NJ: Lawrence Erlbaum.

Digital Magazine. 2010. "Homelessness 2.0: How Technology Helps the
Homeless." December 10, 2010. https://www.borndigital.com/2010/12/10/
homelessness-20-how-technology-helps-the-homeless.

DiLeo, David L. 2016. "How We've Learned to Embrace Homelessness." In *Ending
Homelessness: Why We Haven't, How We Can,* edited by Donald W. Burns and
David L. DiLeo, 141–58. London: Lynne Rienner Publishers.

District Court. 2018. "Search Warrant." State of Minnesota, Minneapolis Police:
Nicholas Pierlert. November 16, 2018. https://kstp.com/kstpImages/repository/cs/
files/Cross%20Search%20Warrant.pdf.

Doe v. Miller, 298 F. Supp. 2d 844, 869 (S.D. Iowa 2005).

Dolan, Karen, with Jodi L. Carr. 2016. *The Poor Get Prison: The Alarming Spread of Criminalization of Poverty*. Institute for Policy Studies, March 4 2015. https://ips-dc.org/the-poor-get-prison-the-alarming-spread-of-the-criminalization-of-poverty/.

Donley, Amy M., and James D. Wright. 2012. "Safer Outside: A Qualitative Exploration of Homeless People's Resistance to Homeless Shelters." *Journal of Forensic Psychology Practice* 12: 288–306.

Dougherty, Conor. 2020. *Golden Gates: Fighting for Housing in America*. New York: Penguin Press.

Du, Susan. 2018. "American Indian Leaders Try to Mend Messy Schism at the Wall of Forgotten Natives." *City Pages*, December 11, 2018. http://www.citypages.com/news/american-indian-leaders-try-to-mend-messy-schism-at-the-wall-of-forgotten-natives/502405471.

Du, Susan. 2021. "Minneapolis Park Board Ends Encampment Permits, Asks Other Agencies to Take Lead on Homeless." *Star Tribune*, February 5, 2021. https://www.startribune.com/minneapolis-park-board-ends-encampment-permits-asks-other-agencies-to-take-lead-on-homeless/600019460/?ref=nl&om_rid=1617810889&om_mid=2345340361.

Du, Susan. 2018. "The Wall of Forgotten Natives: Inside Minneapolis' Largest Homeless Encampment." *City Pages*, September 19, 2018. http://www.citypages.com/news/the-wall-of-forgotten-natives-inside-minneapolis-largest-homeless-encampment/493651661.

DuBois, Ellen Carol, and Lynn Dumenil. 2018. *Through Women's Eyes: An American History with Documents*, 5th edition. Boston: Bedford/St. Martin's.

Dunbar-Ortiz, Rozanne. 2014. *An Indigenous Peoples' History of the United States*. Boston: Beacon.

Dunn, Jennifer L. 2010. *Judging Victims: Why We Stigmatize Survivors and How They Reclaim Respect*. Boulder, CO: Lynne Rienner Publishers.

Dunn, Jennifer L., and Melissa Powell-Williams. 2007. "'Everybody Makes Choices': Victim Advocates and the Social Construction of Battered Women's Victimization and Agency." *Violence against Women* 13: 977–1001.

DuPré, Lindsay. 2019. "Being, Longing, and Belonging." In *Research & Reconciliation: Unsettling Ways of Knowing Through Indigenous Relationships*, edited by Shawn Wilson, Andrea V. Breen, and Lindsay Dupré, 1–4. Toronto: Canadian Scholars.

Duwe, Grant, Donnay, William, and Tewksbury, Richard. 2008. "Does Residential Proximity Matter? A Geographic Analysis of Sex Offense Recidivism." *Criminal Justice and Behavior* 35: 484–504.

Early, Justin Reed. 2013. *Street Child: A Memoir*. Self-published.

Eastham, Linda A. 2011. "Research Using Blogs for Data: Public Documents or Private Musings?" *Research in Nursing & Health* 34: 353–61.

Editorial Board. 2017. "PD Editorial: Sex Offenders Who Are Homeless Are the Greater Risk." *The Press Democrat*, August 1, 2017. https://www.pressdemocrat.com/article/opinion/pd-editorial-sex-offenders-who-are-homeless-are-the-greater-risk/?sba=AAS.

Egerstrom, Lee. 2019. "Navigation Center Filled; Outdoor Homeless Encampments Cleared." *The Circle: Native American News and Arts*, January 3, 2019. http://thecirclenews.org/cover-story/navigation-center-filled-outdoor-homeless-encampments-cleared/.

Ellemers, Naomi. 2018. "Gender Stereotypes." *Annual Review of Psychology* 69: 275–98.

Ellis, Emma Grey. 2020. "For Homeless People, Covid-19 Is Horror on Top of Horror." *WIRED*, April 2, 2020. https://www.wired.com/story/coronavirus-covid-19-homeless/.

Ellickson, Robert C. 1996. "Controlling Chronic Misconduct in City Spaces: Of Panhandlers, Skid Rows, and Public-Space Zoning." *Yale Law Review* 105: 1165–248.

Ellwood, David T. 1989. *Poor Support*. Boston: Harvard University Press.

Endres, Danielle, and Samantha Senda-Cook. 2011. "Location Matters: The Rhetoric of Place in Protest." *Quarterly Journal of Speech* 97: 257–82.

Erlbaum, Janice. 2006. *Girlbomb: A Halfway Homeless Memoir*. New York: Villard.

Evans, Marissa. 2019. "Navigation Center Prepares to Close, While Some Remain without Housing." *Star Tribune*, June 4, 2019. https://www.startribune.com/navigation-center-prepares-to-close-monday-while-some-remain-without-housing/510765282/.

Evenstad v. City of West St. Paul, US District Court, District of Minnesota, Case No. 0:017-CV-04067-JRT-DtS (2018).

Fabian, Maria, with Fred Smith. 2013. *Invisible Innocence: My Story as a Homeless Youth*. CreateSpace Independent Publishing Platform.

Fabj, Valeria, and Matthew J. Sobnosky. 1995. "AIDS Activism and the Rejuvenation of the Public Sphere." *Argumentation and Advocacy* 31: 163–84.

Fahnestock, Jeanne. 1999. *Rhetorical Figures in Science*. New York: Oxford University Press.

Farrugia, David. 2011. "Youth Homelessness and Individualised [sic] Subjectivity." *Journal of Youth Studies* 14: 761–75.

Feagin, Joe R. 1975. *Subordinating the Poor: Welfare and American Beliefs*. New York: Prentice Hall.

Felmlee, Diane, and Robert Faris, 2016. "Toxic Ties: Networks of Friendship, Dating, and Cyber Victimization." *Social Psychology Quarterly* 79: 243–62.

Felmlee, Diane, Paulina Inara Rodis, and Amy Zhang. 2020. "Sexist Slurs: Reinforcing Feminine Stereotypes Online." *Sex Roles* 83: 16–28.

Ferroro, Nick. 2018a. "Sex Offender Who Sued West St. Paul to Get $85K in Settlement. He Now Lives in St. Paul." *Pioneer Press*, June 11, 2018. https://www.twincities.com/2018/06/11/sex-offender-who-sued-west-st-paul-to-get-84g-in-settlement.

Ferroro, Nick 2018b. "West St. Paul Easing Tight Restrictions for Convicted Sex Offenders." *Pioneer Press*, February 28, 2018. https://www.twincities.com/2018/02/28/west-st-paul-easing-tight-restrictions-for-convicted-sex-offenders/.

Fetherling, George. 2001."Preface." In *The Vintage Book of Canadian Memoirs*, edited by George Fetherling, vii-x. Toronto: Vintage Canada (Random House Canada).

Fink, Amber. 2006. "Every Reasonable Means: Due Process and the (Non) Enforcement of a Restraining Order in *Gonzales v. Town of Castle Rock.*" *Law & Inequality: A Journal of Theory and Practice* 24: 375–97.

Flaccus, Gillian, and Michael Hill. 2020. "Surging Virus, Plummeting Temperatures Challenge Shelters." *Associated Press*, December 24, 2020. https://foxbaltimore.com/news/coronavirus/surging-virus-plummeting-temperatures-challenge-shelters?fbclid=IwAR0apnBwI-B2yCw_WmBVl3SzeZy-qfDu0ZxKTsUv04oDlZrMgAmKeKhCowU.

Fleming, David. 2008. *City of Rhetoric: Revitalizing the Public Sphere in Metropolitan America.* Albany, NY: SUNY Press.

Foote, Caleb. 1956. "Vagrancy-Type Law and Its Administration." *University of Pennsylvania Law Review* 104: 603–50.

Forte, James A. 2002. "Not in My Social World: A Cultural Analysis of Media Representations, Contested Spaces, and Sympathy for the Homeless." *Journal of Sociology and Social Welfare* 29: 131–58.

Foucault, Michel. 1986. "Of Other Spaces." *Diacritics* 16: 22–27.

FOX 9 News. 2018. "Minneapolis Homeless Encampment Organizer Under Investigation for Dealing Heroin at Camp." November 24, 2018. https://www.fox9.com/news/minneapolis-homeless-encampment-organizer-under-investigation-for-dealing-heroin-at-camp.

Freedom House First Meeting. 2020, November 10. https://www.stpaul.gov/sites/default/files/2020-11/11.10.20%20WEST%207TH-FORT%20ROAD%20FEDERATION%20Fnl_1.pdf.

Freedom House Second Meeting. 2021, May 28. https://www.youtube.com/watch?v=DAzERo5gc64.

Freedom House Letters. 2021. https://www.stpaul.gov/sites/default/files/2021-05/Freedom%20House%20moe%20comments%20received%205.27.21.pdf.

Fuller, Thomas. 2020. "Isolation Helps Homeless Population Escape Worst of Virus." *New York Times*, December 23, 2020. https://www.nytimes.com/2020/12/23/us/coronavirus-homeless.html.

Furst, Randy. 2020. "Study: Nearly 20,000 homeless on Average in Minnesota." *Star Tribune*, March 26, 2020. https://www.startribune.com/study-nearly-20-000-homeless-on-average-in-minnesota/569093852/.

Gage, Camille. 2021. Personal Interview, March 23, 2021.

Gage, Camille. 2020. Personal Correspondence, November 24, 2020.

Gatollari, Mustafa. 2021. "German City Builds Power Sleeping Pods to Keep Its Homeless Warm." *Distractify*, January 23, 2021. https://www.distractify.com/p/ulmer-nest-homeless-sleeping-pods?fbclid=IwAR2bvcGpuWc9WHvUkT7s22AsXm0oX2DLDRvCQ1IWeMhx9rlQmgcfpul15Fw.

Gaulden, Michael. 2017. *My Way Home: Growing up Homeless in America*. Salt Lake City, Utah: WiDó Publishing.

Giles, Timothy D. 2007. *Motives for Metaphor in Scientific and Technical Communication.* New York: Baywood Publishing/Routledge.

Gnawa, Leo. 2016. *Homeless Lives Matter: Homelessness My Story.* CreateSpace Independent Publishing Platform.

Goffman, Erving. 1961. *Asylums: Essays on the Social Situation of Mental Patients and Other Inmates.* New York: Anchor Books.

Goffman, Erving. 1963. *Stigma: Notes on the Management of Spoiled Identity.* New York: Touchstone Books.

Gonda, Jeffrey D. 2015. *Unjust Deeds: The Restrictive Covenant Cases and the Making of the Civil Rights Movement.* Chapel Hill: University of North Carolina Press.

Gotham, Kevin Fox. 2000. "Urban Space, Restrictive Covenants and the Origins of Racial Segregation in a US City, 1900-50." *International Journal of Urban and Regional Research* 24: 616–33.

Grabill, Jeffrey T. 2009. "Shaping Local HIV/AIDS Services Policy through Activist Research: The Problem of Client Involvement." *Technical Communication Quarterly* 9: 29–50.

Grandbois, Donna. 2005. "Stigma of Mental Illness Among American Indian and Alaska Native Nations: Historical and Contemporary Perspectives." *Issues in Mental Health Nursing* 26: 1001–124.

Gray, Alex. 2018. "Here's How Finland Solved Its Homelessness Problem." *World Economic Forum*, February 13, 2018. https://www.weforum.org/agenda/2018/02/how-finland-solved-homelessness/.

Gunkel, David J., and Gunkel, Ann Hetzel. 1997. "Virtual Geographies: The New Worlds of Cyberspace." *Critical Studies in Mass Communication* 14: 123–37.

Gutierrez, Grace. 2019. "Denver Civil Rights History." Center for Visual Arts, Metropolitan State University of Denver, March 18, 2019. https://www.msudenver.edu/cva/about/blog/denver-civil-rights.shtml.

Guest, Greg, Kathleen M. MacQueen, and Emily D. Namey. 2012. *Applied Thematic Analysis.* Los Angeles: Sage Publishing.

Gurak, Laura J. 1997. *Persuasion and Privacy in Cyberspace: The Online Protests over Lotus MarketPlace and the Clipper Chip.* New Haven, CT: Yale University Press.

Hansen, Moya. 2007. "Five Points, Denver Colorado." *Black Past*, January 18, 2007. https://www.blackpast.org/african-american-history/denvers-five-points/.

Har, Janie. 2019. "Shelter Uproar Highlights Strife in Expensive San Francisco." *AP News*, April 22, 2019. https://apnews.com/3a5aaa8ed10d46ba9fd84fe8242ada49.

Hargraves v. Capital City Mortgage Corp., 140 F.Supp.2d 7 (2000).

Harlow, Tim. 2020. "Fire Breaks Out at Downtown St. Paul Homeless Encampment." *Star Tribune*, December 18, 2020. https://www.startribune.com/fire-breaks-out-at-downtown-st-paul-homeless-encampment/573427651/.

Harris, Alexa. 2012. "Move, Get Out the Way." In *Women of Color and Social Media Multitasking*, edited by Keisha Edwards Tassie and Sonja M. Brown Givens, 69–89. Lanham, MD: Lexington Books.

Hayles, Katherine N. 2005. *My Mother Was a Computer: Digital Subjects and Literary Texts*. Chicago, IL: University of Chicago Press.

Healey, Judith Koll. 2020. "Kenwood Homeless Encampment Is Not What It Seems." Letter to the Editor, *Star Tribune*, July 10, 2020. https://www.startribune.com/kenwood-homeless-encampment-is-not-what-it-.seems/571712042/?ref=nl&om_rid=1617810889&om_mid=915721673.

Hebron, Rich. 2018. *Homeless but Human: Life in a Shelter*. Chicago: Blue Byron Books.

Hekman, Susan. 1991. "Reconstituting the Subject: Feminism, Modernism, and Postmodernism." *Hypatia* 6: 44–63.

Herbert, Steve, and Elizabeth Brown. 2006. "Conceptions of Space and Crime in the Punitive Neoliberal City." *Antipode* 38: 755–77.

Hirschel, David, Eve Buzawa, April Pattavina, and Don Faggiani. 2007. "Domestic Violence and Mandatory Arrest Laws: To What Extent Do They Influence Police Arrest Decisions." *Journal of Criminal Law and Criminology* 98: 255–98.

Hobot, Joe. 2018. "There Is an Encampment in Minneapolis Populated by Indigenous People—and It Is Growing." *News From Indian County*, September 14, 2018. https://www.indiancountrynews.com/index.php/news/editorial-letters/14609-there-is-an-encampment-in-minneapolis-populated-by-indigenous-people-and-it-is-growing.

Hollenbaugh, Erin E. 2011. "Motives for Maintaining Personal Journal Blogs." *Cyberpsychology, Behavior, and Social Networking* 14: 13–20.

Homeless Hub. 2019a. "Trauma and Victimization." https://www.homelesshub.ca/about-homelessness/legal-justice-issues/trauma-and-victimization.

Homeless Hub. 2019b. "Youth." https://www.homelesshub.ca/about-homelessness/population-specific/youth.

HostingTribal.com. 2020. "How Many Blogs Are There? We Counted Them All!" https://hostingtribunal.com/blog/how-many-blogs/#gref.

"Housing First." 2021. https://www.homelesshub.ca/about-homelessness/homelessness-101/housing-first.

Hudson v. Hudson. US Court of Appeals, Sixth Circuit, 475 F.3d 741 (2007).

Humphreys, Ashlee. 2016. *Social Media: Enduring Principles.* New York: Oxford University Press.

Inoue, Vicky. 2016. "Dianna: 'I Was on the Street for 30 Years.'" *Street Sheet*, December 15, 2006. http://www.streetsheet.org/read-our-full-issues/read-an-issue/2016-november-15-2-2/.

Invisible People. 2020. "Tent Cities in America." https://invisiblepeople.tv/tent-cities-in-america/.

James, Susan Donaldson. 2009. "Sex Offender Begs for More Jail Time." ABC News, July 14, 2020. https://abcnews.go.com/Business/story?id=8083584&page=1.

Jasinski, Jana L., Jennifer K. Wesely, James D. Wright, and Elizabeth E. Mustaine. 2010. *Hard Lives, Mean Streets: Violence in the Lives of Homeless Women*. Lebanon, NH: Northeastern University Press/University Press of New England.

Jennings, Francis. 2010. *The Invasion of America: Indians, Colonialism, and the Cant of Conquest*. Chapel Hill: University of North Carolina Press.

Jo, Yonggeol, Minwoo Kim, and Kyungsik Han. 2019. "How Do Humans Access the Credibility of Weblogs: Qualifying and Verifying Human Factors with Machine Learning." *Human Computer Interaction Paper 674*, May 4–9, 2019, Glasgow, Scotland: 1–12.

Johansen, Bruce E. 2012. "Series Editor's Foreword." In *Land and Spirit in Native America* edited by Joy Porter, xi-xiii. Santa Barbara, CA: Praeger

John Doe 1, John Doe 2, and John Doe 3 v. City of Apple Valley, United States District Court, District of Minnesota, Case No: 0:20-cv-00499-PJS-DTS, February 12, 2020.

Johnsen, Sarah, Paul Cloke, and Jon May. 2005. "Day Centres [sic] for Homeless People: Spaces of Care or Fear?" *Social and Cultural Geography* 6: 787–811.

Johnson v. McIntosh [M'Intosh], 21 US (8 Wheat.) 543 (1823).

Johnson, Jenell. 2010. "The Skeleton on the Couch: The Eagleton Affair, Rhetorical Disability, and the Stigma of Mental Illness." *Rhetoric Society Quarterly* 40: 459–78.

Jones, Kristin. 2018. "The Thread that Ties Segregation to Gentrification." *The Colorado Trust*, May 8, 2018. https://www.coloradotrust.org/content/story/thread-ties-segregation-gentrification.

Jones, Michael, and Irit Alony. 2008. "Blogs—The New Source of Data Analysis." *Issues in Informing Science and Information Technology* 5: 433–46.

Jorge, Kaylin. 2020. "COVID-19 Has Made Its Way into the Homeless Shelter at Nashville Fairgrounds." FOX17 WZTV Nashville, April 29, 2020. https://fox17.com/news/local/covid-19-has-made-its-way-into-the-homeless-shelter-at-nashville-fairgrounds.

Juarez, Roy, Jr. 2018. *Homeless by Choice: A Memoir of Love, Hate, and Forgiveness*. IMPACTtruth, Inc.

Karp, Brianna. 2011. *The Girl's Guide to Homelessness: A Memoir*. Harlequin.

Kasprow, Wesley, and Robert Rosenheck. 1998. "Substance Use and Psychiatric Problems of Homeless Native American Veterans." *Psychiatric Services* 49: 345–50.

Kattari, Shanna K., and Stephanie Begun. 2017. "On the Margins of Marginalized: Transgender Homelessness and Survival Sex." *Journal of Women and Social Work* 32: 92–103.

Katz v. United States, 389 U.S. 347 (1967).

Kelling, George L., and James Q. Wilson. 1982. "Broken Windows: The Police and Neighborhood Safety." *The Atlantic*, March 1982. https://www.theatlantic.com/magazine/archive/1982/03/broken-windows/304465/.

Keyes et al. v. School District No. 1, Denver, Colorado, 413 U.S. 189 (1973).

Kidd, Sean A. 2007. "Youth Homelessness and Social Stigma." *Journal of Youth and Adolescence* 36: 291–99.

Kim, Catherine. 2020. "During the Covid-19 Pandemic, Nowhere Is Safe for Homeless People." *Vox News*, March 18, 2020. https://www.vox.com/2020/3/18/21183812/covid-19-coronavirus-homeless.

Koerber, Amy. 2018a. *From Hysteria to Hormones*. University Park, PA; Penn State University Press.

Koerber, Amy. 2018b. "From Hysteria to Hormones and Back Again: Centuries of Outrageous Remarks About Female Biology." *Rhetoric of Health and Medicine* 1: 1–2, 179–92.

Koerber, Amy. 2001. "Postmodernism, Resistance, and Cyberspace: Making Rhetorical Spaces for Feminist Mothers on the Web." *Women's Studies in Communication* 24: 218–40.

Kornfield, Meryl. 2019. "Florida's Sex Offender Population is Again. Where Can They Live Out Their Silver Years?" *Miami Herald*, June 20, 2019. https://www.miamiherald.com/news/state/florida/article231296693.html.

Kozol, Jonathan. 1988. *Rachel and Her Children: Homeless Families in America*. New York: Three Rivers Press.

Kressel, Shirley. 2000. "Privatizing the Public Realm." *New Democracy World.* http://newdemocracyworld.org/old/space.htm.

Kuehn, Bridget M. 2020. "Homeless Shelters Face High COVID-19 Risks." *JAMA: News from the Centers for Disease Control and Prevention*, June 9, 2020. https://jamanetwork.com/journals/jama/fullarticle/2766884.

Kurtz, Howard. 1987. "Welfare Hotel Occupants at Eve of Political Storm in New York." *Washington Post*, September 15, 1987. https://www.washingtonpost.com/archive/politics/1987/09/15/welfare-hotel-occupants-at-eye-of-political-storm-in-new-york/8658e5e0-c603-4f32-a1f3-d3199ce0052d/.

Kyllo v. United States, 533 US 27 (2001).

Lamatt, Rose. 2011. *Is Life One Big Goodbye: One Homeless Woman's Survival Story*. CreateSpace Independent Publishing Platform.

Largent, Mark A. 2002. "'The Greatest Curse of the Race': Eugenic Sterilization in Oregon, 1909–1983." *Oregon Historical Quarterly* 103: 188–209.

Lee, Jessica. 2019. "Minneapolis Homeless Navigation Center Closes, Even as Need Remains Acute." *MinnPost*, June 4, 2019. https://www.minnpost.com/metro/2019/06/minneapolis-homeless-navigation-center-closes-even-as-need-remains-acute/.

Lee, Sharon. 2021. "Tiny House Villages: A Crisis Solution to Homelessness." Low Income Housing Institute. https://lihi.org/wp-content/uploads/2019/05/Tiny-House-Presentation-updated-May-2019.pdf.

Lefebvre, Henri. 1991. *The Production of Space*. Translated by D. N. Smith. Cambridge, MA: Blackwell.

Levenson, Jill S. 2008. "Collateral Consequences of Sex Offender Residence Restrictions." *Criminal Justice Studies* 21: 153–66.

Levenson, Jill, Alissa R. Ackerman, Kelly M. Socia, and Andrew J. Harris. 2013. "Where for Art Thou? Transient Sex Offenders and Residence Restrictions." *Criminal Justice Policy Review* 26: 319–44.

Levenson, Jill, Kristen Zgoba, and Richard Tewksbury. 2007. "Sex Offender Residence Restrictions: Sensible Crime Policy or Flawed Logic?" *Federal Probation* 71: 2–9. https://www.ncjrs.gov/App/Publications/abstract.aspx?ID=243306.

Lewis, Sophie, Samantha L. Thomas, R. Warwich Blood, David J. Castle, Jim Hyde, and Paul A. Komesaroff. 2011. "How Do Obese Individuals Perceive and Respond to the Different Types of Obesity Stigma that They Encounter in Their Daily Lives?: A Qualitative Study." *Social Science & Medicine* 73: 1349–56.

Liebow, Elliot. 1993. *Tell Them Who I Am: The Lives of Homeless Women.* New York: Penguin Books.

Lima, Nádia Nara Rolim, et al. 2020. "People Experiencing Homelessness: Their Potential Exposure to COVID-19." *Psychiatry Research* 288: 112945. https://www.ncbi.nlm.nih.gov/pmc/articles/PMC7151321/.

Link, Bruce G., and Jo C. Phelan. 2001. "Conceptualizing Stigma." *Annual Review of Sociology* 27: 363–85.

Link, Bruce G., Jo Phelan, Ann Stueve, Robert E. Moore, Michaeline Bresnahan, and Elmer Struening. 1995. "Public Attitudes and Beliefs about Homelessness." In *Homelessness in America*, edited by James Baumohl, 143–48. Phoenix, AR: Oryx.

Lobo, Susan, and Margaret Mortensen Vaughan. 2003. "Substance Dependency among Homeless American Indians." *Journal of Psychoactive Drugs* 35: 63–70.

Loehwing, Melanie. 2010. "Homelessness as the Unforgiving Minute of the Present: The Rhetorical Tenses of Democratic Citizenship." *Quarterly Journal of Speech* 96: 380–403.

Long, Elenore. 2008. *Community Literacy and the Rhetoric of Local Publics.* Anderson, SC: Parlor Press.

Lowe, Nicole. 2016. *Never Let Me Go: A Memoir.* CreateSpace Independent Publishing Platform.

Lucie's Place. 2020. "Blog." https://www.luciesplace.org/blog.

Lurie, Nancy Oestreich. 1971. "The World's Oldest On-Going Protest Demonstration: North American Indian Drinking Patterns." *Pacific Historical Review* 40: 331–32.

McCoy, Terrence. 2019. "'This Is Not Me': The Rise of Tent Encampments Is Changing the Face of American Homelessness." *Washington Post*, March 22, 2019. https://www.washingtonpost.com/news/local/wp/2019/03/22/feature/homeless-living-in-a-tent-blocks-from-the-u-s-capitol-and-working-full-time/.

McKerrow, Raymie E. 1999. "Space and Time in the Postmodern Polity." *Western Journal of Communication* 63: 271–90.

Mahoney, Martha. 1991. "Legal Images of Battered Women: Redefining the Issue of Separation." *Michigan Law Review* 90: 1, 5–6, 65–76, 78–79.

Malos, Ellen, and Gill Hague. 1997. "Women, Housing, Homelessness and Domestic Violence." *Women's Studies International Forum* 20: 397–409.

Mandanipour, Ali. 2019. "Rethinking Public Space: Between Rhetoric and Reality." *Urban Design* 24: 38–46.

Maranes, Allan. 2021. "60 Minutes: Heartbreak Hotel" with Ed Bradley. YouTube Video:16:19. https://www.youtube.com/watch?v=JyQROzKO6rQ.

Marback, Richard. 1998. "Detroit and the Closed Fist: Toward a Theory of Material Rhetoric." *Rhetoric Review* 17: 74–92.

Marcus, Isabel. 1994. "Reframing 'Domestic Violence': Terrorism in the Home." In *The Public Nature of Private Violence: Women and the Discovery of Abuse*, edited by Martha Albertson Fineman, 11–35. New York: Routledge.

Margolin, Victor, and Sylvia Margolin. 2002. "A 'Social Model of Design': Issues of Practice and Research." *Design Issues* 18: 24–30.

Martinez, Donna, Grace Sage, and Azusa Ono. 2016. *Urban American Indians: Reclaiming Native Space.* Santa Barbara, CA: Praeger.

Massey, Doreen. 2005. *For Space*. Newbury Park, CA: Sage.

Massey, Douglas S., Len Albright, Rebecca Casciano, Elizabeth Derickson, and David N. Kinsey. 2013. *Climbing Mount Laurel: The Struggle for Affordable Housing and Social Mobility in an American Suburb*. Princeton, NJ: Princeton University Press.

Mauck, Laura. 2001. *Five Points Neighborhood of Denver*. Charleston, NC: Arcadia Publishing.

Mayers v. Ridley, 465 F.2d (D. C. Cir. 1972).

Meerse, Katherine. 2020. Personal Interview, December 29, 2020.

Metraux, Stephen, Caterina G. Roman, and Richard S. Cho. 2017. "Overview: There Is a Direct Correlation Between Homelessness and Crime." In *Homelessness and Street Crime*, edited by Pete Schauer, 65–79. New York: Greenhaven.

Metropolitan Urban Indian Directors (MUID). 2018. "Franklin/Hiawatha Encampment: Wall of Forgotten Natives." https://www.franklinhiawathacamp.org/.

Meyer, Silke. 2016. "Examining Women's Agency in Managing Intimate Partner Violence and the Related Risk of Homelessness: The Role of Harm Minimisation [sic]." *Global Public Health* 11: 198–210.

Miller, Pamela. 2018. "Second Death Is Linked to Minneapolis Homeless Encampment." *Star Tribune*, September 15, 2018. http://www.startribune.com/second-death-linked-to-minneapolis-homeless-encampment/493357271/.

Miller, Carolyn, and Dawn Shepherd. 2004. "Blogging as Social Action: A Genre Analysis of the Weblog." In *Into the Blogsphere: Rhetoric, Community, and Culture of Weblogs*, edited by Laura Gurak and Smilijana Antoljevic, 1–21. University of Minnesota Libraries. https://conservancy.umn.edu/handle/11299/172818.

Miller, Carolyn, and Dawn Shepherd. 2009. "Questions for Genre Theory from the Blogosphere." In *The Internet and the Theory of Genre*, edited by Janet Giltrow and Dieter Stein, 263–90. Amsterdam: John Benjamin.

Miller, Elisabeth. 2019. "Too Fat to be President? Chris Christie and Fat Stigma as Rhetorical Disability." *Rhetoric of Health & Medicine* 2: 60–87.

Miller, Ryan. 2017. "'My Voice is Definitely Strongest in Online Communities': Students Using Social Media for Queer and Disability Identity-Making." *Journal of College Student Development* 58: 509–25.

Minnesota Department of Corrections. 2007, April. "Residential Proximity & Sex Offender Recidivism in Minnesota." https://mn.gov/doc/assets/04-07SexOffender-Report-Proximity_tcm1089-272769.pdf.

Minnesota et al. v. Mille Lacs Band of Chippewa Indians et al. 526 U.S. 172 (1999).

Minneapolis Sanctuary Movement. 2021. https://minneapolissanctuary.org.

Minnesota Statutes 629.341. 2020. "Allowing Probable Cause Arrests for Domestic Violence." https://www.revisor.mn.gov/statutes/cite/629.341.

Minnesota Statutes 518V.01. 2020. "Domestic Abuse Act." https://www.revisor.mn.gov/statutes/cite/518B.01.

Minor, Nathaniel. 2018. "Three Takeaways from the 2018 Denver Point-in-Time Homeless Survey." CPR News, June 15, 2018. https://www.cpr.org/2018/06/15/three-takeaways-from-the-2018-denver-point-in-time-homelessness-survey/.

Mitchell, Don. 1997. "The Annihilation of Space by Law: The Roots and Implications of Anti-Homelessness Laws in the United States." *Antipode* 29: 303–35.

Mitchell, Don. 2003. *The Right to the City: Social Justice and the Fight for Public Space*. New York: Guilford Press.

Mitchell Hamline School of Law Symposium. 2019. "Residency Restrictions: Wise or Unwise?" February 28, 2019. Personal Observation.

Moen, Mike. 2019. "A Look Back on Francis Drake Hotel's History." MPR News, December 26, 2019. https://www.mprnews.org/story/2019/12/26/a-look-back-on-drake-hotels-history.

Molloy, Cathryn. 2015. "Recuperative Ethos and Agile Epistemologies: Toward a Vernacular Engagement with Mental Illness Ontologies." *Rhetoric Society Quarterly* 45: 138–63.

Molloy, Cathryn. 2019. *Rhetorical* Ethos *in Health and Medicine: Patient Credibility, Stigma, and Misdiagnosis*. New York: Routledge.

Monet, Jenni. 2018. "City Camp Is Site of Native American Homelessness, Heroin . . . and Hope." *The Guardian*, October 19, 2018. https://www.theguardian.com/us-news/2018/oct/19/native-american-homeless-heroin-minneapolis.

Montana Little Shell of Chippewa Indians. 2020. https://www.facebook.com/Montana-Little-Shell-Tribe-of-Chippewa-Indians-116712845070717.

Morris, A. Thomas. 1988. "The Empirical, Historical and Legal Case Against the Cautionary Instruction: A Call for Legislative Reform." *Duke Law Journal* 37: 154–73.

Moses, Joy, 2020. "State of Homelessness: A Look at Race and Ethnicity." National Alliance to End Homelessness, May 27, 2020. https://endhomelessness.org/state-of-homelessness-a-look-at-race-and-ethnicity/?gclid=EAIaIQobChMIsfXWqv6T7AIVDdbACh2AjAT8EAAYASAAEgJmI_D_BwE.

Mosites, Emily, Erin M. Parker, and Julie Stoltey. 2020. "Assessment of SARS-CoV-2 Infection Prevalence in Homeless Shelters—Four U.S. Cities, May 27–April 5, 2020." *Morbidity and Mortality Weekly Report CDC*. https://www.ncbi.nlm.nih.gov/pmc/articles/PMC7206983/.

Mountford, Roxanne. 2003. *The Gendered Pulpit: Preaching in American Protestant Spaces*. Carbondale: Southern Illinois University Press.

Mountford, Roxanne. 2001. "On Gender and Rhetorical Space." *Rhetoric Society Quarterly* 31: 41–71.

Mulligan v. Panther Valley Property Owners Association, 766 A.2d. 1186, 1189–91 (N. J. Super Ct. App. Div. 2001).

Mullins, Gretchen P. 1994. "The Battered Woman and Homelessness." *Journal of Law and Policy* 3: 237–55.

Murphy, Todd. 2018. *Homeless: A Day in the Life*. CreateSpace Independent Publishing Platforms.

Murphy-Scott, Dick. 2019. *Homeless Guy with a Laptop*. Amazon.com Services LLC.

Murray, Liz. 2010. *Breaking Night: A Memoir of Forgiveness, Survival, and My Journey from Homelessness to Harvard*. New York: Hyperion.

Murray, Suellen. 2008. "'Why Doesn't She Just Leave?' Belonging, Disruption, and Domestic Violence." *Women's Studies International Forum* 31: 65–72.

Myhra, Laurelle L., and Elizabeth Wieling. 2014. "Psychological Trauma among American Indian Families: A Two-Generational Study." *Journal of Loss and Trauma* 19: 289–313.

National Alliance to End Homelessness. 2020a. "Changes in the HUD Definition of 'Homelessness.'" https://endhomelessness.org/resource/changes-in-the-hud-definition-of-homeless/.

National Alliance to End Homelessness. 2020b. "Homelessness and Racial Disparities." https://endhomelessness.org/homelessness-in-america/what-causes-homelessness/inequality/.

National Alliance to End Homelessness. 2020c. "Rapid Re-Housing." https://end-homelessness.org/ending-homelessness/solutions/rapid-re-housing/.

National Alliance to End Homelessness. 2020d. "State of Homelessness: 2020 Edition." https://endhomelessness.org/homelessness-in-america/homelessness-statistics/state-of-homelessness-2020/.

National Alliance to End Homelessness. 2020e. "Youth and Young Adults." https://endhomelessness.org/homelessness-in-america/who-experiences-homelessness/youth/.

National Coalition for the Homeless. 2014. "Vulnerable to Hate: A Survey of Hate Crimes & Violence Committed against Homeless People in 2013," June 2014. https://nationalhomeless.org/wp-content/uploads/2014/06/Hate-Crimes-2013-FINAL.pdf.

National Conference of State Legislatures. 2019. "Youth Homelessness Overview." https://www.ncsl.org/research/human-services/homeless-and-runaway-youth.aspx.

National Domestic Violence Hotline. 2020. "Domestic Violence Statistics." https://www.thehotline.org/stakeholders/domestic-violence-statistics/.

National Domestic Violence Hotline. 2021. "50 Obstacles to Leaving." https://www.thehotline.org/resources/50-obstacles-to-leaving/.

National Congress of American Indians. 2021. https://www.ncai.org.

National Law Center on Homelessness & Poverty. 2019a. "Alone without a Home: A National Review of State Laws Affecting Unaccompanied Youth." https://nlchp.org/alone-without-a-home-2019/.

National Law Center on Homelessness & Poverty. 2019b. "No Safe Place: The Criminalization of Homelessness in U.S. Cities." https://nlchp.org/wp-content/uploads/2019/02/No_Safe_Place.pdf.

National Law Center on Homelessness & Poverty. 2017. "Tent City, USA. 2017. The Growth of America's Homeless Encampments and How Communities Are Responding." https://nlchp.org/wp-content/uploads/2018/10/Tent_City_USA_2017.pdf.

National Law Center on Homelessness & Poverty and The National Coalition for the Homeless. 2017. "Feeding Intolerance: Prohibitions on Sharing Food with People Experiencing Homelessness," November 2017. https://www.nationalhomeless.org/publications/foodsharing/Food_Sharing.pdf

National Law Center on Homelessness & Poverty and The National Coalition for the Homeless. 2009. "Homes Not Handcuffs: The Criminalization of Homelessness in U.S. Cities," July 2009. http://nationalhomeless.org/publications/crimreport/ CrimzReport_2009.pdf.

Navratil, Liz. 2021. "Minneapolis Starts Program to Disavow Racial Covenants." *Star Tribune*, March 3, 2021. https://www.startribune.com/ minneapolis-starts-program-to-disavow-racial-covenants/600029949/.

Nelson, Emma. 2020. "St. Paul to Open Day Shelter in W. 7th Neighborhood." *Star Tribune*, November 8, 2020. https://www.startribune.com/st-paul-to-open-day-shelter-in-w-7th-neighborhood/573010391/?ref=nl &om_rid=1617810889&om_mid=1988882889.

Nesterak, Max. 2018. "Council OKs Plan to Move Minneapolis Homeless Camp onto Red Lake Land." MPR News, September 26, 2018. https://www.mprnews.org/ story/2018/09/26/minneapolis-homeless-camp-move-red-lake-nation-land.

Nesterak, Max. 2019a. "In the Midst of a Housing Shortage, Minneapolis Struggles to Help Homeless." MPR News, August 6, 2019. https://www.mprnews.org/ story/2019/08/06/minneapolis-homeless-struggles.

Nesterak, Max. 2019b. "What Worked, What Didn't, with Experimental Shelter in Minneapolis?" MPR News, May 21, 2019. https://www.mprnews.org/ story/2019/05/21/what-worked-what-didnt-with-experimental-shelter-in-minnea-polis.

Newcomb, Steven. 2004. "On the Words 'Tribe' and 'Nation.'" *Indian Country Today*, December 8, 2004. https://indiancountrytoday.com/archive/ on-the-words-tribe-and-nation-NUTfP-tyU0uqza8cle2BSg.

Noguchi, Yuki. 2021. "Vaccinating Homeless Patients Against COVID-19: 'All Bets Are Off.'" NPR/MPR News, February 17, 2021. https://www.npr.org/sections/health-shots/2021/02/17/964219973/ vaccinating-homeless-patients-against-covid-19-all-bets-are-off.

Ockerman, Emma. 2019. "The Homelessness Crisis Is Getting So Bad That Cities Are Now Building Their Own Camps." *ViceNews*, July 16, 2019. https://www.vice. com/en_us/article/vb9we3/the-homelessness-crisis-is-getting-so-bad-that-cities-are-now-building-their-own-camps.

Olson, Jeremy. 2020. "Teen Sexual Exploitation a Statewide Problem in Minnesota, Survey Finds." *Star Tribune*, January 27, 2020. http://www.startribune.com/teen-sexual-exploitation-a-statewide-problem-in-minnesota-survey-finds/567337082/.

Otárola, Miguel. 2020. "After Summer in Minneapolis Parks, Homeless Seek Other Spaces for Winter." *Star Tribune*, October 9, 2020. https://www.star-tribune.com/after-summer-in-minneapolis-parks-homeless-seek-other-spaces-for-winter/572683522/?ref=nl&om_rid=1617810889&om_mid=1688230345.

"Parents Arrested in Deaths of 4 Children in Hotel Fire." 1986. *New York Times*, July 13, 1986. https://www.nytimes.com/1986/07/13/nyregion/parents-arrested-in-deaths-of-4-children-in-hotel-fire.html.

Park, Patina, and Robert Lilligren. 2018. "Statement by the Metro Urban Indian Directors (MUID) Regarding Natives Against Heroin." December 6, 2018. http:// stmedia.startribune.com/documents/MUID+Statement+on+Natives+Against+Her oin.pdf.

Pendleton, Virginia, Walker Bosch, Margaret Vohs, Stephanie Nelson-Dusek, and Michelle Decker Gerrard. 2020. "Characteristics of People Who Identify as LGBTQ Experiencing Homelessness." Wilder Research, September 2020. https://www.wilder.org/sites/default/files/imports/2018_HomelessnessInMinnesota_LGBTQ_9-20.pdf.

Perdue, Theda, and Michael D. Green. 2010. *North American Indians: A Very Short Introduction.* New York: Oxford University Press.

Perez, Iris. 2019. "With Navigation Center Closed, Another Encampment Grows." Fox News, June 3. 2019. https://www.fox9.com/news/with-navigation-center-closed-another-encampment-grows.

Persons, Mason. 2021. Personal Interview, January 18, 2021.

Peterson, Marina. 2006. "Patrolling the Plaza: Privatizing Public Space and the Neoliberal State in Downtown Los Angeles." *Urban Anthropology and Studies of Cultural Systems and World Economic Development* 35: 355–86.

PEW Trusts. 2017. "A Hidden Population: Youth Homelessness Is on the Rise." https://www.pewtrusts.org/en/research-and-analysis/blogs/stateline/2017/07/07/a-hidden-population-youth-homelessness-is-on-the-rise.

Phelan, Jo, Bruce C. Link, Robert E. Moore, and Ann Stueve. 1997. "The Stigma of Homelessness: The Impact of the Label 'Homeless' on Attitudes Toward Poor Person." *Social Psychology Quarterly* 60: 323–37.

Pietila, Antero. 2010. *Not in My Neighborhood: How Bigotry Shaped a Great American City.* Chicago: Ivan R. Dee.

Pleck, Elizabeth. 2004. *Domestic Tyranny: The Making of American Social Policy Against Family Violence from Colonial Times to the Present.* Urbana: University of Illinois Press.

Plessy v. Ferguson, 163 U.S. 537 (1896).

Porter, Jessica. 2019. "Redlining: How the Five Points Neighborhood Formed Amid Racist Practices in the 1930s." Denver Channel 7 News, March 1, 2019. https://www.thedenverchannel.com/news/black-history-month/redlining-how-the-five-points-neighborhood-formed-amid-racist-practices-in-the-1930s. YouTube video: 2:24. https://www.youtube.com/watch?v=StuMIxqCJMY.

Porter, Joy. 2012. *Land and Spirit in Native America.* Santa Barbara, CA: Praeger.

Prather, Shannon. 2020. "Ramsey County Officials Ask State to Set Up Homeless Shelter." *Star Tribune*, May 14, 2020. https://www.startribune.com/ramsey-county-officials-ask-state-to-set-up-homeless-shelter/570513312/.

Prather, Shannon. 2021. "St. Paul Grapples with Third Encampment Death This Winter." *Star Tribune*, January 20, 2021. https://www.startribune.com/st-paul-grapples-with-third-encampment-death-this-winter/600012850/?ref=nl&om_rid=1617810889&om_mid=2285584841.

Prather, Shannon, and David Chanen. 2020. "St. Paul, Minneapolis Dismantle Encampments as Officials Scramble to House Homeless." *Star Tribune*, December 16, 2020. https://www.startribune.com/st-paul-minneapolis-dismantle-encampments-as-officials-scramble-to-house-homeless/600001979/?ref=nl&om_rid=1617810889&om_mid=2162619849.

Propen, Amy D. 2012. *Locating Visual-Material Rhetorics: The Map, the Mill, & the GPS*. Anderson, SC: Parlor Press.

Propen, Amy D., and Mary Lay Schuster. 2008. "Making Academic Work Advocacy Work: Technologies of Power in the Public Arena." *Journal of Business and Technical Communication* 22: 299–329.

Propen, Amy D., and Mary Lay Schuster. 2017. *Rhetoric and Communication Perspectives on Domestic Violence and Sexual Assault: Policy and Protocol Through Discourse*. New York: Routledge.

Przybyiski, Roger. 2015. "Recidivism of Adult Sexual Offenders." National Criminal Justice Reference Service. https://www.ncjrs.gov/app/publications/abstract. aspx?ID=27108.

Quackenbush, Nicole. 2011. "Speaking of—and as—Stigma: Performativity and Parkinson's in the Rhetoric of Michael J. Fox." *Disability Studies Quarterly* 31. Online journal. https://dsq-sds.org/article/view/1670/1601.

Quester, Nicole 2015. "Refusing to Remove an Obstacle to the Remedy: The Supreme Court's Decision in Town of *Castle Rock v. Gonzales* Continues to Deny Domestic Violence Victims Meaningful Recourse." *Akron Law Review* 40: 391–434.

Raddatz, Kate. 2019. "Minnesota Vikings to Donate $50,000 to Victims of the Drake Hotel Fire." WCCO News, December 30, 2019. https://minnesota.cbs-local. com/2019/12/30/minnesota-vikings-to-donate-50000-to-victims-of-the-drake-hotel-fire/.

Race & Justice News. 2016. "Racial Disparities in Sex Offender Registration." June 13, 2016. https://www.sentencingproject.org/news/race-justice-news-racial-disparities-sex-offender-registration/.

Rai, Candice. 2016. *Democracy's Lot: Rhetoric, Publics, and the Places of Invention*. Tuscaloosa: University of Alabama Press.

Raphael, Jody. 2000. *Saving Bernice: Battered Women, Welfare, and Poverty*. Lebanon, NH: Northeastern University Press/University Press of New England.

Ratcliffe, Krista. 2000. "Eavesdropping as Rhetorical Tactic: History, Whiteness, and Rhetoric." *Journal of Advanced Composition* 20: 87–119.

Ratcliffe. Krista. 2005. *Rhetorical Listening: Identification, Gender, Whiteness*. Carbondale: Southern Illinois University Press.

Reardon, Sean F., and David O'Sullivan. 2004. "Measures of Spatial Segregation." *Sociological Methodology* 34: 121–62.

Reddington, Francis P. 2009. "A Brief History of Rape Law and Rape Law Reform in the United States." In *Sexual Assault: The Victims, the Perpetrators, and the Criminal Justice System*, 2nd edition, edited by Francis P. Reddington and Betsey Wright Kreisel, 319–33. Durham, NC: Carolina Academic Press.

Redfish. 2020. "Interviews: Homeless During COVID-19." YouTube video: 3:47. March 20, 2020. https://www.youtube.com/watch?v=VB164EYhoYI.

Rhomberg, Chris. 1998. "White Nativism and Urban Politics: The 1920s Ku Klux Klan in Oakland, California." *Journal of American Ethnic History* 17: 39–55.

Rice, Jeff. 2012. *Digital Detroit: Rhetoric and Space in the Age of the Network*. Carbondale: Southern Illinois University Press.

Rice, Jenny. 2021. *Distant Publics: Development Rhetoric and the Subject of Crisis.* Pittsburgh: University of Pittsburgh Press.

Rieh, Soo Young, Grace YoungJoo Jeon, Ji Yeon Yang, and Clifford Lampe. 2014. "Audience-Aware Credibility: From Understanding Audience to Establishing Credible Blogs." *Proceedings of the Eighth International AAAI Conference on Weblogs and Social Media*: 436–45.

Roberson, Jahmeilah, and Bonnie Nardi. 2010. "Survival Needs and Social Inclusion: Technology Use Among the Homeless." http://www.artifex.org/~bonnie/351-roberson.pdf.

Roberts, Carey. 2008. "Women Avoid Abuse Shelters Like the Plague." *Renew America*, September 9, 2008. https://web.archive.org/web/20130123071147/http://www.renewamerica.com/columns/roberts/080909.

Roberts, Sam. 1991. "What Led to Crackdown on Homeless." *New York Times*, October 28, 1991. https://www.nytimes.com/1991/10/28/nyregion/what-led-to-crackdown-on-homeless.html.

Robinson, Brandon Andrew. 2020. *Coming Out to the Streets: LGBTQ Youth Experiencing Homelessness.* Berkeley: University of California Press.

Rodriguez, Yanira, and Ben Kuebrich. 2018. "The Tone It Takes: An Eighteen-Day Sit-In at Syracuse University." In *Unruly Rhetorics: Protest, Persuasion, and Publics*, edited by Jonathan Alexander, Susan C. Jarratt, and Nancy Welch, 162–82. Pittsburgh, PA: University of Pittsburgh Press.

Rogers, Julia H., et al. 2021. "Characteristics of COVID-19 in Homeless Shelters." *Annals of Internal Medicine*, January 2021. https://www.acpjournals.org/doi/full/10.7326/M20-3799?journalCode=aim.

Roper, Eric. 2016. "Amid Strife, Little Earth Residents Work for Reform, Harmony." *Star Tribune*, March 22, 2016. https://www.startribune.com/amid-strife-little-earth-residents-strive-for-reform/373019891/.

Roper, Eric. 2021. "Minneapolis Park Board Winds Down Last Encampment, at Minnehaha Park." *Star Tribune*, January 5, 2021. https://www.startribune.com/minneapolis-park-board-winds-down-last-encampment-at-minnehaha-park/600006973/?ref=nl&om_rid=1617810889&om_mid=2235921865.

Roschelle, Anne R. 2019. *Struggling in the Land of Plenty: Race, Class, and Gender in the Lives of Homeless Families.* Lanham, MD: Lexington Books.

Rose, Emma J. 2016. "Design as Advocacy: Using a Human-Centered Approach to Investigate the Needs of Vulnerable Populations." *Journal of Technical Writing and Communication* 46: 427–45.

Rose, Emma J., and Rebecca Walton. 2015 "Factors to Actors: Implications of Posthumanism for Social Justice Work." In *Proceedings of the 33rd Annual International Conference on the Design of* Communication, edited by Kathie Gossett and Angie Mallory, 1–10. New York: Association for Computing Machinery.

Rothstein, Richard. 2017. *The Color of Law: A Forgotten History of How Our Government Segregated America.* New York: Liveright.

Rubino, Joe. 2017. "'Gentrification Moves East': A Hard Look at Economic Displacement in Denver's Most Historic Black Neighborhood." *The Denver*

Post, December 15, 2017. https://www.denverpost.com/2017/12/15/denver-five-points-gentrification/.

Ruddick, Susan M. 1995. *Young and Homeless in Hollywood: Mapping the Social Imaginary*. New York: Routledge.

Rusk, David. 2003. "Denver Divided: Sprawl, Race, and Poverty in Greater Denver." University of Denver and Colorado State University "Bridges to the Future" Project. https://www.law.du.edu/images/uploads/library/evert/DenverDivided.pdf.

Sánchez-Villar, Juan M. 2019. "The Use of Blogs as Social Media Tools of Political Communication: Citizen Journalism and Public Opinion 2.0." *Communication & Society* 32: 39–55.

Sandler, Lauren. 2020. *This Is All I Got: A New Mother's Search for Home*. New York: Random House.

Schneider, Valerie. 2018. "The Prison to Homelessness Pipeline: Criminal Record Checks, Race, and Disparate Impart." *Indiana Law Journal* 93: 421–55.

Schneider, Barbara, and Chaseten Remillard. 2013. "Caring about Homelessness: How Identity Work Maintains the Stigma of Homelessness." *Text & Talk* 33: 95–112.

Schuster, Mary. 2006. "A Different Place to Birth; A Material Rhetoric of Baby Haven, a Free-Standing Birth Center." *Women's Studies in Communication* 29: 1–38.

Schuster, Mary. 2019. *The Victim's Voice in the Sexual Misconduct Crisis: Identity, Credibility, and Proof*. Lanham, MD: Lexington Books.

Selsky, Andrew. 2020. "Homeless at 'Double Risk' of Getting, Spreading Coronavirus." ABC News, March 7, 2020. https://abcnews.go.com/Health/wireStory/homeless-double-risk-spreading-coronavirus-69454275.

Semuels, Alana. 2016. "How Can the U.S. End Homelessness?" *The Atlantic*, April 25, 2016. https://www.theatlantic.com/business/archive/2016/04/end-homelessness-us/479115/.

Sepic, Matt, and Max Nesterak. 2018. "Red Lake Nation, Frey Offer Surprise Option for Homeless Camp in Minneapolis." MPR News, September 21, 2018. https://www.mprnews.org/story/2018/09/21/red-lake-nation-mayor-frey-surprise-option-for-homeless-encampment-minneapolis.

Serres, Chris. 2018a. "After Months of Turmoil, Homeless Camp in Minneapolis Comes to a Peaceable End." *Star Tribune*, December 21, 2018. https://www.startribune.com/minneapolis-homeless-camp-officially-closed-last-residents-leave-amid-massive-outreach-effort/503364632/.

Serres, Chris. 2018b. "Aid Workers, Others at Minneapolis Homeless Camp Say They Are Fearful." *Star Tribune*, http://www.startribune.com/as-deadline-looms-a-hostile-mood-grips-south-minneapolis-homeless-camp/502124841/.

Serres, Chris. 2018c. "American Indian Leaders Condemn 'Deplorable' Actions of Street Outreach Group at Mpls. Homeless Camp." *Star Tribune*, December 7, 2018. http://www.startribune.com/american-indian-leaders-condemn-deplorable-actions-of-street-outreach-group-at-mpls-homeless-camp/502194541/.

Serres, Chris. 2018d. "Fourth Person Dies at Minneapolis Homeless Camp." *Star Tribune*, November 2, 2018. http://www.startribune.com/ fourth-death-linked-to-minneapolis-homeless-camp/499463831/.

Serres, Chris. 2018e. "From Addict to Crusader: A New Leader Emerges in Minnesota's Indian Community." *Star Tribune*, September 16, 2018. https://www. startribune.com/from-addict-to-crusader-a-new-leader-emerges-in-minnesota-s-indian-community/493435851/.

Serres, Chris. 2018f. "Growing Minneapolis Homeless Camp Raises Public Health Alarms." *Star Tribune*, August 14, 2018. http://www.startribune.com/ growing-minneapolis-homeless-camp-raises-public-health-alarms/490743881/.

Serres, Chris. 2019a. "Indian Activists End Occupation of Former Minneapolis Homeless Camp, Vow to Keep Fighting for More Shelter Beds." *Star Tribune,* December 16, 2019. https://www.startribune.com/indian-activists-end-occupa-tion-of-former-minneapolis-homeless-camp-vow-to-keep-fighting-for-more-beds/566251752/.

Serres, Chris. 2019b. "Indian Activists Hunker Down at Site of Former Minneapolis Homeless Camp." *Star Tribune*, December 14, 2019. https://www.startribune.com/ indian-activists-continue-occupation-of-minneapolis-homeless-camp-demand-more-shelter-beds/566211332/.

Serres, Chris. 2019c. "Indian Activists Reoccupy Site of Former Minneapolis Homeless Camp." *Star Tribune*, December 14, 2019. https://www.startribune. com/indian-activists-plan-protest-at-site-of-former-minneapolis-homeless-camp/566197601/.

Serres, Chris. 2020a. "Hundreds of Minnesota Homeless Move to Area Hotels to Prevent Coronavirus from Spreading in Shelters." *Star Tribune*, May 5, 2020. https:// www.startribune.com/hundreds-of-homeles-minnesotans-move-to-area-hotels-as-officials-race-to-prevent-coronavirus-from-spreading-in-shelters/570183632/.

Serres, Chris. 2020b. "Indian Activists Escalate Campaign for More Shelter Beds in Twin Cities." *Star Tribune*, January 2020. https://www.startribune.com/indian-activists-escalate-campaign-for-more-shelter-beds-in-twin-cities/566704411/.

Serres, Chris. 2020c. "Minnesota Sex Offenders Sue Over Residency Restrictions in Apple Valley." *Star Tribune*, February 13, 2020. https://www.startribune.com/min-nesota-sex-offenders-sue-over-residency-restrictions-in-apple-valley/567841772/.

Serres, Chris, and Libor Jany. 2018. "Minneapolis City Leaders Unveil 'Action Plan' for Growing Homeless Encampment." *Star Tribune*, August 24, 2018. http:// www.startribune.com/minneapolis-city-leaders-to-unveil-action-plan-for-tackling-growing-homeless-encampment/491547431/.

Serres, Chris, David Chanen, and Katie Galioto. 2020. "In the Wake of COVID-19, Homeless Face Closed Doors during the Day, Dangerously Crowded Shelters at Night." *Star Tribune*, March 19, 2020. https://www.startribune.com/in-the-wake-of-covid-19-homeless-face-closed-doors-during-the-day-dangerously-crowded-shelters-at-night/568916332/.

Shane, Leo III. 2021. "The Number of Veterans Experiencing Homelessness Rose Slightly Even Before the Coronavirus Pandemic." *Military Times*, March 18. https://www.militarytimes.com/news/pentagon-congress/2021/03/18/

the-number-of-veterans-experiencing-homelessness-rose-slightly-even-before-the-coronavirus-pandemic/.

Shelley v. Kraemer, 334 U.S. 1 (1948).

Shome, Raka. "Space Matters: The Power and Practice of Space." *Communication Theory* 13: 39–56.

Showden, Carisa R. 2011. *Choices Women Make: Agency in Domestic Violence, Assisted Reproduction, and Sex Work*. Minneapolis: University of Minnesota Press.

Sidis v. F-R. Publishing Corporation, No. 400, Circuit Court of Appeals, Second Circuit (1940).

Silva, Catherine. 2016. "Racial Restrictive Covenants: Enforcing Neighborhood Segregation in Seattle." Seattle Civil Rights & Labor History, University of Washington, December 21, 2015. https://depts.washington.edu/civilr/covenants_report.htm.

Shome, Raka. 2003. "Space Matters: The Power and Practice of Space." *Communication Theory* 13: 39–56.

Skolnik, Terry. 2016. "Homelessness and the Impossibility to Obey the Law." *Fordham Urban Law Journal* 43: 741–88.

Smith, Kelly. 2021a. "In an Unprecedented Step, Minnesota Returned 114 Acres to Lower Sioux Indian Community." *Star Tribune*, February 21, 2021. https://www.startribune.com/in-an-unprecedented-step-minnesota-returns-114-acres-to-lower-sioux-indian-community/600025441/?ref=nl&om_rid=1617810889&om_mid=2403858889.

Smith, Kelly. 2021b. "'Tiny House' Indoor Village Opens in March for 100 Homeless Minnesotans." *Star Tribune*, February 23, 2021. https://www.startribune.com/tiny-house-indoor-village-for-the-homeless-opens-march-8-in-minneapolis/600026263/.

Smith v. Maryland, 442 US 735 (1979).

Snead, Lisa. 2009. "Domestic Violence Litigation in the Wake of *DeShaney* and *Castle Rock*." *Texas Journal of Women and the Law* 18: 305–22.

Snow, David A., and Michael Mulcathy. 2001. "Space, Politics, and the Survival Strategies of the Homeless." *American Behavioral Scientist* 45: 149–69.

Socia, Kelly M. 2012. "The Implementation of County Residence Restrictions in New York." *Psychology, Public Policy, and Law* 18: 206–30.

SOMAPI. 2017. "Adult Sex Offender Recidivism." Office of Sex Offender Management Assessment and Planning Initiative. https://smart.ojp.gov/sites/g/files/xyckuh231/files/media/document/adultsexoffenderrecidivism.pdf.

South Burlington County NAACP et al. v. Mount Laurel Township et al., 67 N.J. 151 (1975).

Southwell, Jenni. 2002. "Family Violence and Homelessness: Removing the Perpetrator from the Home." Discussion paper No. 3. Melbourne: Domestic Violence and Incest Resource Center. https://apo.org.au/node/28430.

Speer, Jessie. 2016. "'It's Not Like Your Home': Homeless Encampments, Housing Projects, and the Struggle over Domestic Space." *Antipode* 49: 517–35.

Spewak, Danny. 2019. "'More Homeless Than We Already Were': Donations Pour in for Fire Victims." KARE11 News,

December 26, 2019. https://www.kare11.com/article/news/local/donations-pour-in-for-fire-victims/89-a726034c-4896-4965-ba23-2ed83af9d079.

Stamm, B. Hudnall, Henry E. Stamm, Amy C. Hudhall, and Craig Higson-Smith. 2010. "Considering a Theory of Cultural Trauma and Loss." *Journal of Loss and Trauma* 9: 89–111.

Stark, Louisa R. 1994. "The Shelter as 'Total Institution.'" *American Behavioral Scientist* 37: 553–62.

Statista.com. 2019. "Estimated Rate of Homelessness in the United States in 2019, by State." https://www.statista.com/statistics/727847/homelessness-rate-in-the-us-by-state/.

Stephens, Ronald J., La Wanna M. Larson, and the Black American West Museum. 2008. *African Americans of Denver.* Charleston, SC: Arcadia.

Stern, Shai. 2021. "'Separate, Therefore Equal': American Spatial Segregation from Jim Crow to Kirjas Joel." *Journal of the Social Sciences* 7: 67–90.

Staite, E, N. Zaremba, P. Macdonald, J. Allan, J. Treasure, K. Ismail, and M. Stadler. 2018. "Educational and Psychological Aspects 'Diabulima' [sic] through the Lens of Social Media: A Qualitative Review and Analysis of Online Blogs by People with Type 1 Diabetes Mellitus and Eating Disorders." *Diabetic Medicine* 35: 1329–36.

Stuart, Forrest. 2016. *Down, Out, and Under Arrest: Policing Everyday Life in Skid Row*. Chicago: University of Chicago Press.

Suk, Jeannie. 2009. *How the Domestic Violence Revolution Is Transforming Privacy*. New Haven, CT: Yale University Press.

Suk, Jeannie. 2008. "Taking the Home." *Law and Literature* 20: 291–317.

Svaldi, Aldo. 2017. "Five Points Has the Highest Rent in Denver, but Highlands Ranch Has Highest Rent in Region." *The Denver Post*, April 3, 2017. https://www.denver-post.com/2017/04/03/five-points-highlands-ranch-highest-rents-in-colorado/.

Tassie, Keisha Edward, and Sonja M. Brown Givens, Eds. 2012. *Women of Color and Social Media Multitasking*. Lanham, MD: Lexington Books.

Taylor, Anne. 2011. "Social Media as a Tool for Inclusion." Stiles Associates Inc. Canada. Funded by Human Resources and Skills Development: 1–86.

Taylor, Derrick Bryson. 2021. "George Floyd Protests: A Timeline." *New York Times*, January 6, 2021. https://www.nytimes.com/article/george-floyd-protests-timeline.html.

Tekle, Asmara. 2009. "Safe: Restrictive Covenants and the Next Wave of Sex Offender Legislation." *SMU Law Review* 62: 1817–62.

Texas Statutes, Family Code, Title 4. 2020. "Protective Orders and Family Violence." https://statutes.capitol.texas.gov/Docs/FA/htm/FA.85.htm.

Thistle, Jesse. 2019. *From the Ashes: My Story of Being Métis, Homeless, and Finding My Way*. New York: Simon & Schuster.

Tick Tock Sheptock. 2011. "Homeless Women Being Mistreated at Open Door Women's Shelter." http://streatstv.blogspot.com/2011/02/homeless-women-being-mistreated-at-open.html.

Tipps, Robin T., Gregory T. Buzzard, and John A. McDougall. 2018. "The Opioid Epidemic in Indian Country." *Journal of Law, Medicine & Ethics* 46: 422–36.

Tolson, Andrew. 2010. "A New Authenticity: Communicative Practices on YouTube." *Critical Discourse Studies* 7: 277–89.

Toolis, Erin E., and Phillip L. Hammack. 2015a. "The Lived Experience of Homeless Youth: A Narrative Approach." *Qualitative Psychology* 2: 50–68.

Toolis, Erin E., and Phillip L. Hammack. 2015b. "'This is My Community': Reproducing and Resisting Boundaries of Exclusion in Contested Public Spaces." *American Journal of Community Psychology* 56: 368–82.

Town of Castle Rock, Colorado v. Gonzales, 545 US 748 (2005).

Tremayne, Mark. 2007. "Introduction: Examining the Blog-Media Relationship." In *Blogging, Citizenship and the Future of Media*, edited by Mark Tremayne, 3–20. New York: Routledge.

Treuer, David. 2019. *The Heartbeat of Wounded Knee: Native America from 1890 to the Present*. New York: Riverhead Books.

Tribal Alliance of Sovereign Indian Nations. 2021. https://www.tasin.org/home.

Tsai, Jack, and Michal Wilson. 2020, March 11. "COVID-19: A Potential Public Health Problem for Homeless Populations." *The Lancet: Public Health* 5: E186–E187. https://www.thelancet.com/journals/lanpub/article/PIIS2468-2667(20)30053-0/fulltext.

Turkle, Sherry. 2021. *The Empathy Diaries: A Memoir*. New York: Penguin Press.

Turkle, Sherry. 1995. *Life on the Screen: Identity in the Age of the Internet*. New York: Simon & Schuster.

Tutty, Leslie Maureen, Cindy Ogden, Bianca Giurgiu, and Gilliam Weaver-Dunlop. 2017. "I Built My House of Hope: Abused Women and Pathways into Homelessness." *Violence Against Women* 19: 1498–517.

US v. Jones, 565 US 400 (2012).

US Department of Housing and Urban Development. 2020. "Federal Definitions." https://youth.gov/youth-topics/runaway-and-homeless-youth/federal-definitions.

US Interagency Council on Homelessness. 2021. "Deploy Housing First System Wide," https://www.usich.gov/solutions/housing/housing-first/.

US Interagency Council on Homelessness. 2018. "Homelessness in America: Focus on Families with Children." https://www.usich.gov/resources/uploads/asset_library/Homeslessness_in_America_Families_with_Children.pdf.

US National Archives and Records Administration. 2016. "American Indian Urban Relocation." https://www.archives.gov/education/lessons/indian-relocation.html.

Van Ness, Peter H. 2001. "The Concept of Risk in Biomedical Research Involving Human Subjects." *Bioethics* 15: 364–70.

Varma, Rohit. 2018. "What You Need to Know about Homelessness among Native Americans." https://medium.com/@DrRohitVarma/what-you-need-to-know-about-homelessness-among-native-americans-47189c97e68e.

Vasilogambros, Matt. 2018. "Homeless Will Now Be Asked: Are You Fleeing Domestic Violence?" The PEW Charitable Trusts, January 19, 2018. https://www.pewtrusts.org/en/research-and-analysis/blogs/stateline/2018/01/19/homeless-will-now-be-asked-are-you-fleeing-domestic-violence.

Verteramo, T. Ray. 2019. *Clarity: Memoirs from the Streets of Vegas*. Self-published.

Vrooman, Nicholas. 2013. "The Whole Country Was…One Robe." YouTube video 19:41, November 1, 2013. https://www.youtube.com/watch?v=FZ7WDfmY4XQ&fbclid

=IwAR0Mn9Msu07lurWvqjr8LXqsdsqBJMb9V1HiZpaXI8vnmHByZxRL4Ifr TvE.

Walls, Eugene N., and Stephanie Bell. 2011. "Correlates of Engaging in Survival Sex among Homeless Youth and Young Adults." *Journal of Sex Research* 48: 423–36.

Walsh, Jim. 2018. "'A Blessing,' 'a Family,' and 'a Shame on Minneapolis': Voices from the Hiawatha Avenue Homeless Encampment." *MinnPost*, September 12, 2018. https://www.minnpost.com/community-sketchbook/2018/09/a-blessing-a-family-and-a-shame-on-minneapolis-voices-from-the-hiawatha-avenue-homeless-encampment/.

Warner, Michael. 1991. "The Mass Public and the Mass Subject." In *Habermas and the Public Sphere*, edited by Craig Calhoun, 377–401. Cambridge: MIT Press.

Warnick, Barbara. 1998. "Rhetorical Criticism of Public Discourse on the Internet: Theoretical Implications." *Rhetoric Society Quarterly* 28: 73–84.

Warren, Peter. 2021. "Nonprofit Settled Unveils Designs for Tiny Homes to Combat Homelessness in St. Paul." *Star Tribune*, January 23, 2021. https://www.startribune.com/nonprofit-settled-unveils-designs-for-tiny-homes-to-combat-homelessness-in-st-paul/600014277/.

Warren, Samuel, and Louis Brandeis. 1890. "The Right to Have Privacy." *Harvard Law Review* 4: 193–220.

Warrington, Molly. 2001. "'I Must Get Out': The Geographies of Domestic Violence." *Transactions of the Institute of British Geographers* 26: 365–82.

Washington Courts. 2020. "Domestic Violence Protection Order Process." https://www.courts.wa.gov/dv/?fa=dv_order.ordtypes.

Wasserman, Jason Adam, and Jeffrey Michael Clair. 2010. *At Home on the Street: People, Poverty & a Hidden Culture of Homelessness*. Boulder, CO: Lynne Rienner Publishers.

Waterloo, Sophie, Susanne E. Baumgartner, Jochel Peter, and Patti M. Vankenburg. 2018. "Norms of Online Expressions of Emotion: Comparing Facebook, Twitter, Instagram, and WhatsApp." *New Media & Society* 20: 1813–31.

Webster, Richard A. 2020. "For Homeless in New Orleans, Hotel Living Brings Benefits and Risks Amid Coronavirus Outbreak." *Washington Post*, April 11, 2020. https://www.washingtonpost.com/national/for-homeless-in-new-orleans-hotel-living-brings-benefits-and-risks-amid-coronavirus-outbreak/2020/04/11/66f1ef92-7ae1-11ea-b6ff-597f170df8f8_story.html.

Weinberger, Richard. 2017. "Residency Restrictions for Sexual Offenders in Minnesota: False Perceptions for Community Safety." Association for the Treatment of Sexual Abusers, Minnesota Chapter. https://pdf4pro.com/view/residency-restrictions-for-sexual-offenders-in-minnesota-4c9439.html.

"Welcome to Listening House & Freedom House." 2018/2020. https://listeninghouse.org.

Wenzel, Suzanne L, Barbara D. Leake, and Lillian Gelberb. 2001. "Risk Factors for Major Violence among Homeless Women." *Journal of Interpersonal Violence* 16: 739–52.

Westerfelt, Alex., and Michael Yellow Bird. 1999. "Homeless and Indigenous in Minnesota." *Journal of Human Behavior in the Social Environment* 2: 145–62.

Westervelt, Eric. 2020. "Sprawling Homeless Camps—Modern 'Hoovervilles'—Vex California." National Public Radio, January 13, 2020. https://www.npr.org/2020/01/13/795439405/sprawling-homeless-camps-modern-hoovervilles-vex-california.

Wheeler, Jennifer, and William H. George. 2004. "Race and Sexual Offending." In *Race, Culture, Psychology, & Law*, edited by Kimberly Holt Barrett and William H. George, 391–402. Thousand Oaks, CA: Sage Publications.

"Where Do Homeless Patients Go After Being Treated for COVID-19?" 2020. PBS NewsHour November 25, 2020. https://www.pbs.org/newshour/health/where-do-homeless-patients-go-after-being-treated-for-covid-19.

White, Kari. 2008. "Where Will They Go? Sex Offender Residency Restrictions as a Modern-day Banishment." *Case Western Research Law Review* 59: 161–89.

Wichowski, Dawn, and Laura Kohl. 2013. "Establishing Credibility in the Information Jungle: Blogs, Microblogs, and the CRAAP Test." *Library Staff Publications, Presentations & Journal Articles*, Bryant University, Paper 3: 229–51.

WiiDooKoDaaDiiWag ("They Help Each Other"). https://www.theyhelpeachother.org/.

Wilder Research Center. 2014. "Homeless Children and Their Families: 2012 Minnesota Homeless Study." https://www.wilder.org/sites/default/files/imports/Homeless%20in%20MN%202012%20Children%20Families_5-14.pdf.

Wilder Research Center. 2004. "Homeless in Minnesota." February 2004. https://www.wilder.org/wilder-research/research-library/homelessness-minnesota-2003-study.

Wilkins, Mark Hanna. 1945. "Racial Situation in Denver." *The Crisis*, 139–40. https://books.google.com/books?id=ElsEAAAAMBAJ&pg=PA128&lpg=PA128&dq=The+Racial+Situation+in+Denver+%2B+Mark+Hanna+Watkins&source=bl&ots=igRqATy0HO&sig=ACfU3U3kefA8_-0UMdRbF0JHgUTxaoV63g&hl=en&sa=X&ved=2ahUKEwj7mqPqovbrAhVQV80KHZDqDJAQ6AEwB3oECAEQAQ#v=onepage&q=The%20Racial%20Situation%20in%20Denver%20%2B%20Mark%20Hanna%20Watkins&f=false.

Wilkinson, David, and Mike Thelwall. 2011. "Researching Personal Information on the Public Web: Methods and Ethics." *Social Science Computer Review* 29: 387–401.

Williams, Brandt. 2020. "Fire Survivors Say Relief Isn't Coming Fast Enough." MPR News and the *Albert Lea Tribune*, January 1, 2020. https://www.albertleatribune.com/2020/01/fire-survivors-say-relief-isnt-coming-fast-enough/.

Williams, Jean Calterone. 1998. "Domestic Violence and Poverty: The Narratives of Homeless Women." *Frontiers: A Journal of Women Studies* 19: 143–65.

Williams, Kevin. 2020. "An Ohio City Known for Helping the Homeless Now Questions Its Limits." *Washington Post*, January 1, 2020. https://www.washingtonpost.com/national/an-ohio-city-known-for-helping-now-questions-its-limits-when-the-homeless-come-from-somewhere-else/2020/01/01/d58a38ac-2b26-11ea-bcd4-24597950008f_story.html?utm_campaign=post_most&utm_medium=Email&utm_source=Newsletter&wpisrc=nl_most&wpmm=1.

Williams v. Lee, 358 U.S. 217 (1959).

Wilson, Shawn, and Margaret Hughes. 2019. "Why Research is Reconciliation." In *Research & Reconciliation: Unsettling Ways of Knowing Through Indigenous Relationships*, edited by Shawn Wilson, Andrea V. Breen, and Lindsay Dupré, 5–19. Toronto: Canadian Scholars.

Woelfer, Jill Palzkill, and David G. Hendry. 2011. "Designing Ubiquitous Information Systems for a Community of Homeless Young People: Precaution and a Way Forward." *Personal Ubiquitous Computing* 15: 565–73.

Wright, Talmage. 1992. *Out of Place: Homeless Mobilizations, Subcities, and Contested Landscape.* Albany: State University of New York Press.

Wong, David W. 2008. "Formulating a General Spatial Segregation Measure." *The Professional Geographer* 57: 285–94.

Xie, Jenny. 2017. "10 Tiny House Villages for Homeless Residents Across the U.S.: Case Studies for a Trending Idea." https://archive.curbed.com/maps/tiny-houses-for-the-homeless-villages.

Zoller, Heather M. 2005. "Health Activism: Communication Theory and Action for Social Change." *Communication Theory* 15: 341–64.

Index

as pathway toward permanent
  homelessness, 131;
perceptions of home and family,
  110–13, 128–32;
prevalence, 108, 128–29;
sense of agency for, 113–16, 131–32;
social media and, 133–35, 179–80;
solutions offered for, 186;
terminology choice, 108;

trauma experienced by, 56, 105,
  107–8, 121, 129, 130–31;
trope of family and home for, 128–32
YouTube, 32, 53

Zeiglers (Colorado homeowners), 81–82
Zhang, Amy, 134
Zoller, Heather, 3–4
zoning policies, 76, 77–79, 103,
  176–77, 184–85

About the Author

Mary Schuster is Professor Emerita with the Writing Studies Department and Affiliated Faculty with the Law School at the University of Minnesota–Twin Cities. She has been a volunteer for two organizations that address domestic violence and sexual assault: WATCH, a court monitoring and research organization, which gave her the 2004 volunteer of the year award, and Tubman, which provides safe shelter, counseling, youth programming, and community education for those who have experienced relationship violence and other forms of trauma. She has written several articles and books on sexual assault, disability, and domestic violence, the most recent of which are *The Victim's Voice in the Sexual Misconduct Crisis* (Lexington Books, 2019) and *Rhetoric and Communication Perspectives on Domestic Violence and Sexual Assault* (with Amy Propen, 2017).

www.ingramcontent.com/pod-product-compliance
Lightning Source LLC
Chambersburg PA
CBHW022306280326
41932CB00010B/997